The Bible Study Resource Guide

The Bible Study Resource Guide

Joseph D. Allison

Illustrations by Richard Stump

THOMAS NELSON PUBLISHERS
Nashville • Camden • New York

TO MY WIFE

"Many a woman shows how capable she is,
but you surpass them all" (Prov. 31:29 NEB).

Published in Nashville, Tennessee, by Thomas Nelson, Inc. and distributed in
Canada by Lawson Falle, Ltd., Cambridge, Ontario.

Printed in the United States of America

Library of Congress Cataloging in Publication Data

Allison, Joseph D.
  The Bible study resource guide.

  1. Bible—Study—Bibliography.   2. Bible—Bibliography.   3. Bible—Study.
I. Title.
Z7770.A45   1982 [BS600.2]   016.22   82–18800
ISBN 0-8407-5814-6

Credits

The book introduction for Job (Fig. 6) is taken from *The New Oxford Annotated Bible,* Revised Standard Version, edited by Herbert C. May and Bruce M. Metzger. Copyright © 1973 by Oxford University Press, Inc. Reprinted by permission.

Information about special Bible editions, binding materials and binding styles (pp. 54-58) as well as the Bible type sizes (Fig. 12) are from *How to Sell the Right Bible.* Copyright © 1980 by Thomas Nelson Publishers. Used by permission.

The excerpt from the Bible dictionary entry "Jezreel" (p. 125) is from *The Zondervan Pictorial Bible Dictionary,* edited by Merrill C. Tenney. Copyright © 1963, 1964, 1967 by Zondervan Publishing House. Used by permission.

The excerpt from the Bible encyclopedia entry "Make-Up" (p. 126) is from *Eerdmans' Concise Bible Encyclopedia,* edited by Pat Alexander. Copyright © 1980 by William B. Eerdmans Publishing Company. Used by permission.

The quote from a Bible survey (pp. 141-142) is from *The Old Testament Speaks,* 3rd ed., by Samuel J. Schultz. Copyright © 1980 by Harper & Row. Used by permission.

The quote from a Bible introduction (p. 142) is from *An Introduction to the Old Testament,* rev. ed. by Edward J. Young. Copyright © 1964 by William B. Eerdmans Publishing Company. Used by permission.

The Bible lexicon entry, *"Luchnia"* (pp. 148-149) is from *A Greek-English Lexicon of the New Testament,* 4th ed. by William F. Arndt and F. Wilbur Gingrich. Copyright © by Walter de Gruyter & Co., Berlin. Used by permission.

The study Bible outline of the Book of Romans (top section of Fig. 7) is from *The Scofield Reference Bible.* Copyright 1909, 1917, renewed 1937, 1945 by Oxford University Press, Inc. Reprinted by permission.

The study Bible outline of the Book of Romans from the *Christian Brotherhood Hour Study Edition* (Fig. 7) is originally from the book, *Toward Understanding Romans,* by Boyce W. Blackwelder. Copyright © 1962 by Gospel Trumpet Company. Used by permission.

The quotation on page 94 is from *The Living Talmud* by Judah Goldin. Copyright © 1957 by Judah Goldin. Reprinted by permission of The New American Library, Inc.

Scripture references noted KJV are from the King James Version of the Bible.

Scripture references noted RSV are from the Revised Standard Version of the Bible, copyrighted 1946, 1952, © 1971, 1973.

Scripture references noted NKJV are from The New King James Version. Copyright © 1979, 1980, 1982, Thomas Nelson, Inc., Publishers.

Scripture references noted NIV are from the *Holy Bible: New International Version.* Copyright © 1978 by the New York International Bible Society. Used by permission of Zondervan Bible Publishers.

Scripture references noted NASB are from the New American Standard Bible, © The Lockman Foundation 1960, 1962, 1963, 1968, 1971, 1972, 1973, 1975, 1977, and are used by permission.

Scripture references noted NEB are from *The New English Bible.* © The Delegates of the Oxford University Press and the Syndics of the Cambridge University Press 1961, 1970. Reprinted by permission.

Special Features of this Guide

Terms used throughout the *Bible Study Resource Guide* that may not be familiar to the reader are printed in italics and marked with an asterisk the first time a term appears. This marking indicates that the term is defined in the Glossary at the back of the book.

Throughout this guide there are references to other Bible reference bibliographies. These references are in parentheses as abbreviations accompanied by page numbers. The full publication information for these references is given under the List of Abbreviations.

Contents

Abbreviations

Bible Reference Bibliographies

BLBS—Warren W. Wiersbe, *A Basic Library for Bible Students* (Grand Rapids: Baker, 1981).

BRW—*Recommending and Selling Biblical Reference Works: A Guide for Booksellers* (Grand Rapids: Eerdmans, 1980).

CC—Charles H. Spurgeon, *Commenting and Commentaries* (London: Banner of Truth, 1969).

GHR—George H. Ramsey, *Tools for Bible Study* (Anderson, Ind.: Warner, 1971).

HBE—F. F. Bruce, *History of the Bible in English,* 3rd ed. (New York: Oxford Univ. Press, 1978).

HBS—Grant R. Osborne and Stephen B. Woodward, *Handbook for Bible Study* (Grand Rapids: Baker, 1979).

HSB—John B. Job, *How to Study the Bible* (Downers Grove, Ill: Inter-Varsity, 1973).

ML—Cyril J. Barber, *The Minister's Library* (Grand Rapids: Baker, 1974).

MTBS—Frederick W. Danker, *Multipurpose Tools for Bible Study,* 2nd ed. (St. Louis: Concordia, 1966).

PBS—Wilbur M. Smith, *Profitable Bible Study* (Boston: W. A. Wilde, 1951).

STB—Lewis Foster, *Selecting a Translation of the Bible* (Cincinnati: Standard, 1978).

TBS—Balmer H. Kelly and Donald G. Miller, *Tools for Bible Study* (Richmond, Va.: John Knox, 1956).

English Bible Versions

ASV—American Standard Version
JB—Jerusalem Bible
KJV—King James Version
LB—Living Bible
NAB—New American Bible
NASB—New American Standard Bible
NEB—New English Bible
NIV—New International Version
NKJV—New King James Version
RSV—Revised Standard Version
RV—Revised Version
TEV—Today's English Version

Preface

Chuck came to me with a tough question. After serving as our youth advisors for several years, he and his wife had received a fifty-dollar gift from the youth group, and they wanted to use that money to buy some basic Bible reference books for their home library. "What should I buy first?" he asked.

I knew several things about Chuck and Lucy's needs and interests: They taught a Sunday school class for young married couples in addition to being the youth advisors. Chuck was the Sunday school's assistant superintendent. Lucy attended a women's Bible study each week. She wanted some good devotional reading, while Chuck wanted to do more in-depth Bible study.

Christians now have a wide assortment of Bible study aids, and we can thank God for them. But it's not always easy to know which reference books are best suited to a certain person's study. It's not easy for a pastor to jot down a shopping list of books for a member of the congregation, no matter how well he may know that person's Bible study goals and abilities.

I recommended that Chuck and Lucy start with *Strong's Exhaustive Concordance, Nave's Topical Bible,* and *The Bible Almanac.* These three books would help them do a wide range of lesson preparation, personal Bible study, and devotional reading. Chuck told me they already had a copy of *Nave's,* so I recommended the one-volume *Commentary on the Whole Bible* by Jamieson, Fausset, and Brown—a conservative commentary that offers some helpful insight into key words and phrases of the Bible.

But each person's needs are different. The reference books I recommended for Chuck and Lucy are not what I would recommend for a ministerial student who needs to study the original languages of the Bible (Hebrew, Aramaic, and Greek). Nor would I recommend a word-study commentary to a new Christian, who would enjoy a more devotional treatment in the beginning stages of Bible study.

I have compiled *The Bible Study Resource Guide* to help you decide which Bible study aids are best for you. I have also provided basic information about English versions of the Bible to help in choosing a Bible version for study. In fact, the first four Chapters could be called a consumer's guide to Bible buying.

I have tried to explain simply and clearly how to use each type of Bible reference book. Following this explanation is an annotated list of some of the more useful books in each category, so that you can make your own comparisons. *The Bible Study Resource Guide* does not include every Bible reference book you may have heard mentioned, but you should find most of them here. This book is one you can take from the shelf again and again, not just to find help for a certain phase of Bible study, but to relish the feast of good material that lies ahead for you.

This *Guide* should entice you to keep coming back to the Word for more. "As newborn babes, desire the sincere milk of the word, that ye may grow thereby" (1 Pet. 2:2). As a student finds knowledge and applies it, he hungers for more.

I pray that you will strive to be a true student of God's Word, and I trust that *The Bible Study Resource Guide* will help you become a skillful student.

Joseph D. Allison, Pastor
Park Forest Church of God
Fort Wayne, Indiana

Acknowledgments

 I wish to express my appreciation to the following persons, who helped to make this book possible:

Robert Sanford and Ron Pitkin of Thomas Nelson Publishers; Al Bryant of Word, Inc.; and Mark Hunt of Zondervan Publishing House, who provided advance information about Bibles and reference books that are in process of publication.

Pauline Holsopple of Anchor Room Bookstore and the staff of the Fort Wayne Bible College Bookstore, who loaned me review copies of new Bible reference books.

The library staffs of Concordia Theological Seminary of Fort Wayne and Vanderbilt Divinity School of Nashville, who gave me access to their collections.

Ralph White of Nashville, who reviewed major portions of Chapters 1 and 6 and made a number of helpful comments and corrections.

Sister Joyce Diltz and the religious community of the Crosier Center, who gave me access to their Roman Catholic library along with several days of solitude for writing.

My secretary, Marilyn Mettert, who placed several long-distance calls, photocopied the manuscript, and assisted in other ways.

My wife, Judy, who did much of the bibliographic research and offered countless suggestions, criticisms, and corrections as she typed the manuscript.

My prayer partners, M. Kay Colbert and Charles Harter, who shared the burden of this book in prayer.

And my congregation, who encourage me to use the creative abilities the Lord has given me.

1.
Bible Versions

 We English-speaking people have two ways in which we can read the Bible. (1) We can learn the original languages in which it was written (biblical Hebrew, *koine Greek**, and a smattering of Aramaic), or (2) we can use an English *translation** of the Bible.

A German housewife who would like to read *Gone with the Wind* has similar choices: learn the English language or get a copy in German. But there the similarity would end, for translating the Bible into English is quite different from translating a twentieth-century novel into a foreign language. When you understand the difference, you will understand why we have so many English versions of the Bible.

Someone translating *Gone with the Wind* into German can still refer to first-edition English copies of the novel. However, someone who wants to translate the Bible has no first-edition copies. The best copies available are handwritten, made at least 150 years after the first edition. And the translator finds perplexing differences among these various copies. For example, some manuscripts of John 1:34 say that Jesus is "the Song of God" (KJV,NIV), while other copies say He is "God's Chosen One" (NEB). Which one should be followed in making the translation to English? The copies must be evaluated in order to choose the ones that seem most authentic; we refer to this task of picking and choosing as *textual criticism.** It is quite a sophisticated science.

Anyone who wants to translate *Gone with the Wind* into German is working with two current, known languages, but someone who wants to translate the Bible must deal with ancient languages as well as a modern language. The Bible translator must convert languages that have not been spoken for centuries, languages whose vocabulary and rules of grammar have been lost. Occasionally, he must compare biblical words with words in other ancient languages to discover their meaning. Then he must try to convey that meaning into modern English.

A person translating *Gone with the Wind* into German is handling a literary work, written primarily to entertain. But someone who wants to translate the Bible is handling a spiritual work, which God gave us to explain the way to eternal life. If the translator of the novel fails to grasp all of Margaret Mitchell's meaning, the readers of the novel will still have an enjoyable experience. If the translator of the Bible fails to grasp all of God's meaning, the readers may be sidetracked from the way of salvation. So the Bible translator must be very careful to convey the sense of the original and to avoid including any personal theological views.

English Versions: A Capsule History

English translations ("*versions*"*) of the Bible have been made for almost 1300 years. The work began with Bishop Aldhelm of Sherborne, who translated the Psalms into Old English shortly before his death in the year 709. The Venerable Bede, a learned Christian monk at Jarrow, had translated part of the Gospel of John into Old English when he died in 735. By the tenth century, Old English scholars had translated all of the Gospels and large portions of the Old Testament into their language.[1]

The man responsible for first bringing the entire Bible into English was John Wycliffe of Oxford. Wycliffe felt that the common people needed to understand God's Word, and he knew that reading the Scriptures in their own language would greatly aid their understanding. So from his post as a lecturer at Oxford University, Wycliffe encouraged scholars of the Oxford community to begin the work of translating the Bible into English. He himself is regarded as the translator of the New Testament.

The printing press had not yet been invented, so these men had to "publish" their work as a handwritten manuscript. They completed the translation shortly before Wycliffe's death in 1384. (It's interesting to note that Wycliffe's team did not work from the Hebrew and Greek manuscripts; they used a Latin translation called the Vulgate, made by the Roman Catholic scholar Jerome around A.D. 400. And the manuscripts Jerome used were themselves late copies of the original manuscripts. So Wycliffe's version was a translation of a translation . . . of a copy!)

More than sixty years later (ca. 1450), Johann Gutenberg invented the process of printing with moveable type. Up to this time, printers had carved the printing plate for an entire page of printed matter from a block of wood. This was a slow, tedious process. But Gutenberg learned how to cast metal molds of individual letters of the alphabet, then lock these letters together to make a complete page. After finishing a job, he could rearrange the metal letters to make a new page. This was the miracle of moveable type—the breakthrough that made modern printing possible.

Soon the Christian world was deluged with various editions of the Greek and Hebrew texts, with new editions of the Latin version and new versions

---

1. F. F. Bruce gives a more detailed account of this early translating process in his *History of the Bible in English,* 3rd ed. (New York: Oxford Univ. Press, 1978), pp. 1–11.

in other languages. Martin Luther released his German New Testament in 1522 and the complete German Bible in 1534. Tyndale published his English New Testament in 1526. Miles Coverdale published an entire English Bible in 1535.

The fourteenth century brought many other English versions, including the Matthew's Bible (1537), the Great Bible (1539), the Geneva Bible (1560), and the Bishops' Bible (1568), not to mention the Rheims New Testament (1582) and the Douay Old Testament in 1609-1610 (the last two being Roman Catholic editions).

Then came the King James Version of 1611. We call it the King James Version (KJV) because King James I of England authorized the project. His six teams of translators worked from printed *critical editions** of the New Testament (which had been made using manuscripts no older than the Middle Ages) and from earlier English versions such as Tyndale's translation. For the Old Testament, they used a Hebrew critical edition, consulting a third-century B.C. Greek version known as the *Septuagint** and the earlier English versions. In the preface to their work, the KJV translators said: "We never thought from the beginning that we should need to make a new translation, nor yet to make of a bad one a good one—but to make a good one better. . . ."[2] The "good one" that they hoped to improve was the Bishops' Bible of 1568, which was preferred by the Anglican clergy. But the most popular Bible of the masses was the Geneva Bible of 1560, produced by English scholars who had escaped to Geneva during the persecutions of Queen Mary. It was printed in a handy size and in clear roman type. King James hoped that the new version would satisfy not only the Anglican clergy, but the Puritan reformers and the uneducated public as well.

The King James Version enjoyed several advantages over the earlier English versions of the Bible:

(1) It was sanctioned by the King of England, thus assuring that most English-speaking people could use it. Many previous English versions had been suppressed (e.g., Tyndale's).

(2) It was published after printers had perfected Gutenberg's process, which permitted them to make fairly inexpensive copies of the KJV.

(3) Its translators held various theological views, giving the project a system of "checks and balances" to override sectarian theological biases.

(4) Its translators were masters of the English language; they could phrase their work in prose of exquisite beauty.

Yet not all of the people of England liked the new translation. The Pilgrims would not even allow a copy of the KJV on board the *Mayflower*

---

2. Joseph L. Gardner, ed., *Reader's Digest Atlas of the Bible* (Pleasantville, N.Y.: Reader's Digest Association, 1981), p. 29.

when it sailed for the New World nine years later; they accepted only the Geneva Bible.[3]

Despite this grudging welcome, the KJV came to be accepted as the standard English Bible version of its day—indeed, the standard version of the following centuries.[4]

Lower Criticism

In later centuries, many Bible manuscripts were discovered that were older than the ones used by the KJV translators. Bible scholars have used these older manuscripts to compile critical editions of the Hebrew and Greek Testaments.

This brings us into the arena of *biblical criticism**—the task of evaluating Bible manuscripts and the content of Scripture itself, using a variety of methods (many of which have not been fully tested). A long digression into critical methods is not necessary at this point, but let us focus on textual criticism, which is also called *lower criticism*.*[5]

Imagine that the discipline of biblical criticism is a hotel building with several stories. To take a package to someone who lives on an upper story, delivery men must enter at the ground level and be admitted by a security guard. In this case, the "lower level" with its cautious guard is textual criticism. The "upper levels," where the package is used, are the various methods of studying the content of the Bible (*higher criticism**).

From this simple illustration, you can see that lower criticism is vital to all other types of Bible study. Before we consider the *meaning* of Scripture, we must be sure that we are using a critical text[6] that best preserves what the original writer set down. We must be sure that it is genuine Scripture. Or to use the hotel analogy, we must let the "security guard" (the textual critic) check the contents of the package (manuscript).

In the nineteenth and early twentieth centuries, archaeologists began finding older Bible manuscripts in the Middle East. Researchers found others in neglected corners of their European archives. As textual critics

---

3. Eugene H. Glassman, *The Translation Debate* (Downers Grove, Ill.: InterVarsity, 1981), p. 15.

4. However, note that the King James Version as we have it today is not exactly the King James Version of 1611 (even though the title page of your KJV may say that it is). Publishers have revised the text of the KJV several times, and the Bible now known as the King James Version is a revision made in 1762 by Dr. Thomas Paris of Cambridge and in 1769 by Dr. Benjamin Blayney of Oxford.

5. For a brief description of *higher criticism,* see Chapter 6.

6. The "critical text" is produced by textual critics from a manuscript. Translators then work from the critical text to produce the version we use in our language. For those of us reading English versions the important question is: what text(s) did the translator(s) use?

compared manuscripts, they found that each one had flaws; words or entire phrases were missing, marred, or obviously rewritten. So the textual critics compiled what seemed to be the most authentic material from these manuscripts in order to provide more reliable Bible texts. These reconstructed texts are called critical editions or *critical texts.* The textual critics —the "security guards" of the text—compiled several new critical editions in the two centuries following the translation of the KJV.

The Call for a Revised Version

Serious Bible students began calling for a thorough revision of the KJV, using these critical editions. Lay readers also wanted someone to revise the KJV, but for a different reason—they wanted a Bible version in the modern English language.

The Church of England appointed a group of scholars to make such a revision. The group issued their version of the New Testament in 1881 and the Old Testament in 1885. Together, these became known as the English Revised Version or simply the Revised Version (RV). The Church of England arranged for a group of American scholars who had worked with the committee to issue their own edition of this work. The Americans hoped to modify the translation a bit to better reflect American usage.

While they were doing this, a young German made a stunning discovery. Adolf Deissmann, an instructor at the University of Marburg, was consulting some Greek papyrus letters at Heidelberg University one day in 1895 when he realized that the common *(koine)* Greek language used in these letters resembled New Testament Greek.

Until this time, Bible scholars thought that the New Testament used a *dialect** all its own; in fact, some referred to it as "biblical Greek." They could not discern the meaning of some New Testament words, because they could not check the meaning elsewhere. They had been pouring over the sophisticated writings of classical Greek literature rather than studying the everyday letters of that ancient time, so they had missed the connection between the New Testament and *koine* Greek.

Unfortunately, Deissmann's discovery came too late to help the American team who were finishing their edition of the RV. They published it in 1901, without much benefit of Deissmann's work; they called the new version the American Standard Version (ASV).

Deissmann's discovery, further manuscript finds, and a continuing demand for more accurate and readable Bible translations prompted publication of other English versions after the ASV. In fact, John H. Skilton lists 123 new versions of the New Testament or the entire Bible issued between 1881 and 1973,[7] and several others have come off the press since then. Almost every new version attempts to improve upon the accuracy or style of the versions that have come before. At the end of this chapter, you will find a list of the better English versions now available. Figure 1 compares these versions in graphic form.

Many Versions—A Curse or a Blessing?

Any Christian bookseller is sure to have heard the complaint: "Why must we have so many versions of the Bible? Why can't we agree on one translation, and stop turning out so many 'new and improved' models?" It's a legitimate complaint, because there are certainly some disadvantages to having so many versions of the Bible.

Consider the pastor who reads the text for the morning sermon and sees the furrowed brows of people in the congregation who are using different versions. He might say, "Now the Revised Standard Version renders it this way," or, "The New American Standard Bible throws a different light on that verse by rendering it this way," and so on. Yet some parishioners will still comment after the service, "I liked your point about verse 12—but my Bible doesn't say that!"

A pastor cannot explain the differences among versions every time he preaches. Normally, he must take the version that seems best and plunge ahead with his sermon, disregarding those furrowed brows and complaints. Yet I don't think we would like to return to the days of the Bishops' Bible, when each church had only one large Bible chained beneath the pulpit, so that the laymen could take turns consulting it while the pastor preached!

Another disadvantage of having so many versions is the incompatibility of Bible study aids. For example, you cannot buy a concordance that will work with all versions of the Bible. Each concordance is based on the KJV, the RSV, or some other version. If you remember part of a verse from the KJV and try to find the whole verse in an RSV concordance, the RSV's wording may be different enough to confuse you. You encounter similar problems in the use of commentaries based on a version different from that of your Bible. Or try using a modern Bible dictionary as you study the KJV, and look for words like *sackbut* or *adamant*—you won't find them!

We might list other disadvantages to having many versions of the Bible, but the problems are not insurmountable. A congregation can overcome the problem of using different versions in a worship service by having pew Bibles of the same version. The worshipers can still refer to their own ver-

---

7. John H. Skilton, ed., *The New Testament Student at Work*, vol. 2 (Nutley, N. J.: Presbyterian and Reformed, 1975), pp. 217–220.

Figure 1—Comparison of Versions

VERSION	DATE	TEXT USED	NUMBER OF TRANSLATORS
AMERICAN STANDARD VERSION	1901	O.T.—Jacob ben Chayim's text (1524-1525)* N.T.—Westcott & Hort's critical ed. (1881)	30
AMPLIFIED BIBLE	O.T. 1965 N.T. 1958	O.T.—Rudolf Kittel's *Biblia Hebraica*** N.T.—Westcott & Hort's critical ed. (1881)	12
JERUSALEM BIBLE	1966	Translation of *La Bible de Jerusalem,* with aid of Latin Vulgate and various Greek and Hebrew texts.	28
KING JAMES VERSION	1611	O.T.—Jacob ben Chayim's text (1524-1525),* consulting the LXX N.T.—T. Beza's *Textus Receptus*	47
LIVING BIBLE	1971	ASV (Paraphrase)	1
NEW AMERICAN BIBLE	1970	O.T.—Eclectic text N.T.—Eclectic text	64
NEW AMERICAN STANDARD	1971	O.T.—Rudolf Kittel's *Biblia Hebraica*** N.T.—Nestle's critical 23rd ed.	58
NEW ENGLISH BIBLE	1970	O.T.—Rudolf Kittel's *Biblia Hebraica*** N.T.—Eclectic text	50
NEW INTERNATIONAL VERSION	O.T. 1978 N.T. 1973	O.T.—Rudolf Kittel's *Biblia Hebraica*** N.T.—Eclectic (Nestle's & Aland/ Black/Metzger critical ed.)	108
NEW KING JAMES BIBLE	O.T. 1982 N.T. 1979	O.T.—Jacob ben Chayim's text (1524-1525)* consulting the LXX † N.T.—F.H.A. Scrivener's *Textus Receptus*	119
REVISED STANDARD VERSION — RSV—2nd Edition	O.T. 1952 N.T. 1946 — 1971	O.T.—Rudolf Kittel's *Biblia Hebraica*** N.T.—Westcott & Hort's critical ed. (1881)	32
TODAY'S ENGLISH VERSION	O.T. 1974 N.T. 1966	O.T.—Rudolf Kittel's *Biblia Hebraica*** N.T.—Aland/Black/ Metzger critical ed.	1 Assisted by translators from American Bible Society and others

* Revised in the Antwerp Polyglot (1569-1572).
** Third edition (1937), based on the Leningrad Manuscript (A.D. 1008) of the Masoretic Text edited by Aaron ben Moshe ben Asher.
† With the *Biblia Hebraica Stuttgartensia,* a revision (1967, 1977) of Kittel's *Biblia Hebraica.*
Copyright © 1982 Joseph D. Allison

sions, of course, but they can follow the pew Bible as the pastor reads the sermon text. An individual can overcome the problem of incompatible study aids by choosing one version for serious study and then buying the study aids designed for that version.

For a moment, let us consider the other side of the issue. Are there any *advantages* to having many English versions of the Bible? Indeed there are.

First, the various versions can balance one another theologically. I mentioned earlier that a translator should avoid bringing personal theological views into the work, but if you compare different versions very carefully you will find a theological perspective in each one. Figure 2 shows how several translators have rendered a few key texts. Notice the theological stance of each one. Also notice how limited your understanding of each verse would be if you had only one version to consult.

Second, the various versions can offset weaknesses in the methods of translation. The two basic methods of translation are *formal equivalence** and *dynamic equivalence.* * A translator who tries to achieve formal equivalence will pick words and phrases that closely parallel the original manuscripts; the object is to give you an English-language "mirror image" of the Hebrew and Greek originals—the same thought pattern, the same level of sophistication, even the same cadence (rhythm of reading) that you would find in the original text. However, English is quite unlike Hebrew or Greek; so when a translator tries to give you formal equivalence, the English must be forced into a Hebrew or Greek mold. The result is a version that may be hard to understand.

A translator who tries to achieve dynamic equivalence will try to express the original *meaning* in English—even if it means restructuring the whole thought pattern of the passage. The weakness of this method is that the translator may misunderstand the full meaning of the original and give a distorted or partial view of what the passage really says. Another problem with this method is that the dynamic-equivalence translator usually will try to express these ideas in a current, modern idiom. Thus the version will be out of date in a few years, as the idioms and clichés pass from use.[8]

To get the full impact of a Bible passage, read a formal-equivalence version beside a dynamic-equivalence version. Two dynamic-equivalence versions may give two radically different views of a passage! (See the comparison in Figure 3.)

---

8. Some people call any dynamic-equivalence version a "paraphrase," as Eugene H. Glassman does in his book, *The Translation Debate.* But "paraphrase" is a misleading term. Strictly speaking, a paraphrase takes a translated version and restates it in other, simpler words in the same language. In this respect, *The Living Bible* is a true paraphrase, because the translator (Kenneth Taylor) took one English version and rephrased it in English terms. His editors did check his work against the Greek and Hebrew manuscripts; but for the most part *The Living Bible* is the ASV in modern clothing—a paraphrase.

Figure 2—Differing Theological Views

Ref.	Protestant	Roman Catholic
Matthew 19:9	...If a man divorces his wife for any cause other than unchastity, and marries another he commits adultery (NEB).	...Whoever divorces his wife (lewd conduct is a separate case) and marries another commits adultery ... (NAB).

Protestant translators usually feel this verse has an "exception clause"—i.e., they feel Jesus condemns any remarriage after divorce *except* when the divorce was caused by infidelity. The Roman Catholic translators of the NAB disagree. According to the NAB, Jesus condemned *any* divorce and remarriage as a form of adultery; the translators think that He singled out divorce for infidelity as one case of this, not an exception to this. (The *Jerusalem Bible* translators go one step further. They give a footnote to refer us to 1 Cor. 7:11, which they believe shows how to deal with this special case—i.e., if one partner commits adultery, the couple should separate but not divorce one another.)

Ref.	Conservative	Liberal
Matthew 3:15	"Permit it to be so now, for thus it is fitting for us to fulfill all righteousness ..." (NKJV). "Let it be so for the present; we do well to conform in this way with all that God requires" (NEB).	"For the present," Jesus answered, "let it be so, for the right thing for us to do is to do everything a good man ought to do" (Barclay). "It is right for us to meet all the Law's demands—let it be so now" (Phillips).

Here the translators wrestle with a tough theological question: Why was Jesus baptized? The Greek text literally says that He was baptized "to fulfill all righteousness," but what does that mean? Barclay answers with a conundrum—in effect, he says that the righteous thing to do is whatever a righteous man should do. Phillips says that righteousness is meeting "the Law's demands," but that would not be true here. Nothing in the Law of Moses demanded that a person be baptized. It seems better to keep the vague language of the Greek text, even though it doesn't answer all our questions.

Ref.	Conservative	Liberal
Luke 13:11	A woman was there who had an evil spirit in her that had kept her sick ... (TEV).	... A woman ... who had been ill from some psychological cause (Phillips).

Here each translator has interpreted what he thinks the Greek phrase *pneūma asthenia* (lit., 'spirit of infirmity') means in this verse. Robert Bratcher, chief translator of the TEV, believes the woman was afflicted by an 'evil spirit' — which is the traditional view. But J. B. Phillips believes she was 'ill from some psychological cause' — in keeping with the liberal view that illnesses are not caused by evil spirits.

Figure 3—Differing Textual Bases and Translation Methods

Ref.	Textus Receptus	Westcott-Hort Type
Luke 17:36	"Two men will be in the field: the one will be taken and the other left" (NKJV).	*Omitted* (NIV)

In this case, the Westcott-Hort type of critical edition completely omits a verse found in the "Received Text." The verse does not appear in some very early Greek manuscripts, but it does appear in early medieval copies.

Ref.	Textus Receptus	Westcott-Hort Type
1 John 5:7	For there are three who bear witness in heaven: the Father, the Word, and the Holy Spirit and these three are one (NKJV).	And the Spirit is the witness, because the Spirit is truth (RSV).

Here the Westcott-Hort type of critical edition rejects a verse that Erasmus had in the third (1522) edition of the *Textus Receptus*. This verse is also missing from the earliest Greek manuscripts, but it appears in Greek texts from the early medieval period.

Ref.	Formal Equivalence	Dynamic Equivalence
Gen. 1:1-2	In the beginning God created the heaven and the earth. And the earth was without form, and void; and darkness was upon the face of the deep. And the spirit of God moved upon the face of the waters (KJV).	When God began to create the heavens and the earth, the earth was a desolate waste, with darkness covering the abyss and a tempestuous wind raging over the surface of the waters (Goodspeed).

The KJV's familiar phrasing of this passage is very majestic, yet it carefully follows the word order and literal meaning of the Hebrew text. Goodspeed attempts to render the Hebrew *idea* into English, without being bound to the word order or the literal meaning. So he occasionally departs from the Hebrew text to give an interpretation that he feels is more plausible. Thus, Goodspeed renders *rūach Elohīm* (lit., "wind of God" or "Spirit of God") as "a tempestuous wind."

Ref.	Formal Equivalence	Dynamic Equivalence
Acts 3:16	And His name, through faith in His name, has made this man strong, whom you see and know. Yes, the faith which comes through Him has given him this perfect soundness in the presence of you all (NKJV).	By faith in the name of Jesus, this man whom you see and know was made strong. It is Jesus' name and the faith that comes through him that has given this complete healing to him, as you all can see (NIV).

The Greek word order of this verse seems awkward to English-language readers, because it is so different from our own. The formal-equivalence version follows the Greek; but the dynamic-equivalence version rearranges the phrasing to give us a smoother rendition. The two versions convey the same meaning; but in this case, the dynamic-equivalence version is a bit easier to read.

The advantage of having many versions is that they help to convey the meaning of the Bible to various dialects of the English-speaking world. The English language as spoken in the hills of eastern Tennessee has its own jargon and shades of meanings, quite different from what you would find on the streets of London. This is why the English Revised Version of 1881 was not suitable for the United States, and it explains why a separate British edition of the Living Bible is published today. Each translation has its intended audience, and the translators phrase their work in the dialect of that audience.

We should thank God for our generous supply of English Bible versions. With them, we can discover the subtle nuances of the ancient Bible manuscripts, even if we cannot read Greek and Hebrew. We can plumb the depths of Bible theology even if we have not outlined a theology of our own. We can read and understand the Word of God in our own language, in terms we use in everyday conversation. Only when we understand the Word can the Word change our lives.

Selecting Versions to Study

Several writers have offered guidelines for selecting Bible versions to use in personal study. Lewis Foster does this quite clearly and helpfully in his book, *Selecting a Translation of the Bible* (Cincinnati: Standard, 1978). See especially Chapter 4 of that book, entitled "Setting Up a Standard: The Essentials of Bible Selection." You will find another good set of guidelines in "The Study of Modern English Versions of the New Testament," Chapter 12 in *The New Testament Student at Work,* vol. 2, ed. John H. Skilton (Nutley, N.J.: Presbyterian and Reformed, 1975). I especially like Skilton's list of test passages, which he suggests for comparing the versions' styles of writing and theological views.

If you have a more scholarly bent, see "Bible Versions," Chapter X in Frederick W. Danker's *Multipurpose Tools for Bible Study,* 2nd ed. (St. Louis: Concordia, 1966). Danker does not give specific guidelines for selecting a version, but he does provide an in-depth analysis of some of the more important English versions. Unfortunately, he could not include the NASB, the NIV, the Jerusalem Bible, and other versions published after 1966.

Let me also suggest some guidelines for selecting a Bible version. As I do, remember that as your personal needs change from time to time, so will your method of Bible study. You should always be alert to find the Bible version(s) best suited to the type of study you are doing. Bible study methods will be described in more detail in the last chapter. But for now, consider these basic methods:

1. *Devotional Bible Study.* This is undoubtedly the most popular type of

Bible study, and the most misunderstood! Some Christians think a "devotional" study is an unstructured, unplanned type of study that "sets the mood" for personal worship. They open the Bible almost at random, read a few verses, and then start to pray. This is Bible *reading,* but it is not Bible *study.* And it certainly is not devotional study.

In simplest terms, a *devotion* is a private act of worship. Your daily devotional time should include private prayer and meditation, and devotional Bible study can be a fruitful part of this. A devotional study also *applies* the Word to your personal life. It seeks a "crossing point" between Scripture and your current life concerns. Among other things, devotional Bible study should shed scriptural light on your problems and give you direction to resolve those problems. It is not an exhaustive or definitive method of study, but it should be systematic. (See Chapter 12 for more specific instructions.)

For the devotional method, you should select a Bible version that is clear and easy to understand. A dynamic-equivalence version, or a *paraphrase,** will be easier to read than a formal-equivalence version. Avoid a version that inserts alternate readings into the text, such as the Amplified Bible, because it is harder to follow.

Select a version that *accurately reflects the original meaning* of the Hebrew and Greek texts. If you can't read Hebrew or Greek, here are a couple of clues to help you: (a) Avoid a version that uses generous amounts of modern slang. A slang expression may convey a vivid idea to you, but it's not likely to be the full idea that the Bible writers had in mind. (b) Avoid a version that inserts the translator's explanation of a verse into the text itself. This amounts to a commentary on the Bible. The Good News Bible has many examples of this.

2. *Inductive Bible Study.* This is the second most popular type of Bible study. You can apply the inductive method to several different types of study—e.g., a word study, a topical study, or a theological study. It is most often used for studying an entire book of the Bible or an entire chapter.

When you use the inductive method, you begin by gathering and analyzing specific facts; then you draw general truths from them. For example, if you chose to do a word study of *salvation* you might look up several key Bible references to the word *salvation,* compare those references, and then draw conclusions about what the Bible teaches on this subject. This would be an *inductive* method of Bible word study. (See Chapter 12 for details about using this method for studying an entire book.)

For the inductive method, again choose a Bible version that is clear and accurate. In addition, choose one that *breaks poetry sections into stanzas and prose sections into paragraphs.* Why is this important? Because stanzas will show you the parallel lines of Hebrew poetry, so you can study the word meanings revealed by Hebrew *parallelism.** Paragraphs will help you find complete theme thoughts, especially in complex theological books such as Romans. The King James Version does not provide stanza and paragraph format, only verses.[9] The Living Bible breaks up prose into paragraphs, but it does not give stanzas of poetry. (Its loose translation of the Hebrew has destroyed the parallelism.) Other modern versions such as the New King James Version (NKJV), RSV, the New English Bible (NEB), the NASB, and the NIV provide both stanzas and paragraphs.

3. *Deductive or Synthetic Bible Study.* This is probably the least popular approach because it takes the most time. The deductive method may also be used in several types of Bible study—e.g., a book study, a historical study, or a biographical study.

When you use the deductive method, you survey the *whole* unit under consideration (a book, a history, a biography) to grasp the significance of the whole. Ask questions such as, "What lesson can we learn from this person's life?" or, "What was Paul's purpose in writing this letter?" and so on. Then you go back and examine the various parts of that unit (chapters, events, doctrines) in the light of the whole. (See Chapter 12 for further instructions.)

For deductive study, you again want a version that is clear and accurate. Stanza and paragraph divisions will help, but they are not crucial. However, be sure to select a version that *preserves the unity of the book you are studying.* Some modern versions, such as the RSV, set aside sections of Scripture that the translators did not find in the oldest manuscripts (e.g., see Acts 8:37, Acts 24:7, and 1 Pet. 5:2). Others rearrange entire chapters to follow new theories of how the Scriptures were written (see the Book of Revelation in the Anchor Bible). This scrambling of Scripture can be confusing in a deductive study.

These three basic methods of Bible study—devotional, inductive, and deductive—can help you achieve your particular Bible study goals. But be sure to select a Bible version that will help you meet that goal. In fact, your Bible study will be richer if you use more than one version.

A Word about the Apocrypha

Protestant readers may not be familiar with the term *Apocrypha.** The Apocrypha (sometimes called Deuterocanonicals) is a set of

---

9. The Geneva Bible of 1560 was the first complete English Bible to break up the Scriptures into chapters and verses to help readers find a passage more easily. But these divisions are arbitrary; they often divide the Scripture in mid-sentence or mid-thought. We continue to use them because they now have four hundred years of tradition behind them.

ancient books or additions written between the time of the Old Testament and the New. All but one of these books (Second Esdras) appeared in the Septuagint, the standard Greek version of the Old Testament that was compiled in the third century B.C. Jerome translated the Apocrypha for his Latin Vulgate version of the Bible, even though he denied the authority of these books in his introduction to the Vulgate. He inserted these books throughout the Old Testament, as the Septuagint translators had done.

Coverdale's English Bible (1535) brought the apocryphal books together and placed them between the Old and New Testaments. The King James Version (1611) followed this pattern.

However, the Puritans and other Protestant groups removed the Apocrypha from their English versions. Protestants excluded these books because they had been written at such a late date, because they were not considered part of the Old Testament by Jews themselves (Council of Jamnia, A.D. 90), and because they often contradicted the teachings of the rest of Scripture.[10] So the first edition of the King James Version included the Apocrypha, but later editions of the KJV omitted them.

Roman Catholics (who accept the Apocrypha as Scripture), Anglicans, and certain other Christians still read and use the Apocrypha. The NEB, certain editions of the RSV, and all Roman Catholic versions contain the Apocrypha. Commentaries on the Apocrypha are also available, and I will note some of them in Chapter 6.

ANNOTATED BIBLIOGRAPHY

Here is a list of some of the best current English versions of the Bible. (I have also included a few versions of the New Testament alone.) They are listed alphabetically by the title of the version, since the titles are more commonly known than the translators. When several different publishers produce a certain version, I have noted only the publisher and the date of the first edition. I have omitted older or less popular versions, such as the ASV or Moffatt's.

Amplified Bible. Grand Rapids: Zondervan, 1965.

While most modern versions put alternate readings in footnotes or italics at the end of each verse, the *Amplified* inserts alternates into the text itself. The Lockman Foundation compiled this version to give Bible students a quick way of tracing the various possible readings of each verse. It uses brackets, parentheses, and italics to insert the various readings. This tends to clutter the text, making the *Amplified Bible* confusing to use.

---

10. See Coverdale's comments about the Apocrypha, quoted by Bruce, HBE, pp. 60,61.

The Complete Bible: An American Translation, trans. J. M. Powis Smith, Edgar J. Goodspeed, et al. Chicago: Univ. of Chicago Press, 1939.

This is commonly called the "Goodspeed version" because Goodspeed's translation of the New Testament was issued first. Drs. Smith and Goodspeed (both of the University of Chicago) followed the *Masoretic Text** of the Old Testament, compared with other ancient texts; they used a critical edition of the Greek New Testament by Brooke F. Westcott and F.J.A. Hort. For this reason, they depart from the readings of the KJV at many points (since the KJV uses only the Masoretic Text of the O.T. and the *Textus Receptus** of the N.T.). This version includes the Apocrypha, translated by Dr. Goodspeed. Smith and Goodspeed have produced a readable dynamic-equivalence version that deftly avoids many of the dated idioms that flaw other versions.

Good News Bible. New York: American Bible Society, 1974.

Robert G. Bratcher prepared a translation of the New Testament into simple English for people who were learning English as a second language. The American Bible Society published this translation in 1966 with the title *Good News for Modern Man.* The Bible Society pressed on to make a translation of the full Bible. Again, their primary goal was to make a simple version for people who know English only as a second language. It is not as true to the Hebrew and Greek manuscripts as a study Bible should be, but it conveys the basic sense of the Scriptures. This translation is also called *Today's English Version* (TEV).

Jerusalem Bible. Garden City, N.Y.: Doubleday, 1966.

Beginning in 1948, the Ecole Biblique et Archeologique in Jerusalem published a massive new French translation of the Bible. The Roman Catholic scholars at this noted institute in Jerusalem used recent manuscript discoveries such as the Dead Sea Scrolls to produce volume after volume of the translation, with a full complement of scholarly notes.

In 1956, a one-volume edition appeared with abridged notes. The *Jerusalem Bible* is an English translation of that French work. More precisely, it is an English translation of the notes; the Scripture itself is a new translation from the Hebrew and Greek. The notes interpret Scripture in light of Roman Catholic dogma, but they do not use the Scriptures as "proof texts" for dogma. The *Jerusalem Bible* includes the Apocrypha, of course.

King James (Authorized) Version. London: Robert Barker, 1611.

This is the standard against which all other English versions of the Bible are measured. The KJV is still the version most widely used by Protestant Christians, even though "simplicity and clarity are not always its chief merits" (MTBS, 179). Many scholars reject the KJV because its translators used rather late copies of the Hebrew and Greek manuscripts, copies that may have been defective at some points. Yet most conservative scholars agree that "the differences [between the manuscripts used by the KJV translators and those used later] are not that great and the KJV is extremely faithful to the text then available" (STB, 50). The American Bible Society editions and one study edition of the KJV, *The Open Bible*

(Nashville: Thomas Nelson, 1976), explain or revise the more archaic words to aid the reader, since the English language has changed considerably from the time when the KJV was first published.

Living Bible. Wheaton: Tyndale, 1971.

This version is truly a paraphrase, since the work was done from the ASV, an existing English version of the Bible. The project started when Kenneth Taylor, an editor at Moody Press, began paraphrasing portions of the New Testament into simple English for his children. Eventually, Taylor founded Tyndale House Publishers to publish his work as he continued paraphrasing the Bible. *The Living Bible* is such a loose paraphrase that it often departs from the meaning of the original. Barber says, "This is not and should not be regarded as an accurate version of the Holy Scriptures. When seen as such, it is a deservedly famous work!" (ML, 49).

New American Bible. New York: P. J. Kennedy and Sons, 1970.

This is the climax of nearly three decades of work that began in 1941 when the Confraternity of Christian Doctrine sponsored a new translation of the New Testament by the Catholic Biblical Association of America. This Roman Catholic work was translated from the Latin Vulgate version. The Association then began work on the Old Testament, using the Hebrew Masoretic Text. Their Old Testament translation (in three volumes) came off the press by 1969. The translators then returned to the Greek manuscripts to revise their New Testament and combined it with the Old Testament to form this completely new version. (*Do not* confuse this with the New American Standard Bible, an evangelical Protestant work.) A few Protestant translators and editors collaborated on the NAB, but the text still bears a distinctly Roman Catholic flavor.

New American Standard Bible. Wheaton: Foundation Press, 1971.

Dissatisfied with the RSV's supposed revision of the ASV, the Lockman Foundation of La Habra, Calif., began work on this independent revision of the ASV in 1959. The NASB is more of a formal-equivalence version than the RSV; it is more careful to preserve the meaning of each word and phrase of the original text. But for that same reason, it does not read as easily as the RSV. Cyril J. Barber and other conservative reviewers praise the NASB as "perhaps the most accurate and reliable translation presently available" (ML, 49), but F. F. Bruce and more liberal reviewers believe the RSV is a better translation overall (HBE, 259).

New English Bible. Oxford and Cambridge: Oxford and Cambridge Univ. Presses, 1970.

The Church of England, the Church of Scotland, and most other major church groups in the British Isles jointly sponsored this translation project, which was intended to be an authoritative revision to use alongside the KJV. The translators used the Masoretic Text of the Old Testament and an *eclectic text** of the New Testament; they strived for a dynamic-equivalence version. They used British expressions that can be hard for American readers to grasp. For this reason, the NEB is seldom used in the United States. "The NEB's freedom in translation often becomes a paraphrase. It introduced many speculative changes which have not necessarily clarified the original message" (STB, 56).

New International Version. Grand Rapids: Zondervan, 1978.

The New York Bible Society sponsored this new translation, using newer critical editions of the Hebrew and Greek manuscripts. The Bible Society's translators tried to preserve the traditional sense of the text, while using the dynamic-equivalence approach, and reviewers seem quite happy with the result. Bruce says, "The language is dignified, readable and easily understood" (HBE, 266). The NIV seems to be an effective wedding of modern scholarship and articulate writing.

New King James Version. Nashville:Thomas Nelson, 1982.

Some versions made from the older (and supposedly better) Bible manuscripts have yielded rather unorthodox readings of Scripture. Disturbed by this trend, the editors at Nelson assembled a team of conservative Bible scholars to make the *New King James Version.* This team used a *majority text** reading of the ancient manuscripts for the Old Testament—i.e., they followed the readings given by *most* of the Bible manuscripts, whether they were the oldest manuscripts or not. (See section on "Critical Editions" in Chapter 10.) They used the *Textus Receptus* for the New Testament. Foster says, "It is an attempt to update the wording of the King James, but to retain its beauty and degree of literalness" (STB, 44).

The New Testament: A New Translation. 2 vols., trans. William Barclay. London: Collins, 1968, 1969.

Barclay says, "In making this translation I have had two aims in view. The first is to try to make the New Testament intelligible to the man who is not a technical scholar . . . . The second was to try to make a translation which did not need a commentary to explain it" (p. 5). He seems to have achieved the first goal, because this version is easy for any layman to understand. But to achieve the second goal, Barclay inserted his own commentary into the text. This can mislead the reader. (See Fig. 3.) Use this version only with a formal-equivalence version such as the NASB or NKJV to screen Barclay's ideas.

New Testament in Modern English, trans. J. B. Phillips. New York: Macmillan, 1958.

British writer J. B. Phillips began this work by making a new version of Paul's epistles for his soldier friends in World War II. C. S. Lewis then encouraged Phillips to translate the rest of the New Testament. "As I see it," Phillips said in his foreword, "the translator's function is to understand as fully and deeply as possible what the New Testament writers had to say and then, after a process of what might be called reflective digestion, to write it down in the language of the people of today" (p. viii). Phillips' version gives you one of the best dynamic-equivalence readings of the New Testament. A revised edition was published in 1973.

Revised Standard Version. Camden, N.J.: Thomas Nelson, 1952.

The National Council of the Churches of Christ ordered this revision of the ASV, using Hebrew and Greek manuscripts that were older than those available to the ASV translators in the late 1800s. However, the translators soon abandoned the idea of revising the ASV and set out to make an entirely new translation.

Although the RSV is easier to read than the ASV or the KJV, many conservative readers complain that it distorts the chief doctrines of the Bible. They charge that the RSV "waters down" the messianic prophecies of the Old Testament and obscures the connection of certain Old Testament passages quoted in the New Testament. Yet the RSV translators insist that they made their changes because of what they found in the ancient manuscripts, not because of their own theological views. See F. F. Bruce for a good discussion of this controversy (HBE, 194–203). Most evangelical reviewers cite this version, but few will recommend it. A revised edition was published in 1971.

2.
Annotated and Study Bibles

Nearly every edition of every version of the Bible has some sort of "helps" for the reader. They range all the way from *cross-references** (references to other Bible verses that will help you understand the meaning of a particular verse) to a full-fledged *commentary** (an explanation of what the verse means, according to the editor of the particular Bible edition in hand). Bibles with such study aids are called "annotated Bibles," "reference Bibles," "study Bibles," etc. For the sake of simplicity, we will group them into two main categories—*annotated Bibles** (with cross references and a few simple notations for *alternate readings** and *textual variants**) and *study Bibles** (with more elaborate notes, an introduction and outline of each Bible book, and articles to broaden your understanding of the Bible).

How "Helps" Were Added

Before we review the common features of annotated and study Bibles, it will be helpful to take a brief journey into history to see how we came to have so many kinds of Bible "helps."

The year is 1604. The place is Hampton Court, the residence of King James I of England. The king has assembled the leading churchmen of his realm to discuss the current state of affairs in the Church of England.

Puritan leader Dr. John Reynolds of Oxford states that dissent within the church might be calmed if all the people had a standard Bible translation. As it is, they may be using the Bishops' Bible, the Geneva Bible, Tyndale's translation, or several other versions that can be bought or smuggled into the country.

Richard Bancroft, Bishop of London, does not like the idea of a new translation. "If every man's humor were followed, there would be no end of translating," he says.

But the idea appeals to King James, who says, "I wish some special pains were taken for a uniform translation . . . to be read in the whole church, and none other."

Seeing that he is about to be overruled, Bishop Bancroft urges the king to ban any notes from the new translation, because it is the *margin notes** of the Geneva Bible which have been so unacceptable to the Anglican leaders. James readily agrees and even refers to the Geneva Bible notes as "partial, untrue, seditious, and savoring too much of dangerous and traitorous conceits."

He points out, for example, the Geneva Bible's note on Exodus 1:19, which says that the Hebrew midwives had a right to disobey the Egyptian king. Then he turns to 2 Chronicles 15:19, where the Geneva Bible notes that King Asa's idolatrous mother should have been executed for her beliefs. (King James surely felt the barb of that comment, since his own mother had been executed for her zealous Roman Catholic beliefs.)[1] So the stipulation that no marginal notes should be added to the new version was clear.

Now we step forward in time to the year 1611, and we enter the London shop of Robert Barker, King James' royal printer. Bound copies of the massive new Bible are stacked on a table to dry. In one corner, an apprentice leafs through one of the finished volumes and his eyes scan the printed pages, each having two columns of Scripture—and a small marginal column of notes!

How can this be?

If we peer over the apprentice's shoulder as he comes to the preface of the book, we find the answer. The preface says that the translators found it necessary to add marginal notes for "wordes and sentences" that seemed to present "difficultie and doubtfulnesse" to the reader.[2] As successive editions of the KJV came from the press, the editors and printers would add more "helps" to the margin: cross-references, alternate readings, variant spellings, even an interpretative comment now and then (despite King James' distaste for them).

Taking another step forward in time to 1701, we see the royal printer's assistants rearrange their Bible printing plates to add yet another feature—a *chronology.* * They are inserting a date for every major event described in the Bible, beginning with the Creation (to which they give a date of 4004 B.C.).

Most of these dates come from a set of books entitled *Annales Veteris et Novi Testamenti,* by Archbishop James Ussher.[3] The archbishop has computed these dates by taking Christ's birth as the year "O" and working backwards, according to the number of years that the Old Testament

1. F. F. Bruce, ed., *History of the Bible in English,* 3rd ed. (New York: Oxford Univ. Press, 1978), pp. 96, 97.

2. Quoted by Frederick W. Danker, *Multipurpose Tools for Bible Study,* 2nd ed. (St. Louis: Concordia, 1966), p. 178.

3. Like most scholarly works of that day, its title is in Latin. It literally means, *Annals of the Old and New Testaments.*

gives for each event of history (e.g., the length of a person's life, the length of Israel's Captivity). The chronology is fascinating. And since there is no copyright law in eighteenth-century Europe, other printers soon pick up the chronology for their own Bible editions.

There are several other stops we might make on this trip through the history of "helps," but for brevity's sake we will move ahead to the summer of 1901. The place is the northern shore of Long Island, New York. Dr. Cyrus I. Scofield, pastor of the Congregational Church at East Northfield, Massachusetts, and Arno C. Gaebelein, editor of a religious paper entitled *Our Hope,* are taking a stroll along the shore this evening. It is a restful break from the week-long Bible conference that Dr. Scofield is holding at a nearby park in Sea Cliff, Long Island. Dr. Scofield has been teaching the *dispensational** view of Bible history, focusing on the return of Christ and His *millennial** reign. Mr. Gaebelein describes the scene for us.

> It was a beautiful night. Our walk along the shore of the Sound lasted until midnight. For the first time he mentioned the plan of producing a Reference Bible, and outlined the method he had in mind. He said he had thought of it for many years and had spoken to others about it, but had not received much encouragement. . . . He expressed the hope that the new beginning . . . in Sea Cliff might open the way to bring about the publication of such a Bible with references and copious footnotes.[4]

This new reference Bible will focus attention on the prophetic teachings of Scripture; it will interpret the full sweep of Bible history, from Creation to Final Consummation, in light of the dispensational formula. Gaebelein and Scofield soon persuade several like-minded men to finance the project. They appoint seven consulting editors to help with the work. And in 1903, Dr. Scofield resigns from the East Northfield pastorate to devote more time to the task.

Finally, in 1909, the *Scofield Reference Bible* is published by Oxford University Press in New York City. It is the first modern reference Bible, and it sets up a standard of scholarship that all subsequent reference Bibles must follow. In his preface to the book, Dr. Scofield writes:

> . . . What the present book does is to present the great subjects concerning which God has revealed the future, and to assemble and analyze that revelation so that any reader of the book will find himself fully introduced to these great and important themes.

---

4. Arno C. Gaebelein, *The History of the Scofield Reference Bible* (New York: Loizeaux Brothers, 1943), p. 47.

The final effect . . . is to leave the mind overwhelmingly impressed with the divine origin and authorship of these ancient oracles. Writing in widely separated ages, under wholly different circumstances, . . . the production of one continuous, harmoniously developed testimony is proof unanswerable that, although He employed many penmen, God alone is the Author of the prophetic testimony.[5]

If we had walked into a New York City bookstore late that year to compare Scofield's reference Bible with the other Bibles then available, we would have been impressed by the contrast. Other Bibles usually contained a narrow column of cross-references, alternate readings, and a chronology on each page. The *Scofield Reference Bible* had that material in *center column notes**; but it also had a lengthy introduction to each book of the Bible, *footnotes** explaining difficult passages, an index to all of the introductions and footnotes, an index of proper names, an index of Bible subjects, a concordance, and a set of Bible maps.

Dr. Scofield and his colleagues had made the Bible a textbook for study. They had given the Bible reader a set of tools for delving into the great themes of Bible teaching, even if he did not agree with their interpretation of that teaching.

By every measure, the *Scofield Reference Bible* formed a watershed in Bible publishing; it raised the Bible buyer's expectations to a much higher plane. And it is fair to say that every full-fledged study Bible published since then has had to provide more "helps" for the reader, in light of Dr. Scofield's achievement.

What Should We Expect?

Bible publishers are prone to make impressive claims for the "helps" in the new editions they bring out. They customarily get endorsements (signed recommendations) from leading pastors and evangelists to support their claims for a particular Bible. Often we find the same people stating that two different Bibles are "the best" in some respect. A well-known evangelical writer recently said that a particular study Bible was "like a Bible correspondence school course." Another said that he could preach from a certain study Bible without any prior study, because that particular edition "lays it (the teaching of a passage) all out for me." With such competing claims, it's hard for the layman to know what study Bible is best for him.

What features should we expect to find in a reference Bible? That depends on whether the Bible is an annotated Bible or a study Bible.

---

5. Ibid., p. 55.

Annotated Bibles

Although the annotated Bible gives only the most simple notes to the text, it should give us a basic apparatus for understanding the Scripture. We should expect an annotated Bible to contain:

1. *Alternate Readings*—The editors should provide any important alternative way of reading a certain verse. This might be: (a) a different *translation* of the verse, if its meaning is obscure; (b) a different *reading* of the verse—i.e., something added or omitted in certain Bible manuscripts; or (c) a different *interpretation* of the verse—i.e., different from what the text literally says. See Figure 4 (p. 38) for examples.

2. *Cross-references*—We should expect to find frequent references to other Bible verses about the same topic. Some Bible editors will refer us to other verses that contain the same key word used in a different way. But this concordance-type cross-reference will not aid our study as much as a topical reference does. See Figure 5 (p. 40) for examples of useful cross-references.

3. *Book Introductions*—Even the simplest type of reference Bible should give us some introduction to each book of the Bible. It should tell something about the contents of the book, who wrote it, and what significance it has for modern readers. Some annotated Bibles group these introductions in a separate article, rather than placing them at the start of each book. See Figure 6 (p. 42) for an excerpt from a typical introduction.

4. *A Selective Concordance*—This feature is included at the back of the Bible. The concordance is a list of important words that occur in Scripture, arranged in alphabetical order, with references to the verses that contain each word. An *exhaustive concordance* would list all of the words of the Bible and all of the verses that contain each word, but a *selective concordance* will list only the most important words of Scripture (perhaps a few hundred) and will show only a few verses that contain each word. (An exhaustive concordance is too big to include in any reference Bible, so when we refer to the concordance in the back of a Bible we can safely assume it is a selective concordance.) See Chapter 5 for instructions on how to use a concordance.

Although some Bibles contain a chronology of Bible events, we should not expect to find one in every reference Bible. Bible scholars now know that we cannot fix dates for most Bible events, even using Archbishop Ussher's simple method.

Ussher's chronology assumed that the Bible gives all of its dates in consecutive order, without any overlapping. But other historical records from the same period do not follow this pattern. They leave gaps in family records; they drop out events that seemed less important; they fail to mention overlaps in people's lives.

Figure 4—Alternate Readings
From the New International Version

Type of Alternate	Scripture Passage	Footnote
Different Translation	Jesus replied, "Friend, do what you came for" (Matt. 26:50).	Or, *"Friend, why have you come?"*
	"You believe at last!" Jesus answered (John 16:31).	Or, *"Do you now believe?"*

These two examples show that even a short Greek phrase can be very difficult to translate. When the translators have some doubt about the exact meaning, they put the most likely translation in the Scripture passage itself and give an alternate translation in a note.

Type of Alternate	Scripture Passage	Footnote
Different Reading (from an ancient manuscript)	But Jesus turned and rebuked them, (Luke 9:55).	Some MSS add, *And he said, "You do not w what kind of spirit you are of, for the Son of Man did not come to destroy men's lives, but to save them."*
	He appointed twelve—designating them apostles—that they might be with him and that he might send them out to preach (Mark 3:14).	Some MSS omit, *designating them apostles.*

The many ancient manuscripts of the Bible often disagree with one another. When they do, a translator will follow the reading considered most reliable, but then give a footnote to show an alternate found in some of the ancient manuscripts. (Note: *MSS* is a symbol for "manuscripts.")

Type of Alternate	Scripture Passage	Footnote
Different Interpretation (i.e., other than what the verse literally says).	While Jesus was in one of the towns, a man came along who was covered with leprosy ... (Luke 5:12).	The Greek word probably designated other related diseases also.
	A second time they summoned the man who had been blind. "Give glory to God," they said ... (John 9:24).	A solemn charge to tell the truth (see Joshua 7:19).

Here are examples of verses that do not give the full impact of what is being said, just by a literal reading. Rather than "padding" the text with a further explanation, the translators provide the explanation in a footnote.

Donald J. Wiseman notes that several archaeological finds do not jibe with Ussher's dates.[6] For example, the Flood evidence unearthed by Sir Leonard Woolley at Ur is older than Ussher's Flood date of 2300 B.C., and artifacts from ancient sites such as Jericho are much older than Ussher's Creation date of 4004 B.C.

So if we simply add or subtract the dates given in the Bible (which Ussher did), we will not get a reliable set of calendar dates. And while archaeologists use some ingenious methods to assign dates to the artifacts they find, these methods are not precise enough to give us reliable calendar dates, either. Most Bibles no longer carry Ussher's chronology, and they provide nothing else to replace it.

Study Bibles

These Bible editions offer more in-depth interpretative notes, along with articles, tables, and charts that help us understand the Scriptures as we have them today. In addition to the four features that we should expect in an annotated Bible, a good study Bible will also contain the following:

1. *In-Depth Introductions*—The study Bible should give us an introduction to each book of the Bible. It should tell us not only the theme of the book but also (a) the author, (b) the approximate date it was written, (c) the place and occasion of its writing, and (d) to whom the book may have been addressed.

2. *Outlines of the Books*—The study Bible should sketch the major themes of each book and show in outline form how each passage relates to the major themes. This is especially important for books of complicated structure, such as Paul's epistles.

3. *Interpretative Notes*—The study Bible should provide some notes about the significance of certain passages. It need not give us a full-fledged commentary on the Scriptures, dissecting every verse. But it should emphasize the meaning of key verses to help us comprehend the central message.

4. *An Article on Archaeology*—Over the past 150 years, the science of archaeology has transformed our understanding of the Bible. The discoveries of archaeologists have an impact on what Bible editors say in their introductions and interpretative notes; so the editors should provide at least one supplemental article to explain how archaeology has influenced their work.

5. *An Article on Bible Texts and Transmission*—By Bible *texts,* we mean the ancient Hebrew and Greek texts of Scripture. By *transmission,*

---

6. Donald J. Wiseman, "The Chronology of the Bible," *The Holman Study Bible* (Philadelphia: A. J. Holman, 1962), p. 1215.

Figure 5—Useful Cross References
From The Open Bible: New American Standard Version

Scripture Passage	Cross-Reference
Better is a poor man who walks in his integrity than he who is perverse in speech and is a fool (Prov. 19:1).	But as for me, I shall walk in my integrity; Redeem me, and be gracious to me (Psa. 26:11).
	He who walks in his uprightness fears the LORD, But he who is crooked in his ways despises Him (Prov. 14:2).
	A righteous man who walks in his integrity—How blessed are his sons after him (Prov. 20:7).

These cross-reeference notes take us to three passages on the same topic as the key passage—i.e., the topic of integrity. Not all of these verses contain the word *integrity.* (Prov. 14:2 calls it "uprightness.") Not all of them use the same Hebrew word ("integrity" = *tom*; "uprightness" = *yosher*). Yet they all address the same issue, and so they are related.

Scripture Passage	Cross-Reference
And He said, "What have you done? The voice of your brother's blood is crying to Me from the ground" (Gen. 4:10).	And to Jesus, the mediator of a new covenant, and to the sprinkled blood, which speaks better than the blood of Abel (Heb. 12:24).
	And when He broke the fifth seal, I saw underneath the altar the souls of those who had been slain because of the word of God, and because of the testimony which they had maintained; and they cried out with a loud voice, saying, "How long, O Lord, holy and true, wilt Thou refrain from judging and avenging our blood on those who dwell on the earth?" (Rev. 6:9,10).

These two cross-references carry us from an Old Testament event to the New Testament consequences of that event. We might also follow the Old Testament problem (sin) to the New Testament consequences (redemption or punishment) by using a simple concordance to trace a key word like *blood;* but it would be a tedious task. The same would be true if we used a topical Bible; we would need to sort through dozens of unrelated verses on *blood* before finding this connection. But the Bible editors make the connection for us.

Scripture Passage	Cross-Reference
And Jesus uttered a loud cry, and breathed His last (Mark 15:37).	And Jesus cried out again with a loud voice, and yielded up *His* spirit (Matt. 27:50). And Jesus, crying out with a loud voice, said, "Father into Thy hands I commit My spirit." And having said this, He breathed His last (Luke 23:46).

Here is yet another type of cross-reference, called a "Gospel parallel." The four Gospels (Matthew, Mark, Luke, and John) often report an incident or teaching from Jesus' life in very similar terms. In fact, many scholars think Matthew and Luke consulted Mark's Gospel as they wrote their report, so they sometimes borrowed his wording. When we put these parallel passages side by side, we see the similarities; but we also notice some striking differences. For example, these cross-references show that if Matthew and Luke did consult Mark's Gospel, they added some further details. And Luke adds a quotation of Jesus—something only an eyewitness could provide; either Luke saw the crucifixion or he consulted someone who did.

(NOTE: In your Bible you will not find cross-reference passages printed in full, as we have done here. They will appear simply as references—e.g., "Matt. 27:50; Luke 23:46"—for you to look up for yourself.)

we mean the way the ancient texts were copied and edited as scribes handed them down ("transmitted") them to us. Knowing about this process helps us understand why we have so many textual variants.

6. *A Chart of Weights, Measures, and Money*—The people who lived in Bible times did not use the *meter,* the *kilometer,* the *hour,* the *dollar,* or other standards of measurement that are in use today. They used units such as the *ephah,* the *shekel,* and the *league.* Bible editors should provide charts to translate these foreign units of measurement into terms we can understand.[7]

7. *A Topical Index*—This feature differs from a concordance in that the concordance gives only the words that appear in the Scriptures, while the topical index lists general topics we might wish to study. The actual word for that topic may not even appear in the Scriptures. For example, the word *abortion* does not appear in the KJV, but the topic is discussed; so a topical index to the KJV might list the term *abortion* with a few key

---

7. Sometimes a Bible version will try to make this conversion for us, as when the *Living Bible* inserts modern money equivalents into the Parable of the Ungrateful Servant (Matt. 18:24,28). The problem with this approach is that our monetary values change; so inflation makes the comment obsolete in just a few years. It's easier for the publisher to update the conversion charts, rather than revise the Scripture each time the book is reprinted, so the charts are likely to be more reliable.

**Figure 6—Book Introduction
From an Annotated Bible: Job**

THE BOOK OF JOB

The book of Job does not attempt to explain the mystery of suffering or to "justify the ways of God with men." It aims at probing the depths of faith in spite of suffering. The ancient folktale of a patient Job (1.1–2.13; 42.7–17; Jas. 5.11) circulated orally among oriental sages in the second millennium B.C. and was probably written down in Hebrew at the time of David and Solomon or a century later (about 1000–800 B.C.). An anonymous poet of the sixth or fifth century B.C. used it as a setting for the discussion between an impatient Job and his three friends (3.1–31.40) and the Lord's discourses from the whirlwind (38.1–42.6). A later poet contributed Elihu's speeches (32.1–37.24).

The storyteller asked, "Does [man] fear God for nought?" (1.9). The poet echoed the question, "What is the Almighty, that we should serve him? And what profit do we get if we pray to him?" (21.15). Unlike the hero of the folktale who is rewarded materially for his virtues, the Job of the poem demands justice, and his final challenge shows that he regards religion and morality as man's claim for happiness (29.1–31.40). Job renounces his defiance only after the Lord asks, "Will you condemn me that you may be justified?" (40.8). Job is satisfied without self-vindication by an experience of immediate communion with God, not unlike that of the great prophets: "Now my eye sees thee" (42.5).

In the poetic language of the book, God is at work in the universe, even "to bring rain on a land where no man is" (38.26), and he is aware of evil (personified by the monsters Behemoth and Leviathan, 40.15–41.34). At the same time, he cares for Job so fully that he reveals himself personally to him and shares with him the vision of his cosmic responsibilities. A God who confesses his burdens to man is a God who is profoundly involved in the destiny of man. He is not an impassive force. In the presence of holiness and creative love, virtuous man surrenders his pride in adoration. In his own way the poet conveyed a view of sin which transcends morality, the awareness of which is possible only in the context of faith.

THERE WAS A MAN IN THE LAND OF Uz, whose name was Job; and that man was blameless and upright, one who feared God, and turned away from evil. ² There were born to him seven sons and three daughters. ³ He had seven thousand sheep, three thousand camels, five hundred yoke of oxen, and five hundred she-asses, and very many servants; so that this man was the greatest of all the people of the east. ⁴ His sons used to go and hold a feast in the house of each on his day; and they would send and invite their three sisters to eat and drink with them. all; for Job said, "It may be that my sons have sinned, and cursed God in their hearts." Thus Job did continually.

6 Now there was a day when the sons of God came to present themselves before the LORD, and Satanᵃ also came among them. ⁷ The LORD said to Satan, "Whence have you come?" Satan answered the LORD, "From going to and fro on the earth, and from walking up and down on it." ⁸ And the LORD said to Satan, "Have you considered my servant Job, that there is none like him on the earth, a blameless and upright man, who fears God and turns

Source: Herbert G. May and Bruce M. Metzger, eds., *The New Oxford Annotated Bible* (New York: Oxford Univ. Press, 1973), p. 613.

42

verses on that topic. The same might be true of *depravity, fanaticism, incarnation,* and many other topics of interest. Some study Bibles call this feature a "cyclopedic index" or an "encyclopedic index" because they also provide a brief description or definition of each topic.

8. *An Index of Proper Names*—Since most selective concordances do not include the names of Bible people, we cannot use them to find the sections of Scripture that pertain to a certain person. For this purpose we need an index of names—an alphabetical list with one or more Scripture references for each name. Some Bible editors give a combined listing of people's names and place names, while other editors give only one or the other. Some give all the proper names, while others give only a selected list. Some publish this index as a separate section, and others incorporate it into their topical index. We may need to examine the Bible carefully to find this feature, but it is a valuable thing to have.

Each study Bible has its own unique features which often make strong selling points for that particular edition. These things might lead a person to choose one study Bible over the rest. But the eight features listed above are basic tools that should be found in any study Bible.

Buying a Reference Bible

Chapter 4 contains some guidelines for buying Bibles of any kind, but let me mention here some special advice for shopping for a reference Bible.

1. *Notice the theological stance of the editor(s).* Some study Bibles were edited by a committee of scholars, from a broad range of theological backgrounds (e.g., *The Holman Study Bible* and *The New Oxford Annotated Bible*). This helps to insure that they will not use the study Bible as a soapbox for a particular set of doctrines, but it also means that the editors may equivocate on certain touchy issues such as the Virgin Birth or the divine inspiration of Scripture to satisfy the majority on their committee.

On the other end of the spectrum are study Bibles edited by one scholar or by a few scholars from the same school of thought (e.g., *The Scofield Reference Bible* and *Walter Martin's Cult Reference Bible*). Their position on certain issues of theology will be clear, and if you happen to agree with that point of view you will be quite happy with such a book. But this type of study Bible may not suggest other points of view, and it may pass over some important issues.

Generally, it's better to select a study Bible that is edited by a committee of scholars from a fairly wide spectrum of theological backgrounds—who agree on the basic tenets of Christian doctrine. *The Open Bible* and *The*

Ryrie Study Bible are two conservative, evangelical study Bibles of this type.

2. *More "helps" do not necessarily make a better Bible.* A new Christian may eagerly compare several study Bibles at the bookstore counter, then choose to buy the one with the most sophisticated study apparatus because he thinks he needs all the "helps" he can get. Then he tries to use the Bible and is disappointed. The "helps" are so complicated and clumsy to use that the budding Bible student gets frustrated, puts the Bible on the shelf, and forgets it. My wife once received such a study Bible as a gift. It has an elaborate color-coded system of cross references—beautiful to look at but exasperating to use. Usually, a few easy-to-use aids will help our Bible study more than an elaborate system of aids.

3. *Consider the version itself as a study aid.* We saw in Chapter 1 that Bible translators have given us many English versions in an effort to render the Scriptures in clear, contemporary terms. So when we compare study Bibles, we should look at the text itself as well as the notes and other "helps" that grow out of the text. Evaluate the version in light of the kind of study you plan to do. (Remember the criteria for selecting versions given in Chapter 1.)

How to Use "Helps"

Let's assume that you have chosen an annotated or study Bible. How should you use it, to get the most from its system of "helps"?

Since each Bible has its own unique features, take time to read the publisher's preface and/or introduction. The editor(s) will describe the special features of this book and tell why they were included. You may find suggestions here for a method of study, drawing on each of the aids that are available. Sometimes a Bible publisher will furnish a separate booklet (e.g., *The Open Bible Owner's Guide)* to describe these features in fuller detail and to explain how you can use them all. At any rate, pay careful attention to the "front matter" in your reference Bible; it will get you started on the right foot.

Suggestions for using some of the specific features are listed below:

1. *Alternate Readings*—As explained earlier, an alternate reading in the margin or footnotes shows a different translation, a different reading (from certain ancient manuscripts), or a different interpretation of the verse. Figure 4 shows some examples of alternate readings from the NIV.

Be sure to check these notes so you will get the full impact of each passage. Reread the verse, inserting or deleting the material that you find in the alternate readings. See how the alternates affect the meaning of the verse. (It's best to do this before following the cross-references.)

2. *Cross-references*—A cross-reference note refers us to another pas-

sage of Scripture that has the same key word or deals with the same topic as the passage at hand. Figure 5 gives some examples, showing the sorts of information that cross-references may provide.

Take time to look up cross-references, especially when you are making an inductive Bible study. They may fill in some crucial gaps of information about the subject under consideration.

3. *Book Introductions*—When making a deductive Bible study (i.e., trying to discern the overall content of a Bible book or a Bible character's life), we can check our conclusions by reading the study Bible's introduction to the Bible book that is involved. The introduction is like the printed program for a drama; it alerts us to the writer's purpose, the themes, and the significance of some secondary themes within the works (like subplots on the stage). The book outlines (see below) are also vital tools for deductive study; they describe the biblical "plot" in even more detail.

Inductive Bible study, which is gaining popularity among neighborhood Bible study groups, does not seem to take much account of these introductions. Inductive study is a bit like stringing pearls: the reader examines one bit of information after another, adding them to a "string" of understanding about the topic of interest. So the attention is focused on discrete bits of data—a verse here, a phrase there—looking for similarities that may tie together insights found scattered throughout the Word. The inductive student seldom consults a book introduction, yet the introduction may cast useful light on the work.

Consider the man who has been chosen to give the baccalaureate address for a graduating college class. He decides to do an inductive study on *wisdom* and, following his Bible's cross-references, he comes to Ecclesiastes 2:15,16:

> Then said I in my heart, As it happeneth to the fool, so it happeneth even to me; and why was I then more wise? Then I said in my heart, that this also is vanity. For there is no remembrance of the wise more than of the fool for ever; seeing that which now is in the days to come shall all be forgotten. And how dieth the wise man? as the fool.

That's not a very encouraging word for young men and women who have worked hard to attain knowledge and develop wisdom! The speaker examines the surrounding verses for some explanation of this passage, but finds no help. So he turns back to his Bible's introduction to the Book of Ecclesiastes and finds a statement like this:

> This is the book of man "under the sun," reasoning about life; it is the best man can do, with the knowledge that there is a holy God, and that He will bring everything into judgment . . . [The book's] conclusions are just in de-

claring it "vanity," in view of judgment, to devote life to earthly things . . . but the "conclusion" (12:13) is legal, the best that man apart from redemption can do, and does not anticipate the Gospel. . . .[8]

This puts the troublesome verses in better perspective. With this view of the book's general thrust, the inductive student can better grasp the meaning of a particular passage. It may even become the choicest "pearl" in his inductive strand, because of what he learns from the study Bible's introduction!

4. *Book Outlines.*—Use these outlines especially when engaged in a deductive study; they clearly display the themes of the book or the key events of a character's life, giving you an overview of the subject under study.

When studying a book that is theologically complex (e.g., Rom. or 1 Cor.), be sure to compare the outline at hand with another from a study Bible prepared by editors of a different theological persuasion. Such a comparison may reveal two different perspectives on the message of the book. (See Fig. 7.)

5. *Interpretative Notes*—These notes may give some helpful insights, but they often present the editors' theological stance as well. They may discuss the nuances of certain words, the cultural setting of the passage, how the original audience may have understood what is being said, and so on. But when the interpretative notes begin to discuss "hidden meanings" or to make dogmatic pronouncements, they have become a commentary on the text.

In any case, remember that these notes are merely the editors' interpretations of Scripture; they are not Scripture itself. So do not assume that an interpretative note is the final, infallible word on a given passage.

6. *Supplemental Aids.* The other features listed earlier—such as the article on archaeology or the table of weights and measures—will not be vital to your Bible study every time you open the Word. Refer to them only when you need them.

For example, if the editors' introduction to Genesis raises a question in your mind about how the Jews preserved this great book through so many centuries, turn to your study Bible's article on Bible texts and their transmission. Or if you wonder whether archaeologists have found evidence of the miraculous victory won by Joshua's armies at Jericho (Joshua 6), turn to your study Bible's article on archaeology. Perhaps you are reading about Peter's finding a four-drachma coin in the mouth of a fish (Matt. 17:24-27), and you wonder how much that coin would be worth today. Look at your study Bible's table of monetary values for the answer.

---

8. C. I. Scofield, ed., *The Scofield Reference Bible* (New York: Oxford Univ. Press, 1945), p. 696.

Figure 7—Study Bible Outlines: Romans

The Scofield Reference Bible

The Epistle, exclusive of the introduction (1.1–17), is in seven parts:

I. The whole world guilty before God, 1.18–3.20.

II. Justification through the righteousness of God by faith
The Gospel remedy for guilt, 3.21–5.11.

III. Crucifixion with Christ
The resurrection life of Christ, and the walk in the Spirit
The Gospel provision for inherent sin, 5.12–8.13.

IV. The full result in blessing of the Gospel, 8.14–39.

V. Parenthesis: The Gospel does not abolish the covenant
promises to Israel, 9.1–11.36.

VI. Christian life and service, 12.1–15.33.

VII. The outflow of Christian love, 16.1–27.

Source: C. I. Scofield, ed., *The Scofield Reference Bible*
(New York: Oxford Univ. Press, 1945), p. 1191.

The Christian Brotherhood Hour Study Edition

I.	Introduction	1:1–17
II.	The Universal Need for Righteousness	1:18–3:20
III.	The Character of God's Kind of Righteousness	3:21–4:25
IV.	The Results of God's Kind of Righteousness	5:1–8:39
	1. Justification and peace with God	5:1–21
	2. Freedom from the dominion of sin	6:1–23
	3. A new relation to law	7:1–25
	4. Participation in the life of the Spirit	8:1–39
V.	The Problem of Jewish Unbelief	9:1–11:36
VI.	The Practical Application of Righteousness	12:1–15:13
VII.	Resumé of Paul's Previous Ministry and Future Intentions	15:14–33
VIII.	Conclusion	16:1–27

Source: James E. Massey, ed., *The Christian Brotherhood
Hour Study Edition* (Nashville: Thomas Nelson,
1979), p. 32.

The differences between these two outlines may not be apparent at first. But if you look more closely, you will see some disagreements because of the editors' different theological views: The first is dispensational and the second is not; while Dr. Scofield says that "the Gospel does not abolish the covenant promises to Israel," Dr. Massey gives this section a less dogmatic title. The second espouses Wesleyan holiness doctrine and the first does not; while Dr. Massey says our new life in Christ brings "freedom from the dominion of sin," Dr. Scofield simply feels that the Gospel makes "provision for inherent sin." Be alert to these doctrinal viewpoints by comparing outlines in two or more study Bibles. (Note: I rearranged Scofield's outline into a normal outline pattern to make the comparison easier.)

These supplemental aids can help to bring the Scriptures to life. Use these aids and the other features of your reference Bible as tools to uncover what God's Word is saying to you today.

ANNOTATED BIBLIOGRAPHY

The annotated and study Bibles listed below are arranged in order—alphabetically by the editor's surname, by title if the editor's name is not given. Nearly all of these books are still under copyright protection, so they have not been reprinted by other publishers, as some Bible versions have been. The phrase "red-letter edition" means that the words of Christ are printed in red.

Criswell, W. A., ed. *The Criswell Study Bible*. Nashville: Thomas Nelson, 1979.
    Of all the study Bibles based on the KJV, this one seems most useful for the layman. The notes do not delve into complex theological issues; instead, they clarify the obscure passages and apply the Scriptures to everyday concerns. It is a very practical book. *The Criswell Study Bible* gives a detailed introduction and outline for each book, subheadings for major sections of the text, and cross-references for nearly every verse. The supplemental study aids include a six-page chart of the prophecies of Christ, a five-page table of Bible weights and measures, a glossary that explains major Bible concepts and doctrines, and a subject index to major notes—an index that tells you where in this Bible's footnotes you will find major discussions of doctrinal and practical issues. This study Bible gives a thoroughly conservative (some would say "fundamentalist") interpretation of Scripture.

Dake, F. J., ed. *Dake's Annotated Reference Bible*. Lawrenceville, Ga.: Dake Bible Sales, 1963.
    This book is much more than an "annotated Bible"; its lengthy margin notes give a veritable commentary on the text. The editor inserts an outline into the text through the use of frequent subheadings, and he gives numerous cross-references. The Cyclopedic Index at the back of the book is another handy feature. This is a monumental work for one man. Unfortunately, the notes are printed in small type, making them hard to read, and the author's comments can be a bit fanciful —especially with regard to prophecy. *Dake's Annotated Reference Bible* uses the KJV.

Good News Bible: Catholic Study Edition. Nashville: Thomas Nelson, 1979.
    Probably the first study edition of the Good News Bible, this Roman Catholic work has only minimal study aids. The introductions to the books are sketchy; the footnotes are sparse; there are relatively few subheadings to show the themes of the text. The editors have grouped the apocryphal books together between the Testaments, which is not the traditional Catholic order. Despite these weaknesses, the work is a first in supplying study aids for the TEV and in offering Catholic readers a simple, easy-to-use reference Bible.

Lindsell, Harold, ed. *The Lindsell Study Bible.* Wheaton: Tyndale, 1980.

Conservative evangelical writer Harold Lindsell (former editor of *Christianity Today* magazine and author of the controversial book *The Battle for the Bible*) compiled this study edition of the *Living Bible*. In his introductory comment, Dr. Lindsell declares that its study notes are "written from the standpoint of conservative theological scholarship" (p. xiv), and the book fulfills that promise. In the introduction to each book of the Bible, Dr. Lindsell sets up a dialogue between liberal and conservative views on matters of authorship, date, and so on.

The Master Study Bible. Nashville: Holman, 1981.

This bulky NASB study Bible has over one thousand pages of study aids, including a Bible encyclopedia, a concordance, and Gospel parallels compiled by A. T. Robertson. It offers several helpful articles from noted writers of the past, such as "How to Study the Bible," by R. A. Torrey and "The Languages of the Bible," by William F. Albright. The introduction and outline of each book are also helpful. This volume should be quite popular in evangelical circles as the NASB becomes more widely accepted. Red-letter edition.

May, Herbert G., and Bruce M. Metzger, eds. *The New Oxford Annotated Bible.* New York: Oxford Univ. Press, 1973.

The editors aptly call this an "annotated Bible," rather than a study Bible, because they have kept the interpretative notes and other study aids to a minimum. They use the revised (1971) edition of the RSV and the RSV Apocrypha. They provide a brief introduction to each book of the Bible, commenting on its author, title, date, contents, and literary genre. They usually reflect a liberal view of *literary criticism** in these introductions (e.g., see the introductions to Genesis, Isaiah, and the epistles of Peter). The editors also follow the practice (used in standard RSV editions) of putting certain portions of Scripture in small italic footnotes because they doubt the authenticity of these passages (e.g., Acts 8:37 and 1 Pet. 5:2). *The New Oxford Annotated Bible* groups the books of the Apocrypha at the end of the Bible. The editors use brief footnotes to give alternate readings, cross-references, and an outline of the contents. This annotated Bible carries the *nihil obstat** and *imprimatur** of the Roman Catholic Church.

Nave, Orville J., and Anna Semans Nave. *Nave's Study Bible.* Wheaton: Creation House, 1977.[9]

This is one of the oldest study Bibles still in print. Developed in the late 1800s, it uses the KJV text with alternate readings from the RV. *Nave's Study Bible* has generous cross-references in the margin and links many Old Testament messianic prophecies with their fulfillment in the New Testament. Nave's footnotes are very brief; the Dictionary-Concordance is keyed to refer back to the footnotes. Nave includes the Ussher chronology, but the publishers have inserted question marks after many of the dates. Although this work is a classic, it is too out-of-date to be of much use.

---

9. Also available from (Grand Rapids, Mich.: Baker, 1979) and (Nashville: Broadman, 1978).

The Open Bible. Nashville: Thomas Nelson, 1978.

Compiled by a team of evangelical scholars, this reference Bible has two strong study features: a Biblical Cyclopedic Index at the *front* of the Bible, and a series of Christian Life Study Outlines in the footnotes of the N.T. The Cyclopedic Index lists over eight thousand biblical subjects including names, events, and doctrines, giving a brief definition or explanation of each one and a list of Scripture references keyed to page numbers in *The Open Bible*. The Christian Life Study Outlines, compiled by Dr. Porter L. Barrington, are like a miniature course in theology. They are presented as a unit at the beginning of the New Testament, and then repeated as fifteen separate study lessons in footnote form. *The Open Bible* is available with the KJV or NASB; the KJV *Open Bible* updates some of the version's more archaic words. Red-letter edition.

Ryrie, Charles C., ed. *The Ryrie Study Bible*. Chicago: Moody, 1979.

Dr. Ryrie of Dallas Theological Seminary takes a solidly conservative position in the study notes of this Bible. For example, in his introductory notes he makes a strong defense of Moses' authorship of the Pentateuch and Isaiah's authorship of the entire Book of Isaiah—points at which most other study Bibles are noncommittal. He gives extensive footnotes and detailed outlines of the Bible books. His comments on prophecy are strongly dispensational and *premillennial*.* An interesting feature is Dr. Ryrie's "Synopsis of Bible Doctrine" in the back of the book—an outline of key Bible doctrines presented in systematic style with Scripture references. This study Bible is available with the KJV or NASB text. Red-letter edition.

Sandmel, Samuel, ed. *The New English Bible: Oxford Study Edition*. New York: Oxford Univ. Press, 1976.

This annotated edition of the NEB resembles *The New Oxford Annotated Bible* (RSV) but the study aids are completely different. The introductions and annotations of this book are much more brief, and the editors have not given an outline of each book (not even broad chapter outlines, as found in *The New Oxford Annotated Bible)*. The notes emphasize more modern, liberal views such as the *documentary theory**, a triple authorship of Isaiah, and a denial that Paul wrote 2 Thessalonians. Most of the supplemental articles are too sketchy to be helpful (except for the article entitled "Literary Forms of the Bible"), and all of them reflect liberal literary criticism of the Scriptures. The *Oxford Study Edition* includes the Apocrypha and carries the imprimatur of Bishop Bernard J. Flannagan.

Scofield, C. I., ed. *The New Scofield Reference Bible*. New York: Oxford Univ. Press, 1967.

The editorial committee for this revised edition (headed by E. Schuyler English) made several changes in Scofield's work to make it more useful to modern readers. They revised the archaic spellings of the KJV text at many points. They expanded the introduction to each Bible book to discuss its author and date and to give a brief outline. They simplified the numbering system for the footnotes. And they expanded the footnotes, when necessary, to deal with questions about Scofield's interpretation of prophecy. The revisers also removed Ussher's chronology from the center column, "because of the lack of evidence on which to fix dates" (p. vi). However, they were careful to preserve and explain Scofield's comments on the dispensations of history.

Thompson, F. C., ed. *The New Chain-Reference Bible.* Indianapolis: B. B. Kirkbride, 1934.

This ingenious work combines the features of a topical Bible and a simple cross-reference Bible. Instead of referring you to a few selected cross-references on a particular topic, the editor sends you to a "chain" of marginal cross-references on the topic. Notes along the left-hand margin give the "pilot reference"—the Scripture verse where a cross-reference "chain" on that topic begins. Notes along the right-hand margin give the "forward reference"—the verse that is the next link in a "chain" you might be following. In the back of the Bible, the editor gives a Text Cyclopedia, where he has assembled each entire chain of references and listed the chains by topic in alphabetical order (much like a topical Bible). The *Chain-Reference Bible* uses the KJV.

3.
Topical Bibles

In the summer of 1969, I went from door to door selling Bibles and Bible reference books in Mount Holly, North Carolina.

One of the most popular books I sold was *Nave's Topical Bible*. As I recall, the sales pitch that we used for *Nave's* went something like this:

"Mrs. Jones, did you realize that the Bible you see Billy Graham holding when he preaches on TV is a *Nave's Topical Bible*?[1]

That statement got people's attention. Aside from the fact that they respected Billy Graham as a preacher, folks wanted to know why anyone would use a topical Bible instead of a regular Bible. They were bound to ask, "What's a *topical* Bible?" And then I would tell them.

At the risk of still sounding like a salesman, let me explain what a topical Bible is.

A regular Bible presents the Scriptures in traditional *canonical** order, beginning with Genesis and ending with the Book of Revelation. A topical Bible presents the Scriptures in topical order; that is, it alphabetically lists several hundred Bible-related topics, quoting the Scriptures related to each topic. Figure 8 shows a sample entry from *Nave's* for the topic "Seven". Notice that it cites a wide range of Scriptures connected with that topic. Also notice that the topical Bible does not print all of the Scripture references in full; it quotes only the most significant ones and gives references for the rest. (One verse might relate to a half-dozen topics, so it is impractical to print it in full every time. If the editors did that, the topical Bible would occupy several volumes!)

A topical Bible can be a great time-saver for any Bible student. Instead of poring over cross-references or concordances for hours on end, you can have at your finger tips the pertinent passages on just about any Bible topic you would like to study.

In spite of its great usefulness, some people have never heard of the topi-

---

1. I do not know how the company determined that Billy Graham preached from *Nave's Topical Bible*. After hearing him quote translations other than the KJV (which *Nave's* uses), I am sure he does not always preach from *Nave's*. But the dust jackets on two editions of *Nave's* carry Dr. Graham's statement that "outside of the Bible this is the book I depend on more than any other."

Figure 8—Topical Bible Entry: "Seven"

cries of them which have reaped are entered into the ears of the Lord of sabaoth.

See MASTERS; WAGES.

SERVICE. See ALTRUISM.

SETH. Son of Adam, Gen. 4:25,26; 5:3,8; 1 Chr. 1:1; Luke 3:38. Called SHETH, 1 Chr. 1:1.

SETHUR, one of the twelve spies, Num. 13:13.

SEVEN. Interesting facts concerning the number. **DAYS:** Week consists of, Gen. 2:3; Ex. 20:11; Deut. 5:13,14. Noah in the ark before the flood, Gen. 7:4,10; remains in the ark after sending forth the dove, Gen. 8:10,12. Mourning for Jacob lasted, Gen. 50:10; of Job, Job 2:13. The plague of bloody waters in Egypt lasted, Ex. 7:25. The Israelites compassed Jericho, Josh. 6:4. The passover lasted, Ex. 12:15. Saul directed by Samuel to tarry at Gilgal, awaiting the prophet's command, 1 Sam. 10:8; 13:8. The elders of Jabesh-gilead ask for a truce of, 1 Sam. 11:3. Dedication of the temple lasted double, 1 Kin. 8:65. Ezekiel sits by the river Chebar in astonishment, Ezek. 3:15. The feast of tabernacles lasted, Lev. 23:34,42. Consecration of priests and altars lasted, Ex. 29:30,35. Ezek. 43:25, 26. Defilements lasted, Lev. 12:2; 13:4. Fasts of, 1 Sam. 31:13; 2 Sam. 12:16,18,22. The firstborn of flocks and sheep shall remain with mother, before being offered, Ex. 22:30. The feast of Ahasuerus continued, Esth.1:5. Paul tarries at Tyre, Acts 21:4; at Puteoli, Acts 28:14.

WEEKS: In Daniel's vision concerning the coming of the Messiah, Dan. 9:25. Ten times, Dan. 9:24. The period between the Passover and the Pentecost, Lev. 23:15.

MONTHS: Holy convocations in the seventh month, Lev. 23:24-44; Num. 29; Ezek. 45:25.

YEARS: Jacob serves for each of his wives, Gen. 29:15-30. Of plenty, Gen. 41: 1-32,53. Famine lasted in Egypt, Gen. 41:1-32,54-56; in Canaan, 2 Sam. 24:13; 2 Kin. 8:1. Insanity of Nebuchadnezzar, Dan. 4:32. Seven times, the period between the jubilees, Lev. 25:8.

MISCELLANY OF SEVENS: Of clean beasts taken into the ark, Gen. 7:2. Abraham gives Abimelech seven lambs, Gen. 21:28. Rams and bullocks to the number of, required in sacrifices, Lev. 23:18; Num. 23:1; 29: 32; 1 Chr. 15:26; Ezek. 45:23. Blood sprinkling seven times, Lev. 4:6; 14:7; oil, 14:16. Seven kine and seven ears of corn in Pharaoh's vision, Gen. 41:2-7. The Israelites compassed Jericho seven times, on the seventh day sounding seven trumpets, Josh. 6:4. Elisha's servant looked seven times for appearance of rain, 1 Kin. 18:43. Naaman required to wash in Jordan seven times, 2 Kin. 5:10. Seven steps in the temple seen in Ezekiel's vision, Ezek. 40:22,26. The heat of Nebuchadnezzar's furnace intensified sevenfold, Dan. 3:19. The light of the sun intensified sevenfold, Isa. 30:26. The threat-

ened sevenfold punishment of Israel, Lev. 26:18-21. Silver purified seven times, Psa. 12:6. Worshiping seven times a day, Psa. 119:164. Seven chamberlains at the court of Ahasuerus, Esth. 1:10; seven princes, Esth. 1:14. Seven counsellors at the court of Artaxerxes, Ezra 7:14. Seven maidens given to Esther, Esth. 2:9. Symbolical of many sons, Ruth 4:15; 1 Sam. 2:5; Jer. 15:9; of liberality, Eccl. 11:1,2. Seven magi, Prov. 26:16. Seven women shall seek polygamous marriage, Isa. 4:1. Seven shepherds to be sent forth against Assyria, Mic. 5:5,6. Seven lamps and pipes, Zech. 4:2. Seven deacons in the apostolic church, Acts 6:3. Seven churches in Asia, Rev. 1:4,20. Seven seals, Rev. 5:1. Seven thunders, Rev. 10:3. Seven heads and seven crowns, Rev. 12:3; 13:1; 17:9. Seven kings, Rev. 17:10. Seven stars, Rev. 1:16,20; 3:1; Amos 5:8. Seven spirits, Rev. 1:4; 3:1; 4:5; 5:6. Seven eyes of the Lord, Zech. 3:9; 4:10; Rev. 5:6. Seven golden candlesticks, Rev. 1:12. Seven angels with seven trumpets, Rev. 8:2. Seven plagues, Rev. 15:1. Seven horns and seven eyes, Rev. 5:6. Seven angels with seven plagues, Rev. 15:6. Seven golden vials, Rev. 15:7. Scarlet colored beast having seven heads, Rev. 17:3,7.

SEVENEH, a city in Egypt, Ezek. 29:10 [R.V.]; 30:6 [R.V.]; A.V., SYENE.

SEVENTY. The senate of the Israelites composed of seventy elders, Ex. 24:1,9; Num. 11:16,24,25. Seventy disciples sent forth by Jesus, Luke 10:1-17. The Jews in captivity in Babylon seventy years, Jer. 25:11,12; 29:10; Dan. 9:2; Zech. 1:12; 7:5. See ISRAEL.

Seventy weeks in the vision of Daniel, Dan. 9:24.

SHAALABBIN. See SHAALBIM.

SHAALBIM. A city of Dan, Josh 19:42; Judg. 1:35. One of Solomon's commissary cities, 1 Kin. 4:9. Called SHAALABBIN, Josh. 19:42.

SHAAPH. 1. Son of Jahdai, 1 Chr. 2:47.

2. Son of Caleb, 1 Chr. 2:49.

SHAARAIM. 1. A city of Judah, called also SHARAIM, Josh. 15:36; 1 Sam. 17:52.

2. A city of Simeon, 1 Chr. 4:31.

SHAASHGAZ, a chamberlain of Ahasuerus, Esth. 2:14.

SHABBETHAI. 1. A Levite, assistant to Ezra, Ezra 10:15.

2. An expounder of the law, Neh. 8:7.

3. A chief Levite, attendant of the temple, Neh. 11:16.

SHACHIA, son of Shaharaim, 1 Chr. 8:10.

SHADRACH, called also HANANIAH. A Hebrew captive in Babylon, Dan. 1; 2: 17.49; 3.

SHAGE, father of Jonathan, one of David's guard, 1 Chr. 11:34.

SHAHARAIM, a Benjamite, 1 Chr. 8:8.

Source: Orville J. Nave, ed., *Nave's Topical Bible* (Nashville: Thomas Nelson, 1979).

cal Bible. Why don't the bookstores advertise it more?

The classics in this field, such as *Nave's Topical Bible* and *Torrey's Topical Text Book*, were compiled in the late 1800s—a time when revivals brought to the Lord thousands of new converts who knew very little about the Bible. Christian leaders such as Orville J. Nave (a chaplain in the Civil War) and R. A. Torrey (an evangelist and pastor) worked with these new converts every day and knew firsthand the acute need for easy-to-use Bible study aids. Concordances were bulky, expensive, and hard for new converts to use. They needed something that would quickly guide them to Scriptures that spoke to their own needs. And so the idea of a topical Bible was born.

In checking the library stacks at Vanderbilt Divinity School for topical Bibles, I found at least a dozen books of this sort—all published in the late 1800s.

The demand for topical Bibles seems to have slackened when *Scofield's Reference Bible* and other study Bibles began to appear about the turn of the century. The study Bibles provided their own system of topical references in the margin notes, a topical index, or both; many laymen found that this apparatus was all they needed. So the topical Bibles were moved farther back on the bookseller's shelf. Some bookstores no longer stock topical Bibles; a customer must place a special order for one.

A Multipurpose Tool

The topical Bible can be a versatile Bible study tool. Here are a few of the ways you might use one in your study:

1. *To review all key Scriptures on a certain Bible topic.* This is the chief purpose of a topical Bible and the way in which you will most often use it. Perhaps you want to study the issue of God's influence upon national affairs. Figure 9 shows what you might find under the topic, *Nation.* These Scriptures show how God influenced the history of Israel; how He punished the nation for its sins; how corrupt rulers affected the nation's relationship with God; how the people prayed for God's blessing upon the nation, and so on.

Notice that the entry gives cross-references to other related topics, such as *Sin, national; Government; King;* and *Rulers.* If the student will check these entries, he will find even more scriptural teaching on the subject. And these entries may bring to mind other topics such as *Patriotism* and *Politics,* where he finds even more information.

When making a topical study like this, I jot down on a sheet of paper all the Scripture references that interest me. Then I look up the references that the topical Bible did not quote in full and write those passages on another

Figure 9—Topical Bible Entry: "Nation"

11:1-11. Kindness of, to David, and death, 2 Sam. 10:1,2; 1 Chr. 19:1,2.

2. Probably identical with JESSE, 2 Sam. 17:25.

NAHATH. 1. Son of Reuel, Gen. 36:13, 17; 1 Chr. 1:37.

2. Called also TOAH and TOHU. A Levite, 1 Chr. 6:26,34; 1 Sam. 1:1.

3. A Levite and overseer of the sacred offerings, 2 Chr. 31:13.

NAHBI, a prince of Naphtali, and one of the twelve spies, Num. 13:14.

NAHOR. 1. Grandfather of Abraham, Gen. 11:22-26; 1 Chr. 1:26. In the lineage of Christ, Luke 3:34.

2. Brother of Abraham, Gen. 11:26; Josh. 24:2. Marriage and descendants of, Gen. 11:27,29; 22:20-24; 24:15,24.

NAHSHON. Son of Amminadab, Ex. 6: 23; Num. 1:7; 1 Chr. 2:10. Captain of the host of Judah, Num. 2:3; 10:14; 1 Chr. 2:10. Liberality of, Num. 7:12,17.

NAHUM, one of the minor prophets. Prophesies against the Assyrians; declares the majesty of God and his care for his people, Nah. 1. Foretells the destruction of Nineveh, Nah. chapters 2, 3.

NAIL. Isa. 41:7; Jer. 10:4. Made of iron, 1 Chr. 22:3; of gold, 2 Chr. 3:9. Jael kills Sisera with, Judg. 4:21.

FIGURATIVE. Ezra 9:8; Isa. 22:23,25; Zech. 10:4.

NAIN, a city in Galilee. Jesus restores to life a widow's son in, Luke 7:11.

NAIOTH, a place in Ramah, 1 Sam. 19: 18,19,22; 20:1.

NAME. Value of a good, Prov. 22:1; Eccl. 7:1. A new name given to persons who have spiritual adoption, Isa. 62:2. To Abraham, Gen. 17:5; Sarah, Gen. 17:15; Jacob, Gen. 32:28; Paul, Acts 13:9. Intercessional influence of the name of Jesus, see JESUS, IN HIS NAME.

SYMBOLICAL: Hos. 1:3,4,6,9; 2:1.

NAMES OF JESUS. See JESUS, NAMES OF.

NAOMI. Wife of Elimelech; mother-in-law of Ruth; dwelt in Moab; returns to Bethlehem; kinswoman of Boaz, Ruth chapters 1-4.

NAPHISH, called also NEPHISH. A son of Ishmael, Gen. 25:15; 1 Chr. 1:31.

NAPHTALI. 1. Son of Jacob and Bilhah, Gen. 30:7,8; 35:25. Jacob blesses, Gen. 49:21. Sons of, Gen. 46:24; 1 Chr. 7:13.

2. Tribe of. Census of, Num. 1:42,43; 26: 48-50. Position assigned to, in camp and march, Num. 2:25-31; 10:25-27. Moses's benediction on, Deut. 33:23. Inheritance of, Josh. 19:32-39; Judg. 1:33; Ezek. 48:3.

Defeat Sisera, Judg. 4:6,10; 5:18. Follow Gideon, Judg. 6:35; 7:23. Aid in conveying the ark to Jerusalem, Psa. 68:27. Military operations of, 1 Chr. 12:34,40; against, 1 Kin. 15:20; 2 Kin. 15:29; 2 Chr. 16:4.

Prophecies concerning, Isa. 9:1,2; Rev.7:6.

NAPHTUHIM, the inhabitants of central Egypt, Gen. 10:13; 1 Chr. 1:11.

NARCISSUS, a believer at Rome, Rom. 16:11.

NATHAN. 1. Son of David and Bathsheba, 2 Sam. 5:14; 1 Chr. 3:5; 14:4.

2. A prophet in the time of David. His message to David concerning the building of a temple, 2 Sam. 7:1-17; 1 Chr. 17:1-15. Reproves David for his adultery with Bathsheba and his murder of Uriah, 2 Sam. 12: 1-15. Gives Solomon the name Jedidiah, 2 Sam. 12:25. Assists Bath-sheba in securing to Solomon, her son, the succession to the throne, 1 Kin. 1:10-14,22-27. Assists in anointing Solomon, 1 Kin. 1:32-45.

Kept the chronicles, 1 Chr. 29:29; 2 Chr. 9:29. Assists David in the organization of the tabernacle, 2 Chr. 29:25.

NATHANAEL, becomes a disciple of Jesus, John 1:45-49; 21:2.

NATHAN-MELECH, an idolatrous chamberlain, 2 Kin. 23:11.

NATION. Sins of, Isa. 30:1,2. Chastised, Isa. 14:26,27; Jer. 5:29; 18:6-10; 25:12-33; Ezek. 2:3-5; 39:23,24; Dan. 7:9-12; 9:3-16; Hos. 7:12; Joel 1:1-20; Amos 9:9; Zeph. 3:6,8. Perish, Psa. 9:17; Isa. 60:12.

National adversity, prayer in, Judg. 21: 2-4; 2 Chr. 7:13,14; Psa. 74; Joel 2:12; lamented, Ezra 9; Neh. 1:4-11; Jer. 6:14; 8:11, 20,21; 9:1,2. See SIN, NATIONAL.

Prayer for, Psa. 85:1-7; Lam. 2:20-22; 5; Dan. 9:3-21.

Involved in sins of rulers, Gen. 20:4,9; 2 Sam. 24:10-17; 1 Chr. 21:7-17; of other individuals, as Achan, Josh. 7:1,11-26.

Peace of, Job 34:29; Psa. 33:12; 89:15-18. Promises of peace to, Lev. 26:6; 1 Kin. 2:33; 2 Kin. 20:19; 1 Chr. 22:9; Psa. 29:11; 46:9; 72:3,7; 128:6; Isa. 2:4; 14:4-7; 60:17,18; 65:25; Jer. 30:10; 50:34; Ezek. 34:25-28; Hos. 2:18; Mic. 4:3,4; Zech. 1:11; 3:10; 8:4,5; 9:10; 14:11. Prayer for peace, Jer. 29:7; 1 Tim. 2:1,2. Peace given by God, Josh. 21:44; 1 Chr. 22:18; 23:25; Psa. 147:13,14; Eccl. 3:8; Isa. 45:7. Instances of national peace, Josh. 14:15; Judg. 3:11,30; 1 Kin. 4:24,25. See WAR.

Righteousness exalteth, Prov. 14:34.

See GOVERNMENT; KING; RULERS.

NATURALIZATION, Acts 22:28; Eph. 2:12,19.

NATURAL RELIGION. See RELIGION, NATURAL.

NAUM, an ancestor of Jesus, Luke 3:25.

NAVIGATION, sounding in, Acts 27:28. See COMMERCE; MARINER; NAVY.

NAVEL, treatment of, at birth, Ezek. 16:4.

NAVY. Solomon's, 1 Kin. 9:26; Hiram's, 1 Kin. 10:11; of Chittim, Dan. 11:30,40. See COMMERCE; MARINER; NAVIGATION.

NAZARENE. See NAZARETH.

NAZARETH, a village in Galilee. Joseph and Mary dwell at, Matt. 2:23; Luke 1: 26,27,56; 2:4,39,51. Jesus from, Matt. 21:11; Mark 1:24; 10:47; Luke 4:34; 18:37; 24:19. People of, reject Jesus, Luke 4:16-30. Its name opprobrious, John 1:46.

Source: Orville J. Nave, ed., *Nave's Topical Bible* (Nashville: Thomas Nelson, 1979).

sheet of paper. When I'm finished, I have several sheets of paper with
Scripture passages pertaining to the topic I am studying. I place these beside the passages already quoted in the topical Bible, so that I can review
what the Bible says about that topic. Often this is how I begin my research
for a sermon, a Sunday school lesson, or an article. The topical study
brings several related Scriptures together and provides perspective on
what the entire Word of God says about the topic.

2. *To review the key events of a Bible character's life.* The better topical
Bibles have proper-name entries for most of the men and women mentioned in Scripture. Figure 10 shows an entry for *Andrew.* The entry begins with Scriptures that identify who Andrew was and describe his background. Then the topical Bible gives a list of Scriptures that describe the
important events of Andrew's life in chronological sequence.

The advantage of using a topical Bible rather than a concordance is noticeable when researching Bible characters. A concordance will give you
only the passages that contain the person's name, but the topical Bible includes every passage that refers to the person, even those verses that do not
contain the name (e.g., a concordance lists John 1:40, while a topical Bible
gives John 1:40-42). Furthermore, a concordance will list these passages in
canonical sequence, or the order in which they occur in the books of the
Bible. But that list will not show you the *time sequence* in which the events
occurred. The topical Bible does. For these reasons, the topical Bible's arrangement can be far more useful for biographical study.

3. *To find Scriptures that interpret the significance of a Bible character.*
Were we to study only the events of a Bible person's life, we might miss the
reason why Scripture describes him. The topical Bible gives Scriptures that
both narrate the person's life and that interpret the meaning of that life.
As an example, here are are some of the subheadings listed under *David* in
Nave's Topical Bible:[2]

> Devoutness of . . .
> Justice in the Administration of . . .
> Discreetness of . . .
> Meekness of . . .
> Merciful . . .
> David as Musician . . .
> Poet . . .
> Prophet . . .
> Type of Christ . . .
> Jesus Called Son of . . .
> Prophecies Concerning Him and His Kingdom . . .

---

2. Orville J. Nave, ed., *Nave's Topical Bible* (Nashville: Thomas Nelson, 1979), p. 278.

Fig. 10—Topical Bible Entry: "Andrew"

against, Jer. 11:21-23. Inhabitants of, after Babylonian captivity, Ezra 2:23; Neh. 7:27.

2. Son of Becher, 1 Chr. 7:8.

3. A Jew, who returned from Babylon, Neh. 10:19.

ANATOMY, human, Job 10:11.

ANCHOR, Acts 27:29,30. FIGURATIVE: Heb. 6:19.

ANCIENT OF DAYS, an appellation of Jehovah, Dan. 7:9,13,22.

ANDREW. An apostle. A fisherman, Matt. 4:18. Of Bethsaida, John 1:44. A disciple of John, John 1:40. Finds Peter, his brother, and brings him to Jesus, John 1:40-42. Call of, Matt. 4:18; Mark 1:16. His name appears in the list of the apostles in Matt. 10:2; Mark 3:18; Luke 6:14. Asks the Master privately about the destruction of the temple, Mark 13:3,4. Tells Jesus of the Greeks who sought to see him, John 12:20-22. Reports the number of loaves at the feeding of the five thousand, John 6:8. Meets with the disciples after the Lord's ascension, Acts 1:13.

ANDRONICUS, kinsman of Paul, Rom. 16:7.

ANEM, a Levitical city, 1 Chr. 6:73.

ANER. 1. A Canaanitish chief, Gen. 14:13,24.

2. A Levitical city of Manasseh, 1 Chr. 6:70.

ANGEL. ONE OF THE HOLY TRINITY: Trinitarian authorities interpret the Scriptures cited under this topic as referring to Christ, who according to this view was the divine presence in the wilderness. Called ANGEL, Acts 7:30,35; MINE ANGEL, Ex. 32:34; ANGEL OF GOD, Ex. 14:19; Judg. 13:6; 2 Sam. 14:17,20; ANGEL OF THE LORD, Ex. 3:2; Judg. 2:1; ANGEL OF HIS PRESENCE, Isa. 63:9.

ANGEL. A CELESTIAL SPIRIT: Called ANGEL OF THE LORD, Matt. 1:20,24; 2:13,19; 28:2; Luke 1:11; Acts 5:19; 8:26; 12:7,23; MORNING STARS, Job 38:7; HOSTS, Gen. 2:1; 32:2; Josh. 5:14; 1 Chr. 12:22; Psa. 33:6; 103:21; Luke 2:13; PRINCIPALITIES, POWERS, Eph. 3:10; Col. 1:16. Created, Gen. 2:1; Neh. 9:6; Col.1:16. Of different orders, Isa. 6:2; 1 Thess. 4:16; 1 Pet. 3:22; Jude 9; Rev. 12:7. Immortal, Luke 20:36. Worship God, Neh. 9:6; Phil. 2:9-11; Heb. 1:6. Not to be worshipped, Col. 2:18; Rev. 19:10; 22:8,9. Do not marry, Matt. 22:30; Mark 12:25; Luke 20:35. Are obedient, Psa. 103:20; Matt. 6:10; Luke 11:2; 1 Pet. 3:22; 2 Pet. 2:11; Jude 6. Have knowledge of, and interest in, earthly affairs, Matt. 24: 36; Luke 15:7,10; 1 Tim. 5:21; 1 Pet. 1:12. To be judged by men, 1 Cor. 6:3. See FUNCTIONS OF, below.

Men called angels, 2 Sam. 19:27. Are examples of meekness, 2 Pet. 2:11; Jude 9. Are wise, 2 Sam. 14:17,20; mighty, Psa. 103:20; 2 Pet. 2:11; holy, Matt. 25:31; Mark 8:38; elect, 1 Tim. 5:21; innumerable, Deut. 33:2; 2 Kin. 6:17; Job 25:3; Psa. 68:17 [R. V. omits angels in v. 17]; Heb. 12:22; Jude 14.

Aspects of, Judg. 13:6; Isa. 6:2; Dan. 10:6; Matt. 28:3. See UNCLASSIFIED SCRIPTURES RELATING TO, below.

FUNCTIONS OF: Guard the way to the tree of life, Gen. 3:24. Law given by, Acts 7:53; Gal. 3:19; Heb. 2:2. Medium of revelation to prophets, 2 Kin. 1:15; Dan. 4:13-17; 8: 19; 9:21-27; 10:10-20; Zech. 1:9-11; Acts 8:26; Gal. 3:19; Heb. 2:2; Rev. 1:1; 5:2-14; 7:1-3, 11-17; 8:2-13; chapters 9 to 20; 22:6,16.

Remonstrates with Balaam, Num. 22:22-27. Announces the birth of Samson, Judg. 13; of John the Baptist, Luke 1:11-20; of Jesus, Matt. 1:20,21; Luke 1:28-38; 2:7-15. Warns Joseph to escape to Egypt, Matt. 2:13. Minister to Jesus after the temptation, Matt. 4:11; Mark 1:13; John 1:51; during his passion, Luke 22:43. Present at the tomb of Jesus, Matt. 28:2-6; the ascension, Acts 1:11. Will be with Christ at his second coming, Matt. 25:31; Mark 8:38; 2 Thess. 1:7; Jude 14,15; at the judgment, Matt. 13:39,41,49; 16:27; 24:31; 25:31; Mark 13:27.

MINISTRANT TO THE RIGHTEOUS: Gen. 16:7. And the angel of the LORD found her by a fountain of water in the wilderness, by the fountain in the way to Shur.

Gen. 24:7. He shall send his angel before thee. [Ex. 32:34; 33:2.] 40. The LORD, before whom I walk, will send his angel with thee, and prosper thy way;

Ex. 23:20. Behold, I send an Angel before thee, to keep thee in the way, and to bring thee into the place which I have prepared. 23. For mine Angel shall go before thee, and bring thee in unto the Amorites, and the Hittites, and the Perizzites, and the Canaanites, the Hivites, and the Jebusites; and I will cut them off. Ex. 33:2.

Num. 20:16. And when we cried unto the LORD, he heard our voice, and sent an angel, and hath brought us forth out of Egypt:

1 Kin. 19:5. And as he lay and slept under a juniper tree, behold, then an angel touched him, and said unto him, Arise *and* eat. 6. And he looked, and, behold, *there was* a cake baken on the coals, and a cruse of water at his head. And he did eat and drink, and laid him down again. 7. And the angel of the LORD came again the second time, and touched him, and said, Arise *and* eat; because the journey *is* too great for thee. 8. And he arose, and did eat and drink, and went in the strength of that meat forty days and forty nights unto Horeb the mount of God.

2 Chr. 18:18. Therefore hear the word of the LORD; I saw the LORD sitting upon his throne, and all the host of heaven standing on his right hand and *on* his left.

PSA. 34:7. The angel of the LORD encampeth round about them that fear him, and delivereth them.

PSA. 68:17. The chariots of God *are* twenty thousand, *even* thousands *of* angels: 2 Kin. 6:17. [H. R. V. upon thousands]

PSA. 91:11. For he shall give his angels charge over thee, to keep thee in all thy ways. 12. They shall bear thee up in *their* hands, lest thou dash thy foot against a stone. Matt. 4:6; Luke 4:10,11.

Source: Orville J. Nave, ed., *Nave's Topical Bible* (Nashville: Thomas Nelson, 1979).

4. *To find examples of applied scriptural teaching.* A topical Bible not only gives the passages that refer to a teaching (e.g., *Obedience*), but also a list of passages that show how various persons applied or exemplified that teaching. Here is a list of the Scripture references under *Obedience to God—Exemplified* in *The New Topical Text Book*[3].

> *Noah,* Gen. 6:22.
> *Abram,* Gen. 12:1–4, with Heb. 11:8, Gen. 22:3,12.
> *Israelites,* Exod. 12:28, Exod. 24:7.
> *Caleb,* Num. 32:12.
> *Asa,* 1 Kings 5:11.
> *Elijah,* 1 Kings 17:5.
> *Hezekiah,* 2 Kings 18:6.
> *Josiah,* 2 Kings 22:2.
> *David,* Psa. 119:106.
> *Zerubbabel,* Hag. 1:12.
> *Josep* Matt. 1:24.
> *Wise Men,* Matt. 2:12.
> *Zacharias,* Luke 1:6.
> *Paul,* Acts 26:19.
> *Saints of Rome,* Rom. 16:19.

Obviously, these are not all of the people mentioned in Scripture who were obedient to God, but the list illustrates how a variety of men and women have obeyed God.

5. *To make a systematic study of Bible doctrine.* A topical Bible leads the reader through the most sophisticated teachings of God's Word in an organized, systematic way, much like a teaching outline. In fact, some pastors and Sunday school teachers use an outline from a topical Bible as they teach doctrinal subjects. Here is a good example of the systematic teaching format, again drawn from *The New Topical Text Book*.[4] To save space, the Scripture references given with the outline are not included, but the number of references is indicated in parentheses.

Creditors

Defined (1)
Might Demand
  Pledges (2)
  Security of Others (2)

3. R. A. Torrey, *The New Topical Text Book,* rev. ed. (New York: Revell, 1897), p. 185.
4. Ibid., p. 68.

Mortgages on Property (1)
Bills or Promissory Notes (1)
To Return before Sunset, Garments Taken in Pledge (3)
Prohibited From
Taking Millstones in Pledge (1)
Violently Selecting Pledges (1)
Exacting Usury from Brethren (2)
Exacting Debts from Brethren During Sabbatical Year (1)
Might Take Interest from Strangers (1)
Sometimes Entirely Remitted Debts (3)
Often Cruel in Exacting Debts (3)
Often Exacted Debts
By Selling the Debtor or Taking Him for a Servant (2)
By Selling the Debtor's Property (1)
By Selling the Debtor's Family (3)
By Imprisonment (2)
From the Sureties (2)
Were Often Defrauded (2)
Illustrative Of
God's Claim upon Men (3)
The Demands of the Law (1)

6. *To trace the development of a Bible doctrine.* Most topical Bibles list doctrinal Scriptures in canonical order, under a given topic or subtopic. This allows the reader to trace the gradual unfolding of a doctrine (e.g., *Justification*) under the Old Covenant and the New. First, the reader will find all of the teachings on that subject recorded in the *Pentateuch,* * followed by any references found in the *Historical Books,* * the *Writings,* * or the *Prophets,* and then the references in the Gospels, the Book of Acts, the Epistles, and the Book of Revelation. So he sees God's progressive revelation of that truth throughout Bible times.

What to Expect

Compared to the number of study Bibles available, the selection of topical Bibles will seem scanty indeed. Bible publishers offer us few titles in this category. But watch for these qualities in any topical Bible you may select:

1. *An appropriate selection of topics.* While the classics such as Nave's and Torrey's cover topics that one might normally explore in Bible study (e.g., Bible doctrines, characters, places, events), some of the newer topical Bibles have tried to include rather offbeat or faddish topics to attract the buyer's attention. Some of these books claim to show what the Scriptures say on topics like *Automobile, Atomic Bomb, Computers,* or *Popu-*

lar Music. Scripture may touch on these topics in some secondary way, but it does not give God's definitive Word on them. An editor who gleans some far-fetched collection of Scripture verses for topics of current interest like these is misleading readers; he claims to give an authoritative message from God on matters that the Bible does not specifically address. This type of topic selection will distort your understanding of Scripture today and make your topical Bible obsolete tomorrow.

2. *Adequately broad coverage of topics.* While some topical Bibles include topics that are best omitted, others omit topics which are important to the Bible student. A small topical Bible might suggest that the editors have eliminated several important Bible topics or given only a few references for the topics they do list, in order to meet a stringent size requirement. Some editors will eliminate all proper names. Others will abbreviate the coverage of doctrinal topics, etc.

It's a good idea to make a few spot checks on a topical Bible's coverage before purchasing it. For example, see if it includes entries for important Bible characters such as *Melchizedek, Josiah, Simeon,* and *Stephen.* Notice how many references it gives for major doctrines such as *Redemption, Atonement, Justification, Salvation, Grace,* and *Sanctification.* If there are only a half dozen or so references for each one, the coverage is too superficial. Finally, thumb through the pages, looking for faddish entries such as the ones mentioned earlier. If you find several of these, the editor probably used poor judgment in selecting other topics as well.

3. *Clear, understandable headings.* Space limitations do not permit a topical Bible to quote all of the Scripture passages in full; the editor must omit some readings, give only the references for them, and supply brief headings to explain their content. Skillful editors will provide clear, understandable headings, but sometimes editors are not so adept and give headings that confuse or mislead. These two examples illustrate the point:

> *"Priests*—Emoluments of . . . "
> *"Reprobacy* . . . See *Obduracy."*

A topical Bible must have coherent headings, "handles" that are easy to grasp, if it is to be a useful tool for any Bible student.

ANNOTATED BIBLIOGRAPHY

This list of topical Bibles does not include books of Bible quotations,[5] even though they are also organized topically. Such books contain a more arbitrary selection of Scripture passages; they are quotation an-

---

5. Examples would be Anthony J. Castagno, *Treasury of Biblical Quotations* (Nashville: Thomas Nelson, 1980); *The Words of Jesus* (Nashville: Thomas Nelson, 1982), and Jo Petty, *Apples of Gold* (Norwalk, Conn.: C. R. Gibson, 1965).

thologies, rather like *Bartlett's Familiar Quotations.* And they may not have the Bible's most definitive statements on a given subject. The books listed below provide a more thorough and systematic treatment of Scripture, in topical form.

Holman Topical Concordance. Philadelphia: A. J. Holman, 1979.

This appears to be a revision of *The New Topical Text Book* by R. A. Torrey. (To note the similarity, compare several topics in the two books, such as *Covenant(s); Fear, Godly;* or *Prophecy.)* The basic change is that, while *The New Topical Text Book* arranged subheadings in a philosophically systematic order, the *Holman Topical Concordance* arranges them in alphabetical order. The Holman editors have also added some new topics of interest to modern readers. (See the entry below under R. A. Torrey for further comments.)

Inglis, James. *A Topical Dictionary of Bible Texts.* Grand Rapids: Baker, 1979.

This book was first published in 1861 by Fleming H. Revell under the title *The Bible Text Cyclopedia.* According to my estimate, it covers more than four thousand Bible topics, including some of the more significant proper names. Inglis prints the full Scripture passages (KJV) for doctrinal and "practical" subjects, but gives only the references for all other subjects. At the end of the book, he provides an "Abstract of Subjects"—an index to all the doctrinal and "practical" topics in the book.

Joy, Charles R., ed. *Harper's Topical Concordance,* rev. ed. New York: Harper and Brothers, 1976.

According to the editor, this book contains 2,775 topics with about 33,200 Scripture passages. All of the Scripture texts are printed in full, using rather small type. Nonetheless, it is rather easy to find subjects in this book, because the editor supplies a generous number of cross-references between topics. The book includes headings for special days—i.e., appropriate readings for Lincoln's Birthday, Father's Day, Ash Wednesday, and so on. The book also includes several headings of special interest in the late 1950s, such as (racial) *Integration* and *Segregation.*

Monser, Harold E., ed. *Monser's Topical Index and Digest of the Bible.* Grand Rapids: Baker, 1979.

This book was first published in 1914 by the Cross-Reference Bible Company of New York, under the title *Cross-Reference Digest of Bible References.* It contains the topical listing of Scriptures previously published in Monser's *Cross-Reference Bible.* The most interesting feature of Monser's book is the treatment of proper names from the Bible. Under the entry for each significant proper name (e.g., *Jerusalem* and *Jesus Christ*), Monser gives a list of Scriptures related to that person or place, plus another listing of related topics. For example, under *Jesus Christ* is a listing of all of Jesus' key teaching topics (such as *Teachers, False; Tribulation; Works*). Thus the book is a good resource for studying an important Bible character. However, Monser also includes many insignificant subheadings under the proper names; for example, under *Jesus Christ* you will also find topics such as *Nothing, Raiment,* and *Three Days.*

Nave, Orville J., ed. *Nave's Topical Bible.* Nashville: Thomas Nelson, 1979.[6]

The editor began work on this book during the Civil War, while he served as a chaplain. "The quiet of army garrisons, apart from the rush and distraction of dense communities, has been favorable to its careful preparation," he wrote (p. 5). He used the KJV, with occasional alternate readings from the RV, arranged under more than twenty thousand topics (including all of the proper names found in the Bible). *Nave's Topical Bible* is surely the classic in this field. It does not include some topics of modern interest, such as *Homosexuality* (see *Affections*) and some of its topic headings can mislead modern readers (e.g., *Infidelity* contains only Scriptures about infidelity to God, not marital infidelity). However, it is still the most complete and accessible listing of Scripture topics now available.

Nave, Orville J., ed. *Nave's Topical Living Bible.* Wheaton: Tyndale, 1982.

This new edition of *Nave's Topical Bible* quotes phrases from the popular paraphrase *The Living Bible.* It should become one of the most frequently used reference books on the layman's bookshelf. In fact, it may revive interest in topical Bibles which has been waning for so long.

Pinson, William M., ed. *The Word Topical Bible of Issues and Answers.* Waco: Word, 1981.

This book is very limited in scope, listing KJV Scripture passages for only about three hundred topics. The editor says, "The book majors on ethical and moral issues. Thus, more theological subjects such as faith, heaven, or regeneration are not included nor are personal crisis subjects such as depression, grief, or death found here" (p. 5). *The Word Topical Bible* does focus on social issues such as *Divorce, Gambling,* and *Prostitution,* and it reviews Scripture about these subjects rather helpfully. But the narrow focus of subject matter is sure to limit its usefulness.

Torrey, R. A.[7] *The New Topical Text Book,* rev. ed. New York: Revell, 1897.

This book contains about six hundred Bible topics. The choice of topics seems rather arbitrary, because it includes many topics of minor importance (such as *Raven*) but omits other topics of great importance (such as *Sacraments, Ordinances,* and *Rituals*). *The New Topical Text Book* gives one or two selected Scripture references for each main idea under a topic, but it does not print any Scripture

---

6. Also available from (Grand Rapids: Baker, 1979) and (Waco: Word, 1979). Condensed edition available from (Chicago: Moody, 1979).

7. While many librarians catalog this book under Torrey's name, he did not claim to be the editor or compiler. The title page simply says: *"The New Topical Text Book...* With Introduction on Methods of Bible Study by Rev. R. A. Torrey." In his introduction, Torrey says that the book represents "the results of the hard work of many minds." Nevertheless it has long been tied to Torrey and his reputation, and is listed here under his name.

passages in full. An interesting feature of this book is a supplemental article entitled, "Outline of the Fundamental Doctrines of the Bible," by David Allen Reed

Viening, Edward, ed. *The Zondervan Topical Bible.* Grand Rapids: Zondervan, 1979.

Perhaps the most recent exhaustive topical Bible, this book (like Nave's) contains over twenty thousand topics and subtopics and over one hundred thousand Scripture texts, many of them printed in full. This work also uses the KJV as its basic text, but includes alternate readings from the RV, ASV, and RSV. In that respect it is more complete than Nave's, but its topical headings are as badly in need of updating as Nave's. For topical headings, it often uses archaic KJV terms (e.g., *Viol* instead of *Lyre*; *Copulation* instead of *Sexual Relations*) and other uncommon terms (e.g., *Lasciviousness, Obsequiousness,* and *Surfeitings*). The book also accepts some controversial terms as legitimate topics (see *Intermediate State,* for example).

4.
A Bible Buyer's Guide

Auto shopping is a familiar American pastime. Nearly every family in this country has had the experience of wandering from one car lot to another, comparing price stickers, peering under the hood, and buckling the seat belts for a test drive. After several rounds of this, at least one person in the family becomes the acknowledged expert at auto buying.

Buying Bibles differs from buying cars in several ways. Most Bibles are made to last longer than the typical family car, so a person won't need to look for the "latest model" of the Bible very often.[1] And most people who are interested in buying a Bible do not take time to compare the various Bibles they could choose from, so they are not likely to know what features are available when they enter the bookstore to buy a new Bible. This chapter is designed to help you learn at least as much about buying Bibles as you probably know about buying a two-tone sedan.

Know What You Need

As with buying a car, you can make your most appropriate choice of a Bible when you know what you truly need. That seems simple enough. But many Bible buyers enter a bookstore with only a vague notion of what they really plan to do with their Bible. They are prone to be confused by the wide variety of Bibles they find at the store, and they are likely to be dissatisfied with the Bible they do purchase, when they discover it's not the best tool for the type of study they need to do.

So give it a bit of thought: Why are you buying a Bible, anyway?

Perhaps *you are a new Christian*. You have just surrendered your life to Jesus Christ, and you have no Bible of any kind. You need one that will help you grow in your new life with Christ, ideally one that you can carry with you to school or your job, so you can "feast on the good things of the Lord" at any opportunity throughout the day.

In this case, you would be wise to look for a simple text Bible, perhaps only a New Testament or a New Testament with Psalms. Such a book is small, easy to carry, and inexpensive. It does not have a complex system of

---

1. The useful life of a Bible depends on several factors—its original durability, the frequency of use and handling, exposure to weather, the care with which it is used, and so on. You can usually expect a quality Bible to last at least ten years, even with heavy use.

study notes or cross-references, but as a new Christian most of your study will be devotional. For that, you do not need a sophisticated reference apparatus.

Perhaps *you are an established Christian.* You have served the Lord for a few years and you are eager to gain a deeper understanding of His Word. You may want to learn more so that you can share the gospel with an unsaved friend. You may want to learn what God's Word says about a particular problem that you face on the job, in your neighborhood, or in your family. Perhaps you simply want to grow stronger in the Lord as an individual; you want to put on more spiritual "armor" to be ready for tests that are yet to come (see Eph. 6:11-17). Any of these needs might prompt you to do more serious Bible study. And for that, you will need an annotated Bible or a study Bible that offers more than a few explanatory notes.

Or perhaps *you are a full-time Christian worker.* You may be just beginning your ministry as a pastor, an evangelist, a missionary, a Christian schoolteacher, or some other Christian worker who uses the Bible every day for guidance and instruction. You will need a complete Bible (including the Apocrypha, if you are Roman Catholic, Episcopalian, or a member of some other communion that uses it). An annotated Bible or study Bible is a must for preparing lessons and sermons, for counseling, or for your personal study. Here again you will need to compare the reference Bibles that are available, choosing the version and study apparatus that seem best suited to your daily work.

There is a different set of considerations if *you are buying the Bible as a gift to a friend.* This is harder to do, because you must try to discern what type of Bible will best suit your friend's needs. Does the person fit one of the categories just mentioned—a new Christian, an established Christian who wants to grow, or a full-time Christian worker? This should help you decide what to buy.

Many times when we buy a Bible as a gift, it is to commemorate a special event. Bible publishers produce special editions for such gift-giving occasions. Here are some examples:

Brides' Bibles—Hand-sized Bibles with a separate wedding memory section and family register. Bound in traditional white to commemorate the special occasion, these Bibles are sold essentially as keepsakes rather than for regular use.

Family Bibles—Large Bibles for use in the home, usually with many illustrations and maps and much supplemental material. These Bibles contain a special section for recording family history such as births, deaths, and marriages.

Gifts and Award Bibles—Text Bibles designed for church school presentations and other gift occasions. They usually contain some study helps to aid in church school work.

Babies' New Testaments—Gift New Testaments, often bound in pastel colors, to commemorate births.

Lectern and Pulpit Bibles—Large-sized Bibles printed in large type for easy reading on a pulpit or lectern. These Bibles are sometimes called Desk Bibles.

Pew or Library Bibles—Inexpensive, hardcover Bibles placed in church pews for the use of worshipers, or placed in libraries.[2]

These gift Bibles are beautiful, but they are *not* designed for daily use. As you can tell by the descriptions, most of them are keepsakes instead of actual reading or study editions. They do not have many study aids; the type may be difficult to read; the size of the book may make it awkward to handle (too small or too bulky); the binding is not as durable as with a regular text Bible or study Bible. Consider these facts when you buy a Bible as a gift, and ask yourself whether you are buying it as a keepsake or as a study tool. There is a proper time for each.

Practical Features

"The Bible Selector" (Fig. 11) is printed to save time and confusion when you make your next Bible purchase. We have already discussed two sets of options listed on "The Bible Selector"—versions and study helps—in Chapters 1 and 2. Looking at the rest of this chart, we see some of the other options available to us at the Bible bookseller's.

1. *Overall Size.* Do you really need an entire Bible, or will a portion of Scripture suit your needs? For some purposes, you might want the compactness of a New Testament alone. It can be handily carried in shirt pocket or purse, and it's easy to pack in a suitcase. For devotional reading, it may be all the Bible you need.

2. *Type Size.* Is small type difficult for you to read? What size can you read easily? (Fig. 12 may help you decide.) When selecting a Bible to give to a friend, be careful to choose one with large enough type. If in doubt, select the next size *larger* than the one you think he or she can read.

3. *Color of Type.* Do you prefer a Bible that highlights the words of

---

2. Taken from *How to Sell the Right Bible* (Nashville: Thomas Nelson, 1980), p. 10.

Figure 11—The Bible Selector

Who Will Be Using This Bible?

For What Purpose? (Devotions, Teaching, Preaching, Counseling, etc.)

How Often Will It Be Handled Each Week?

FEATURE	OPTIONS							YOUR CHOICE
Content	N.T. Only		N.T. with Psalms		N.T. and O.T.		N.T. and O.T. with Apocry.	
Version	Amp.	TEV	JB	LB	NASB	NIV	Phillips*	
	Barclay*	Goodsp.	KJV	NAB	NEB	NKJV	RSV	
Study Helps	None (Text Only)		Notes Only	Concordance Only		Annotated Bible	Study Bible	
Cover	Paper	Flexible Cloth	Flexible Kivar	Cloth Boards	Kivar on Boards	Leather		
Type Size	Compact (4 to 6 pt.)		Standard (7 to 10 pt.)		Large Print (11 to 12 pt.)		Giant Print (14 to 16 pt.)	
Color of Type	All Black				Red-Letter		(Words of Christ)	

DECISION:

---

*These versions contain New Testament only.

Christ in red ink? A red-letter edition costs a little more than one with the standard all-black type, but booksellers report that far more people buy red-letter editions. Check the *shade* of red ink that is being used in the red-letter edition; a dark red ink (about the color of fired brick or dried blood) is much easier to read than a light or bright shade of red.

4. *Cover.* How often will this Bible be handled? Several times a day? Once a day? Once a week? The answer should determine what sort of cover material you choose. "The Bible Selector" (Fig. 11) shows six basic types of binding, or covering, ranked from the least durable (paper cover) to the most durable (leather cover). The type of binding is also a fair gauge of expense: the least durable covers are least expensive, while the most durable covers are most expensive.

Because the cover has such a crucial bearing on the useful life of the Bible (and on the amount of money you can expect to pay), a few technical details about the types of cover material and the methods of binding used on various Bibles will be helpful:

Binding Materials

There is a wide variation in durability and overall quality in leather made from the hides of different kinds of animals. And there can be a great deal of quality difference in the skins of two animals of the same species. The quality of the leather also depends to a great degree on the skill of leather artisans, buyers, tanners, dyers, and specialists in fine binding.

The Finest Leather
Morocco (sometimes called natural, genuine morocco, hand-grained morocco, or pin seal morocco)—One of the most luxurious and most durable of all book leathers, morocco comes from the skins of goats bred in the Indian-Pakistani area. The *natural* grain of the leather is brought out in the processing.

High Quality Leathers
Top Grain Cowhide—Full-grained genuine cowhide from the top or outside of the hide. It is an extremely supple, durable leather. (A leather designated simply as "cowhide" may be made from a "split"—a lower level of the hide. This leather is of lesser quality than top grain cowhide.)

Pigskin, Aniline Gloss—A durable leather that has been specially treated to produce a high sheen.

Figure 12—Bible Type Sizes

thou hast brough dom a great sin? me ᴿthat ought n 10 And A-bim′- What sawest thou	7 And they *heir* partners, he other ship, ome and help ame, and filled	3 And say, Y rael, hear the GOD; Thus sai the mountains
Typical Bible type approximately 10 pt.	Large Print approximately 12 pt.	Giant Print approximately 16 pt.

(Most newspapers and books are set in 8 pt. to 10 pt.)

Source: *How to Sell the Right Bible* (Nashville: Thomas Nelson, 1980), p. 9.

Berkshire Leather—One publisher's name for quality pigskin which has been specially tanned to enhance its appearance. (*Note:* The only difference between aniline gloss pigskin and Berkshire leather is in the processing.)

East India Calf (or Water Buffalo Calfskin)—Made either from top grain or a "split" of the hide of a young Asian water buffalo, this cover material usually has ª polished grained surface.

India Calfskin—Similar to East India Calf or Water Buffalo Calfskin, but with a different grain.

Genuine Leather—A leather cover of unspecified origin. The leather may be pigskin or some other quality leather.

Medium Quality Leathers

French Morocco—Genuine leather, usually made from the flesh or underside of sheepskin, embossed in various grains. It is not as durable as top grain leather.

Persian Morocco—Leathers made from hides of hair sheep, usually embossed in all grains.

Reconstituted Materials

Material reconstituted from finely ground leather fibers. In other words, this is recycled leather scraps.

Non-Leather Bindings

Imitation Leather—A durable binding material simulating leather. It consists of an impregnated cloth fibrous base.

Leatherflex—A modern binding material simulating leather. It consists of an impregnated fibrous base with a tough plastic coating. It is washable and highly resistant to soiling, flexing, and abrasion.

Permaleather—A very durable, cloth-based imitation leather. Some publishers call their cloth-based, impregnated binding materials such names as Rexine, Moroccoette and Ariston. (Moroccoette can also be a latex-impregnated *paper* base.) Skivertex, Buksyn, and Durabond are other simulated leathers made from non-woven materials.

Vinyl Binding
Vinyl—A tough, man-made petrochemical material that is both durable and attractive.

Cloth Bindings
Cloth—Woven strands of durable cotton fabric, usually with pyroxylin coating (a protective plastic varnish) as a moisture resistant.

Flexible Denim Finish—A simulated denim with pliable backing, which results in a soft denim appearance.

Buckram—A rich natural cloth which is often hand detailed.

Binding Styles

Flush Cut—A cover style often used on inexpensive Bibles or Testaments, the cover being cut *flush* so that it does not project beyond the page edges.

Limp—A flexible binding with covers projecting slightly beyond the edges of the pages, approximately one-eighth of an inch.

Semi-Limp (sometimes called Semi-Overlapping or Half-Circuit)—A flexible binding style in which the covers overlap the page edges somewhat more than in a limp binding. They are shaped to fold down slightly over the edges, but they do not touch.

Over Boards—Cover material is placed over stiff boards. This is the standard binding for hardcover books. It is often used in Bibles for church pews and libraries.

Padded Cover—A Bible cover which features a thin layer of foam under the cover, giving it a cushioned feel.

Snap-Flap Style—A popular Bible binding style which has an elongated back cover overlapping the front cover and can be fastened. Protects the Bible and is often preferred to zippers.

Zipper Binding—An overlapping binding with a zipper for closing the covers completely, protecting the Bible from dust and wear.[3]

We could also look at other features, such as the various kinds of Bible paper or the way page edges may be decorated (color-stained, gilded, etc.), but these things do not affect the durability, usability, or price of the Bible significantly. Your local bookseller can give you more information about these options, if you want to learn more.

One last piece of advice: Be sure you are happy with your Bible purchase *before* you leave the store. While booksellers are usually willing to accept a "return" if you change your mind about the book, do not ask them to take back a Bible that has visible signs of use, or one that has your name stamped on the cover.

Care of the Bible

You will get much longer service from your Bible if you take special care in handling it. Here are some suggestions for the care of your Bible.

1. *Carefully open a new Bible.* Many people ruin a new Bible (or any other book) by using strong-arm tactics to "break it in"; actually, they break the binding and shorten the useful life of the book. Try the following method to open a new Bible:

(A) Hold the spine of the book in one hand and take the pages (not the covers) in the other hand, with your thumb about halfway up the edge. Gently arch the pages and let them splay loose from your thumb. This helps to loosen page edges that have been stuck together by staining or gilding—a common problem with new Bibles. If you find that many of the pages are stuck together, move your thumb to the top corner of the pages and repeat the process. Then move your thumb to the bottom corner and repeat. (See Fig. 13.)

(B) Change hands and repeat Operation A, arching the pages and letting them splay in the other direction.

(C) Lay the Bible on a flat surface and open it at about the center of the book. *Do not rub a crease along the center,* where the pages meet. Just let the Bible lie open for a couple of minutes, until the pages begin to lie

---

3. The sections on "Binding Materials" and "Binding Styles" were taken from *How to Sell the Right Bible,* pp. 17-20.

Figure 13—How to Open a New Bible

72

down flat by themselves. (This will take longer if the Bible or the room is cold.)

(D) Repeat this *gentle* opening procedure at about one-fourth of the way from the front of the book.

(E) Repeat the procedure at about one-fourth of the way from the back of the book.

(F) As you open the Bible to begin using it, try to let the pages lie flat by themselves. If you must crease the center, do it gently with the edge of your hand (which is broader and softer than a thumbnail). *Never* bend the spine back; this will weaken or break the binding. You will know the binding is broken when you see a crack down the center, where the pages meet; eventually these pages will come loose and start to fall out.

2. *Protect the Bible from dampness.* Rain, snow, or excessive humidity can ruin a fine Bible. Water dissolves the natural oils in leather; it makes glue become brittle; it softens the staining or gilding on page edges. Excessive humidity can also cause mildew.

You can avoid most of these problems by getting a plastic or vinyl slipcover for your Bible. Or you can get a Bible with a snap-flap or zipper binding. Be careful if drinking beverages while reading your Bible. A Bible-reading "coffee klatch" is great for fellowship, but disaster for many a Bible.

3. *If you mark your Bible, use a fine felt-tip pen.* A pencil point or a fountain-pen point will tear most Bible papers. So will many fine-tipped ballpoint pens. Ballpoints also make a furrow on the page, making it harder to read (and easier to tear) the other side of that page.

A fine felt-tip pen seems to work best, because it makes a clear mark without denting the paper. And because it's a fine point, it puts less ink on the page and is less likely to bleed through. (Test it on the corner of some inconspicuous page at the back of your Bible, to see if it bleeds through.)

4. *If the binding wears out, consider having your Bible rebound.* This is especially good advice when you have made notes or markings in the Bible and you want to keep them. Your local Christian bookseller should be able to have the Bible rebound for you. If not, see the Appendix of this book for addresses of firms that do this kind of work. Usually it costs no more to rebind a Bible than to buy a new one.

5.
Concordances

Suppose you are planning to talk with an unsaved friend, to explain how he or she can receive the eternal life that Jesus Christ offers. You are making a list of Scripture passages that you feel will be of special help. You vaguely recall a verse that says, " . . . He is faithful and just to forgive us our sins, and to cleanse us from all unrighteousness." But you can't remember the rest of the verse, and you're not sure where it is found. How do you find it?

One way would be to search through the Bible page by page. There are about 31,000 verses, though, so that approach would take quite a bit of time.

A better way would be to find the verse with the help of a concordance. You open this book and find a key word in the alphabetical list that you remember from the passage—perhaps the word FORGIVE. And under the word *forgive,* you find a listing of all the verses of the Bible that contain the word. Beginning with the Book of Genesis, the list takes you into the New Testament's references to *forgive*, and soon you come across a line that says:

I Jo. 1.9 he is faithful and just to forgive us[1]

You turn to 1 John 1:9, and read the verse in full. This is the way thousands of Bible students use their concordances every day.

A concordance is perhaps the most helpful book you can have in your library, after the Bible itself. You can use it to locate a Bible verse that you need, to compare the various ways a Greek or Hebrew word is translated in the Bible, to examine the biblical development of an important idea or doctrine, or to do several other types of study. The concordance is a guide to the entire Bible, a pathfinder with which you should be well acquainted.

An Interesting History

Bible concordances were being published long before the King James Version came off the press. In fact, the first Bible concordance was compiled before the Bible had been divided into verses! The original pur-

---

1. Robert Young, ed., *Young's Analytical Concordance to the Bible* (Nashville: Thomas Nelson, 1980), p. 367.

74

pose of the Bible concordance was not to help people locate elusive verses.

Cardinal Hugo de Santo Caro wished to compare similar Scripture passages from the Latin Vulgate. So he enlisted the help of several hundred monks to compile *concordantiae* (Latin, meaning "parallels")—that is, lists of Scripture passages that contained the same or similar words. The *concordantiae* were published in 1230.[2]

For the sake of easy reference, the monks used the Bible chapter divisions made by Stephen Langton, the late Archbishop of Canterbury. Cardinal Hugo further divided each chapter into seven equal parts; and each of these was divided into twenty-four subsections, corresponding to the twenty-four letters of the Latin alphabet. The monks did not copy the actual Scripture passages, just a list of these reference codes. Here is an example of what they might have listed under the phrase, "Verily, I say unto you:"

Matthiae V • III • F
Matthiae V • IV • T
Matthiae VI • I • E
Matthiae VI • I • N

This method is better than combing the entire New Testament to find the "Verily" passages of Jesus. Yet without the quoted Scripture passages themselves, the list of *concordantiae* was little more than a curiosity piece. Three Dominican friars in England rectified this problem by supplying the Scripture passages for Cardinal Hugo's list by 1252. (This was still more than three hundred years before the English Bible was to be divided into verses!)

Over the following years, Bible scholars compiled similar *concordantiae* for the Hebrew Old Testament, the Septuagint, and the Greek New Testament. But the first English concordance, compiled by Thomas Gybson, was not published until 1540.[3] Gybson's concordance was of the New Testament only, and referred to passages by chapter numbers only. In 1550, John Marbeck published the first English-language concordance of the entire Bible—still without the benefit of verse division. The title of Marbeck's work is an interesting summary of the purpose that the concordance had assumed by that time:

A Concordance,
that is to say, a work wherein
by the order of the letters of the A.B.C.
you may readily find any word

---

2. Frederick W. Danker, *Multipurpose Tools for Bible Study*, 2nd ed. (St. Louis: Concordia, 1966), pp. 1,2.
3. Ibid., p. 9.

> *contained in the whole Bible,*
> *so often as it is there expressed or mentioned.*[4]

No longer was the concordance merely a list of parallels, much like a "frequency list" (which tells the Bible student how often a certain word or phrase appears in the Bible, and in which books it appears). The concordance had become a ready reference tool, to help the student find and study the occurrences of any significant word in Scripture.

Scottish children of the eighteenth century who lived in pious Presbyterian homes were not allowed to play sports or table games on the Sabbath. But they were permitted a few Bible quizzes or a Bible word hunt. With a long strip of paper in hand, each child would scan the lines of a chosen Bible book, noting every reference to a particular word. Thus it is not surprising that many of the Bible concordances produced after John Marbeck's came from the pens of Scottish scholars.

A lad of Aberdeen named Alexander Cruden became so obsessed with this game that he spent every spare moment making Bible word searches of his own. He worked by day as a bookseller in London, by night as a printer's proofreader. And he rose from bed early each morning to glean further entries for his Bible concordance. One biographer says that he completed his work in a year's time,[5] although that seems rather incredible.

At any rate, in 1737 he published *A Complete Concordance of the Old and New Testaments.* Cruden noted thirteen English Bible concordances that had been published up to that time, including Marbeck's; but his was the first that claimed to be "complete." Even his claim was qualified. He wrote:

> . . . Though it be called in the title-page *A Complete Concordance,* poor
> sinful man can do nothing absolutely perfectly and complete, and therefore
> the word *Complete* is only to be taken in the comparative sense.[6]

Indeed, Cruden overlooked many Bible references in his concordance. He inserted some of them in the two revisions he made before his death in 1770, but even then his concordance was not a thorough listing of all references to all the words of the Bible. It was complete, but not exhaustive.[7]

---

4. Ibid. I have modernized the spellings in this title to convey the sense more clearly.

5. Edith Olivier, *The Eccentric Life of Alexander Cruden* (London: Faber and Faber, 1934), p. 58.

6. Ibid., p. 65.

7. One of the sad ironies of history is that Alexander Cruden spent much of his life in insane asylums for various reasons. Yet his friends regarded him as a genius, a veritable encyclopedia of Bible knowledge. "If Cruden was a madman," his biographer writes, "he was a remarkably clear-headed one . . ." (Olivier, *Eccentric Life,* p. 64).

An Edinburgh bookseller named Robert Young, who had a mastery of ancient biblical languages, issued his *Analytical Concordance to the Holy Bible* in 1862. Young listed the key words alphabetically, as Cruden and other concordance editors had done. But he went one step further and listed the Scripture passages under each word according to the Hebrew or Greek word that it translated. Figure 14 (pp. 78-79) compares an entry from Cruden's concordance with the same entry from Young's concordance, to show how Young displayed the linguistic origin of each word.

In 1890, Dr. James Strong published his *Exhaustive Concordance of the Bible*. Here at last was a concordance designed to list every occurrence of every word in the KJV. This mammoth volume has gone through twenty-four editions, and each time a few entries have been added that were missed in the original effort.

Instead of dissecting the Hebrew and Greek background of each word in the text of the concordance itself, Dr. Strong published two supplemental dictionaries of the Hebrew and Greek words found in the Hebrew and Greek texts that the KJV translators used. He gave each of these words a code number. Then he tagged each citation in the concordance with the proper code number, to show which Hebrew or Greek word occurred in that verse. Thus a student using the *Exhaustive Concordance* could do a Hebrew or Greek word study by following these code numbers to the dictionaries. But he did not have to work around a linguistic apparatus in the concordance itself if he was simply interested in a study of the English text.

With the KJV being the most popular English version of the Bible, *Strong's Exhaustive Concordance* has become the most popular concordance. Bible publishers have brought out other concordances keyed to the newer versions (see the Annotated Bibliography at the end of this chapter), but none of them rival the perennial popularity of Strong's.

Beyond Proof Texting

Bible students most often use a concordance to track down a Bible passage that they partially recall. They remember a fragment and want to find the complete verse. A concordance is ideally suited to this kind of Scripture sleuthing. Yet too much use of the concordance for this purpose becomes a crutch for a lazy mind and inhibits the practice of memorizing Scripture.

Other people fall prey to the temptation of using a concordance for proof texting—poring over Scripture to find some passage to support preconceived notions. Danker nettles our consciences when he says:

. . . For someone on the lookout for a particularly appropriate proof text, a concordance is indispensable. As an example, I Tim. 2:11 is very handy if

Figure 14—Cruden's and Young's Concordances

Alexander Cruden's *Complete Concordance* (1737)

KINSMAN.

Num.   5. 8. if the man have no *k.* to recompense
        27.11. ye shall give his inheritance to his *k.*
Deu.   25.†5. her husband's next *k.* shall go in
         †7. if a man like not to take his next *k.* wife
Ruth   2. 1. Naomi had a *k.* his name was Boaz
       3. 9. thou art a near *k.*
      12. a *k.* nearer than I
      13. if he will perform to thee the part of a *k.* well if not, I will do the part of a *k.* to thee
      4. 1. behold the *k.* of whom Boaz spake, came by
       6. the *k.* said, I cannot redeem it for myself
       8. the *k.* said unto Boaz, buy it for thee
      14. hath not left thee this day without a *k.*
John 18.26. being his *k.* whose ear Peter cut off
Rom. 16.11. salute Herodion my *k.* greet them

KINSMEN.

Ruth   2.20. the man is near of kin one of our next *k.*
1 Chron.15.†5. Uriel and his *k.* two hundred twenty
Psal. 38.11. my lovers and *k.* stood afar off
Mark 3.†21. when *k.* heard, they went to lay hold
Luke 14.12. call not friends, brethren, nor *k.*
Acts 10.24. Cornelius . . . had called together his *k.*
Rom.   9. 3. accursed, for my *k.* according to the flesh
     16. 7. salute my *k.*
            thy *k.* salute you

Robert Young's *Analytical Concordance* (1862)

KINSMAN, (next or near)—
1. *To free, redeem,* גאל *gaal.*
   Num.   5. 8 if the man have no kinsman to recompe.
   Ruth   2.20 the man (is) near. one of our next kins.
         3. 9 spread therefore. for thou (art) a near k.
        3.12 now it is true that I (am thy) near kins.
        3.12 howbeit there is a kinsman nearer than I
        4. 1 the kinsman of whom Boaz spake came by
        4. 3 he said unto the kinsman, Naomi, that is
        4. 6 the kinsman said, I cannot redeem (it)
        4. 8 the kinsman said unto Boaz, Buy (it) for
        4.14 hath not left thee this day without a ki.

2. *Acquaintance* מודע *moda*
   Ruth   2. 1 Naomi had a kinsman of her husband's

3. *Near,* קרוב *qarob.*
   Psa. 38.11 My lovers . . . and my kinsmen stand afar

4. *Flesh, relation,* שאר *sheer.*
   Num. 27.11 unto his kinsman that is next to him of

5. *One of the same race, kinsman, συγγενής suğḡēnes.*

Luke	14.12	neither thy kinsmen, nor . . . neighbours
John	18.26	being (his) kinsman whose ear Peter cut
Acts	10.24	called together his kinsmen and near
Rom.	9.3	my brethren, my kinsmen according to
	16. 7	Salute Andronicus and Junia, my kinsmen
	16.11	Salute Herodion my kinsman. Greet
	16.21	Lucius, and Jason, and Sosipater, my k.

KINSMAN, to do or perform the part of a—
  To free, redeem, אֵל gaal.

Ruth	3.13	if he will perform . . . the part of a kinsman
	3.13	well; let him do the kinsman's part; but
	3.13	if he will not do the part of a kinsman
	3.13	then will I do the part of a kinsman to

Notice that Cruden lists the Scripture references in straight canonical order, making a division only between the singular (*kinsman*) and plural (*kinsmen*). But Young divides the references according to the original Hebrew or Greek word being translated, and he indicated the literal meaning of each word.

Also notice that Young and Cruden each cite twenty four occurrences of the word *kinsman* (or *kinsmen*), but they disagree at points. Cruden cites Deuteronomy 25:5, 7, 1 Chronicles 15:5, and Mark 3:21 because his edition of the KJV listed *kinsman* or *kinsmen* as an alternate reading in the margin of those verses. (The dagger symbol in Cruden's indicates an alternate reading.) Young cites Ruth 4:3 and Romans 16:21, which Cruden seems to have overlooked.

---

the subject of woman's suffrage in the congregation is broached. But to limit the concordance to this function is to sacrifice its magnificent interpretive possibilities.[8]

Proof texting ignores the fact that God gave us the *whole* Bible as His revealed Word; it assumes that any nugget of Scripture contains the whole truth, in and of itself. But the mature Bible student knows that every nugget of Scripture must be compared with the entire vein of the "mother lode." Sound doctrine cannot be built on a single passage of Scripture, because other passages may clarify or modify that passage.

There are many legitimate needs for finding a particular Scripture passage in the course of regular Bible study other than the hot pursuit of a proof text. With that caution in mind, let us consider how to use a concordance most efficently when we search for a particular verse.

You will probably save time if you look for the most unusual word in that portion of the verse which you recall. The concordance's list of passages for that word should be shorter than the rest. Going back to the example at the start of this chapter, let us assume you want to find the Bible verse that says, ". . . He is faithful and just to forgive us our sins and to cleanse us from all unrighteousness."

---

8. Danker, *Multipurpose Tools*, p. 11.

If you have a truly *exhaustive* concordance, you can find the verse under any word in the portion that you remember. But if you turn to the word *He,* you find several thousand references; the word *is* has even more references. Trying to find the verse under either of these headings is "like trying to find a needle in a haystack."

What about the word *forgive*? Strong's concordance lists fifty-three occurrences of *forgive* in the KJV. And if you happen to know that the verse occurs in the New Testament, you reduce that number to twenty-five. That's indeed a more manageable haystack! If your memory is good enough to recall that the word *unrighteousness* is in the verse, the search is even easier. (Strong lists twenty-one occurrences in the entire Bible, seventeen in the New Testament.)

Be sure to check other forms of the key word, if you do not find the desired Scripture passage under the most basic form of that word. For example, Strong's concordance has separate entries for *forgive, forgiven, forgiveness, forgivenesses, forgiveth,* and *forgiving.*[9] So if your memory was a bit hazy about the exact form of this word, you might need to check several forms of the word. (For verbs, check different tenses. For nouns, check different numbers and genders of the word.)

Of course, this sort of Scripture search is still no substitute for memorizing important portions of the Word. We become painfully aware of this when we try to find a verse that has only commonly used words, such as "In the beginning was the Word, and the Word was with God, and the Word was God." This verse is vital to our knowledge of the eternal nature of Christ. Yet if we try to locate it with a concordance, we find that nearly every word occurs hundreds of times in Scripture. The least common word in this verse is *beginning;* and Strong's concordance lists 106 occurences of *beginning.* Better to memorize the verse and the reference (John 1:1)!

If we recall a portion of a verse with only very common words, we may be able to narrow our search by using an *analytical* concordance and looking for a key *phrase* that probably came from a single Hebrew or Greek word. Let's say we wanted to locate the verse from the Christmas story that says, "And they made known abroad the saying which was told them concerning this child."

All of the words are commonly found in the Bible. So let's focus our search on a phrase, such as the verb phrase "made known." This phrase comes either from the Greek word for *make* or from the Greek word for *known.* If we go to Strong's concordance, we find nearly four full pages of references to *make* and its related verb forms.

But if we go to *Young's Analytical Concordance,* we find several bold-

---

9. Young's concordance gives separate entries for various Hebrew and Greek forms of this word, rather than the various forms of the English rendering.

face headings that break up the list, according to different Hebrew and Greek words *and* according to different phrases that are derived from these words:

MAKE (ruler), to—
MAKE as though, to—
MAKE away, utterly to—
MAKE (baldness), to—
 etc.

Immediately we see that the phrase "make known" is not here. So we turn in Young's concordance to *known*, where we find these analytical headings:

KNOWN—
KNOWN, to be—
KNOWN, to be fully—
KNOWN, to be made—
KNOWN, to make (to be)—
KNOWN abroad, to make—
 etc.

And under that last heading we find this single reference:

To make known throughout, thoroughly,
 Luke 2:17 they made known abroad the saying which

So we find the verse. Unfortunately, Young's concordance does not always help us locate a key phrase (for example, it does not have a section for "BEGINNING, in the—" to help us with John 1:1). But its analytical format can help us find many verses with common words by following a phrase.

If you do not recall a bit of the verse itself but you can recall the *subject* of the verse, begin looking under Bible words that may refer to that subject. For example you may recall that 1 John 1:9 deals with God's forgiveness, but you don't recall the exact wording of the verse. One approach is to make a list of Bible words that are related to God's forgiveness:

forgive, forgiveness, *etc.*
grace, gracious, *etc.*
love, lovingkindness, *etc.*
mercy, merciful, *etc.*

Then begin checking the passages listed under these words until you come across 1 John 1:9.

Frankly, this sort of Scripture search is agonizingly slow. If you can remember only the topic of the verse, you may get faster results with a topical Bible, rather than taking this circuitous route with a concordance.

Two Other Uses: Word Study and Topic Study

How else might we use a concordance, besides locating a Scripture reference that we do not fully recall? Here are some ideas.

Word Study

Explore the richness of meaning in a Hebrew or Greek word by using a concordance to find various occurrences of the word in Scripture. Strong's concordance and Young's concordance will help you do this in the KJV.[10] (Unfortunately, the concordances for newer versions seldom furnish the linguistic apparatus you need for this type of study.[11]) Two processes are outlined below for conducting a study of the word *holy* in the Old Testament.

A. If you are using Young's concordance, turn to the standard English entry, HOLY. Beneath it you will find numbered italic subheadings; each one indicates a different Hebrew or Greek term. Here are the first three of the nine subheadings under "HOLY" and "HOLY, to be—":

1. *Kind,* חָסִיד *chasid.*
2. *Separate, set apart,* קָדוֹשׁ *qadosh.*
3. *Separate, set apart,* קַדִּישׁ *qaddish.*

In each case, Young first gives you the *literal meaning* of the term, then the actual Hebrew or Greek *script* of the term, and finally the English *transliteration** of that term.

If you decide to study the Hebrew word *qadosh,* the second of Young's subheadings, you look under that subheading and find a list of fifty-six verses from the KJV, in which the Hebrew word *qadosh* was translated as *holy.* You select a few of these verses for further study and learn that *qadosh* could mean to "separate" a nation from all other nations (Ex. 19:6), to "separate" oneself from other gods to serve the one true God (Lev. 20:7), or to be a place "separated" from all others as a place where God is regularly worshiped (Ps. 65:4) or where religious rituals are per-

---

10. Cruden's concordance does not show the Hebrew or Greek source of a word.

11. Some of the newer versions (e.g., RSV and NEB) were translated from different texts than those the KJV translators used. So we cannot reliably use a KJV concordance to trace the Hebrew or Greek origin of the words or phrases we find in these versions.

formed (Lev. 6:27). Water that was reserved for cleansing rituals was "holy," in the sense that it was separated from the people's normal bathing water (Num. 5:17). The camp of the Israelites was "holy," in the sense that it was separated from all indecent things (Deut. 23:14). The Sabbath day was "holy," in the sense that its activities for the worship of God were separated from everyday activities for the pleasure of man (Is. 58:13). All of these insights and more come from a careful study of the passages that we find under *qadosh* in this concordance.

B. If you are using Strong's concordance, you must do a bit more work to identify the Hebrew words. But the task is not as difficult as you may think. Notice the code number printed at the right-hand side of each Scripture reference in this sample from the entry *holy* in Strong's:

Ex. 3:5 whereon thou standest is $h \cdot$ ground.	6944
12:16 there shall be an $h \cdot$ convocation,	"
16 shall be an $h \cdot$ convocation to you;	"
15:13 thy strength unto thy $h \cdot$ habitation.	"
16:23 of the $h \cdot$ sabbath unto the Lord:	"
19:6 of priests, and an $h \cdot$ nation.	6918
20:8 the sabbath day, to keep it $h \cdot$.	6942
22:31 and ye shall be $h \cdot$ men unto me	6944

These numbers refer you to one of the Bible-language dictionaries that Strong appended to his concordance. A number in regular roman type (as these are) refers to his "Hebrew and Chaldee Dictionary"; a code number in italic type refers to his "Greek Dictionary of the New Testament." So you turn to the "Hebrew and Chaldee Dictionary" to find the Hebrew word designated by the second code number, as follows:

6918, קָדוֹשׁ qâdôwsh, *kaw-doshé;* or
קָדֹשׁ qâdôsh, *kaw-doshé;* from 6942; *sacred*
(ceremonially or morally); (as noun)
God (by eminence), an *angel,* a *saint,* a *sanctuary;*—holy (One), saint.

Strong first gives you the Hebrew script (with a variant script below it), then the English transliteration, followed by a *vocalized spelling* (how to pronounce the word). He indicates that this word comes "from 6942"—i.e., it is derived from the Hebrew word with code number 6942 (*qadash*). Then he gives the literal meaning of the word, "sacred"; and following the semicolon he gives several examples of persons or things that Scripture says are *qadosh.*

Return to his concordance entry *holy* and run your finger down the right-hand side of the column. Each time you encounter the number 6918, you have found a verse that uses *qadosh*. Every time you see the number 6942, you have found a verse that uses *qadash,* the root word of *qadosh*. Knowing this, you can proceed with your study and find insights similar to the ones described in Part A.

The William Carey Library has published two books that can help you in making Greek word studies with Strong's concordance. You will find detailed information about them in Chapter 11; but I will briefly mention here how they work, since they are so closely tied to the concordance.

The Word Study Concordance, edited by George V. Wigram and Ralph D. Winter, is an enlarged edition of an older reference book entitled *The Englishman's Greek Concordance.* This new book (published 1978) lists all the significant Greek words of the New Testament texts used by the KJV translators. It identifies each word by giving the appropriate code numbers from Strong's concordance, plus other numbers that refer to more sophisticated language-study aids. The exciting thing about this book is that it also lists under each word all its occurrences in the New Testament, as Young's concordance does.

Suppose you would like to study the word *understanding,* as found in Luke 2:47. Strong's concordance gives this word the code number 4907. Turning to that number in *The Word Study Concordance,* you find all of the pertinent information about the word and a composite list of the seven New Testament passages that contain the word.

The companion volume, entitled *The Word Study New Testament,* contains the entire text of the KJV New Testament. But it flags each significant word or phrase with its related Strong's code number. So you can read a Scripture passage in this book until you come to a word or phrase that you would like to study, then take the code number to either Strong's concordance or Winters' *Word Study Concordance* to find other passages where it is used.

This ingenious system has a couple of disadvantages. It does not include Old Testament (Hebrew) words, and it requires using two books, possibly three, to do the work you could do more quickly with Young's and your own New Testament.

The main advantage of the system is that it gives further information about the Greek word (e.g., the number of times it is used and its root word) that you will not find in Young's. Also, it directs you to more sophisticated word-study information in lexicons and Greek concordances, described in Chapter 11.

Remember that the purpose of any word study is to grasp the meaning of God's Word for your life. The piling up of linguistic data has little value for Christian living, but applying the truth of these biblical words leads to transformation.

Topical Study

A concordance can help you review quickly and easily what Scripture says on a certain topic, such as divorce. How is this subject treated both in Old Testament writings and in New Testament writings? Did God progressively reveal more of His will concerning divorce as human history proceeded? A concordance can give some insight into the background of such a subject.

Alexander Cruden shows his real genius on a topic such as this. He gives us not only a definition of divorce, but a brief commentary on the subject which weaves together the Bible's key references to divorce.

DIVORCE

Is *the dissolution of marriage, or the separation of husband and wife.* Moses *tolerated* divorces; *His words on this subject are in* Deut. 24:1, 2, 3, 4. When a man hath taken a wife and married her, and it comes to pass that she find no favour in his eyes, because he hath found some uncleanness in her; then let him write her a bill of divorcement, &c. *Commentators are much divided concerning the sense of these words,* because he hath found some uncleanness, *or, as the* Hebrew *has it,* matter of nakedness, in her.

The school of Shammah, *who lived a little before our Saviour, taught that a man could not lawfully be divorced from his wife, unless he had found her guilty of some action which was really infamous, and contrary to the rules of virtue. But the school of* Hillel, *who was Shammah's disciple, taught, on the contrary, that the least reasons were sufficient to authorize a man to put away his wife; for example, if she did not dress his meat well, or if he found any woman whom he liked better. He translated Moses' text thus:* If he hath found any thing in her, or an uncleanness . . . . [12]

Cruden continues with several more paragraphs of explanation. This sort of treatment is seldom found in a topical Bible or other concordance. It makes Cruden's concordance a more fascinating volume, but also a more antiquated one. One soon discovers Cruden's reliance on folklore about natural history, cosmology, and other subjects by reading his discussion of *serpent, tongue, unicorn,* or *world.*

More recent concordances also give insight into Bible topics, usually by way of linguistic background rather than commentary. So their information seems more useful. For example, here is what Young's concordance says about *divorce* and closely related words.

DIVORCE
A cutting off, בְּרִיתוּת *kerithuth.*
    Jer. 3. 8 put her away, and given . . . a bill of divorce

---

12. Alexander Cruden, ed., *A Complete Concordance to the Holy Scriptures* (New York: Revell, n.d.), p. 137.

DIVORCED, to be—
To loose off or away, 'απολύω *apoluō.*
Matt. 5:32 whosoever shall marry her that is divorced

DIVORCED, woman—
To cast out, divorce, גָּרַשׁ *garash.*
Lev. 21.14 a divor. woman, or profane, (or) an harlot
    22.13 priest's daughter be a widow, or divorced
Num. 30.9 of a widow, and of her that is divorced

DIVORCEMENT, (writing of)—
1. *A cutting off,* בְּרִיתוּת *kerithuth.*
Deut. 24.1 let him write her a bill of divorcement
    24.3 and write her a bill of divorcement, and
Isa. 50.1 the bill of your mother's divorcement
2. *A setting or standing off or away,* ἀποστάσιον.
Matt. 5.31 let him give her a writing of divorcement
    19.7 command to give a writing of divorce
Mark 10.4 suffered to write a bill of divorcement

Notice the various actions that divorce implied to the Hebrew or Greek mind—cutting off, setting loose, casting out, sending away. While the Hebrews considered a divorced woman to be a "cast out" woman, the Greeks considered such a woman to be "set loose" or "sent away," given freedom from the marriage bond. What a contrasting image! Reflect upon Young's linguistic notes and you will discern even more about the topic of divorce.

Using a concordance for topical study requires some creative thinking. While the concordance can provide the type of good background we have just sampled, it furnishes only Scripture references that contain a certain word. So to do a true topical study with the concordance, you must imagine several words that might be related to the topic. Again using the example of *divorce,* you might derive these related words:

discord
dissention
enmity
marriage
separation
vows

You can then see what references are listed in a concordance under these words, references that may shed light on the topic.

Also notice any refinements of the Bible's teaching about a certain topic as you follow the concordance list from the Old Testament to the New. For example, scan this list of selected references from the entry *Passover* in *Nelson's Complete Concordance of the Revised Standard Version Bible,* and watch for a development of the theme as history progresses.[13]

it in haste. It is the LORD's p.	Ex	12.11
families, and kill the p. lamb		12.21
is the sacrifice of the Lord's p.,		12.27
...		
"Keep the p. to the LORD your God,	2 Ki	23.21
For no such p. had been kept since		23.22
Josiah this p. was kept to the		23.23
...		
the returned exiles kept the p.	Ez	6.19
they killed the p. lamb for all		6.20
celebrate the feast of the p.,	Eze	45.21
after two days the P. is coming,	Mt	26.02
us prepare for you to eat the p.?"		26.17
I will keep the p. at your house		26.18
...		
release one man for you at the P.	Jn.	18.39
the day of Preparation for the P.		19.14

Several things become evident from this quick reading of the concordance list on *passover*: (1) The Passover ordinance was established at the time of the Jews' Exodus from Egypt. It commemorated the Lord's "passing over" the Jews, withholding the plague of death from them. (2) King Josiah revived the Passover observance. (3) The Jews revived the Passover observance again when they returned from the Babylonian Captivity. (4) Jews in New Testament times still celebrated the Passover. (5) Certain customs grew up surrounding the Passover—e.g., the Roman governor's release of a prisoner as a goodwill gesture.

ANNOTATED BIBLIOGRAPHY

Many Bible concordances were compiled so long ago that their copyright protection has expired. Such books are now in "public domain" —they belong to the public, and anyone may reprint them. So some concordances on this list are available from more than one publisher. In these cases, I have given the information for one current publisher and indicated with a footnote that other publishers also produce that book.

---

13. John W. Ellison, ed., *Nelson's Complete Concordance of the Revised Standard Version Bible* (New York:Thomas Nelson, 1957), pp. 1437-1438.

Cruden, Alexander, ed. *Cruden's Unabridged Concordance.* Grand Rapids: Baker, 1979.[14]

Early in this chapter we noted the significant place of Cruden's work in the history of Bible concordances. Some pastors still feel that Cruden's concordance is best after two hundred years of comparison and criticism. Yet Cruden's is not as complete as Strong's or Young's concordances; it omits some passages where a word appears, and it does not include names. But Cruden's *definitions* of some words make interesting study (see *church* and *salvation,* as examples). Baker's edition contains a sketch of Cruden's life and his "Compendium of the Holy Bible," which summarizes each chapter of Scripture; some publishers omit these features. The chief advantages of Cruden's concordance are its smaller size and lower price, compared to Strong's and Young's. Like them, it is based on the KJV.

Ellison, John W., ed. *Nelson's Complete Concordance of the Revised Standard Version Bible,* 2nd ed. New York: Thomas Nelson, 1978.

This concordance was generated by the Univac I computer, using the text of the RSV. Prior to this time, the task of compiling a concordance might have taken two decades or more; the computer did this work in a matter of hours. *Nelson's Complete Concordance* lists every word of the RSV, except for insignificant or very common prepositions, verbs, and articles (listed at the front). Unfortunately, the concordance does *not* indicate the Hebrew or Greek word that has been translated in each case. Even so, this is a very thorough and useable concordance for the RSV.

Goodrick, Edward W., and John R. Kohlenberger III, eds. *The NIV Complete Concordance.* Grand Rapids: Zondervan, 1981.

This computer-generated concordance contains all key words of the NIV, listing about 250,000 Scripture passages. The editors eliminate most adverbs, prepositions, articles, and other words that occur so often that they are of little help in locating a specific passage. They insert helpful cross-references to take the reader to related verb forms. However, the editors do not indicate the Hebrew or Greek origins of these words, so the concordance is not very helpful for word studies in those languages. Another drawback is the small type, which makes reading difficult.

Morrison, Clinton, ed. *An Analytical Concordance to the Revised Standard Version of the New Testament.* Philadelphia: Westminster, 1979.

This concordance follows the general pattern of Young's *Analytical Concordance,* but it offers some excellent features not found in Young's. Where the RSV

---

14. Also available from (Grand Rapids: Zondervan, 1979), (Old Tappan, N.J.: Revell, 1980), (Old Tappan, N.J.: Spire, 1979), (Waco: Word, 1979), and (Nashville: Broadman, 1972). Abridged editions are available as *Cruden's Compact Concordance* from (Grand Rapids: Zondervan, 1979), and *Cruden's Handy Concordance* from (Grand Rapids: Zondervan, 1979) and (Grand Rapids: Baker, 1979).

has rendered a Greek word rather freely, Morrison lists the verse with the warning that it is rendered "idiomatically"—followed by a more literal rendering in brackets. When the RSV supplies a word not in the Greek, Morrison lists the passage under that heading, but he notes that it is used "contextually." His index-lexicon at the back of the book lists various ways a Greek word is translated in the RSV. While this concordance covers only the New Testament, it should be of real help to anyone using the RSV.

Speer, Jack Atkeson. *The Living Bible Concordance.* Poolesville, Md.: Poolesville Presbyterian Church, 1973.

This computer-generated concordance has an interesting history. In November 1972, the fifty-eight member congregation of Poolesville Presbyterian Church met to pray for the survival of the premature baby son of one of their members, Jack Speer. Speer found great comfort during this time by reading the Living Bible. When his son survived, Speer decided to use his knowledge of computer programming to make a concordance of the LB. With the encouragement and financial backing of the Poolesville congregation, he succeeded. The format of *The Living Bible Concordance* resembles that of *The NIV Complete Concordance* and *Nelson's Complete Concordance*—it simply gives each key word, with a list of passages where that word occurs. It gives no definition of the word, nor its Hebrew or Greek origin. In two appendices, Speer lists the references to insignificant words (articles, prepositions, etc.) and the references to numbers and measurements.

Strong, James, ed. *The Exhaustive Concordance of the Bible.* Nashville: Abingdon, 1979.[15]

This is by far the most popular concordance based on the KJV because it is the most complete concordance. Dr. Strong accounts for every word in the KJV, including insignificant words such as *a, and, it, of,* or *that.* He gives a portion of the verse containing each significant word, (for the very common words such as the ones just mentioned he provides a list of references without actually quoting the passages). In an appendix, he includes "A Comparative Concordance of the Authorized and Revised Versions" (showing every instance in which the RV or the ASV renders a word differently than the KJV does). He also includes a "Hebrew and Chaldee Dictionary" and a "Greek Dictionary of the New Testament," listing all the Hebrew and Greek words translated by the KJV, with their pronunciation and definition. This enables the student to do Greek and Hebrew word studies, even when he has no prior knowledge of those languages. (See the explanation for this process given earlier in this chapter.) Some publishers omit portions or all of this appendix from their editions of Strong's concordance. A more compact edition of this concordance was published by Thomas Nelson Publishers in 1981, under the title *Strong's Concise Concordance.*

---

15. Also available from (Grand Rapids: Baker, 1979), (Nashville: Broadman, 1978), (Iowa Falls: Riverside Book and Bible House, 1979), (Nashville: Thomas Nelson, 1978), and (Waco: Word, 1979).

Thomas, Robert L., ed. *New American Standard Exhaustive Concordance of the Bible.* Nashville: Holman, 1981.

The growing popularity of the NASB made this concordance necessary. It is set up on the pattern of Strong's *Exhaustive Concordance* (even using the same Hebrew and Greek word codes), but the headings and passages are from the NASB. The editors have furnished a "Hebrew-Aramaic Dictionary" and a "Greek Dictionary" at the end of the book, keyed to Strong's word codes in the concordance. The type in these dictionaries is easier to read than that in most editions of Strong's. Also, the word derivations are more reliable than in Strong's dictionaries. This is an excellent study tool for anyone using the NASB.

Young, Robert. *Analytical Concordance to the Bible.* Grand Rapids: Eerdmans, 1960.[16]

This is the latest edition of Young's classic work; other earlier editions are still being published in Great Britain and America. Young's concordance is based on the KJV. It has two advantages over Strong's concordance: (1) It gives a brief definition of every word and a description of every person or place, and (2) it identifies each Hebrew or Greek word in the concordance itself, rather than listing them in a separate section with code numbers. This feature makes Young's easier to use for Greek and Hebrew word studies. However, Young's also has two distinct disadvantages, when compared to Strong's: (1) It does not have references to any word that the KJV translators supplied (the italicized words in the KJV), and (2) it often gives key *phrases* rather than key words, which requires a different approach as explained in this chapter. Despite these disadvantages, many Christian workers feel this concordance is more useful than Strong's.

---

16. Also available from (Nashville: Thomas Nelson, 1980).

6.
Bible Commentaries

And Ezra the scribe stood on a wooden pulpit which they had made for the purpose; and beside him stood Mattithia, Shema, Anaiah, Uriah, Hilkiah, and Maaseiah on his right hand; and Pedaiah, Mishael, Malchijah, Hashum, Hashbaddanah, Zechariah, and Meshullam on his left hand. . . . Also Jeshua, Bani, Sherebiah, Jamin, Akkub, Shabbethai, Hodiah, Maaseiah, Kelita, Azariah, Jozabad, Hanan, Pelaiah, the Levites, helped the people to understand the law, while the people remained in their places. And they read from the book, from the law of God, clearly [Or *with interpretation*]; and they gave the sense, so that the people understood the reading (Neh. 8:4, 7,8, RSV).

This seems to be the first record of a popular Bible commentary, "popular" meaning that it was intended to help the common people, who knew little about their precious heritage of Scripture. They had just returned to Jerusalem after many hard years of captivity in Babylon (586-458 B.C.). During that time, they began to adopt the language of their captors (Aramaic). Now they could scarcely understand what the Hebrew Old Testament said, much less apply it to their current life. They needed a commentary, so Ezra's scribes (Hebrew, *soferim*) "gave the sense" of the Word to the people. As one modern Jewish writer observed, "In their endeavour to cause the people to understand the reading, Ezra and his associates (the *soferim*) had to build bridges between the past and the present . . . [1]

"To build bridges between the past and the present" is a fitting way to describe the task of a Bible commentator! He rephrases the Word in terms that contemporary hearers can understand. He explains how the Word addresses current problems and questions. And he applies the Word to people's needs, discussing the implications of Scripture for their lives today.

Ezra's helpers did that at the Water Gate, and the best Bible commentators continue to do that from their pulpits. Occasionally, a person with this expository gift records his commentary in writing, so that all of us can

---

1. From I. Epstein's foreword to H. Freedman and Maurice Simon, eds., *Midrash Rabbah,* vol. 1 (London: Soncino, 1939), p. x. For this brief history of Jewish commentaries, I am also indebted to Hermann L. Strack, *Introduction to the Talmud and Midrash* (New York: Harper Torchbooks, 1965) and to Judah Goldin, trans., *The Living Talmud* (New York: Mentor, 1957).

enjoy it. These expository studies—written Bible commentaries—are the focus of this chapter.

Jewish Commentaries

To understand better how we came to have the Bible commentaries of today, we should review the history of Jewish Scripture commentaries. The Jewish commentaries set the pattern of Scripture exposition that the early church fathers followed. The rabbis' comments are still quoted in our modern Christian commentaries. So in a real sense, the Jewish commentaries were the direct ancestors of the Christian Bible commentaries we now have.

Ezra's expositors, and Ezra himself, were called "scribes" (*soferim*) because they made new handwritten copies of the ancient Hebrew Scriptures. Since many of the Jews returning from Babylon now spoke Aramaic (a language related to Hebrew, but quite different in some respects), the *soferim* soon began translating the Scriptures into Aramaic as they copied them. These Aramaic translations are called *targums*. The *targums* became the common "Bible" of the post-exilic Jews;[2] probably the scroll that Jesus read in Nazareth was an Aramaic *targum* (Luke 4:10 ff.).

This process of copying and translating the Old Testament into Aramaic was not enough, however. The Jewish worshipers still needed to know how Scripture related to their everyday lives. What might they learn from Scripture that would help them in dealing with their families, their foreign oppressors, and the spiritual struggles within themselves?

To answer such questions, the *soferim* continued to interpret the Scriptures at public readings. In other words, they continued to "give the sense" of the Scriptures as Ezra's assistants had done at the Water Gate. They gave their people an "exposition" (Hebrew, *midrash*) of the Law. They commented on the original meaning of Scripture. Perhaps they explained the sense of ancient Hebrew names. Occasionally, they made "enactments" to apply the Law to contemporary problems. They also stated "preventive measures" to insure that a person did not violate the Law. They pronounced "legal expedients," loopholes in the Law that would permit Jews to conduct necessary activities without violating the Law.[3]

---

2. J. I. Packer, Merrill C. Tenney, and William White, Jr., eds., *The Bible Almanac* (Nashville: Thomas Nelson, 1980), p. 345.

3. Judah Goldin notes an interesting "legal expedient" recorded in the *Mishna*: The sages allowed Jews who lived in adjacent houses surrounding a courtyard to prepare food before the Sabbath and leave it at one of the homes. Then on the Sabbath itself, they could cross the courtyard to carry food into their homes, even though the Law otherwise forbade them from "carrying burdens" on the Sabbath. So the "expedients" were also an important kind of commentary on the Law. (Goldin, *The Living Talmud,* p. 19).

But the scribes did not put their commentary in writing. According to Professor Judah Goldin, "such teaching and legislating as the *soferim* conducted through their schools and councils were carried on orally, in order to carefully distinguish between what was the Written Torah, *Scripture,* and the body of exegesis."[4] After about 270 B.C., certain *soferim* who were especially gifted teachers began to mentally organize and memorize these scribal comments. Instead of repeating a passage of Scripture, interjecting the comments that various scribes had made about it (*midrash*), these "sages" or "teachers" (Hebrew, *tannaim*) began by responding to a question that someone had brought to them. They recited various Scriptures, the scribal comments on those Scriptures, and even Jewish legends or folklore that seemed to have some bearing on the subject. This approach was eventually called "paragraphing" or "study" (Hebrew, *mishna*).

We can scarcely comprehend the stupendous feat of memorization that the *tannaim* achieved. Try to imagine a college lecture hall where the students use no notebooks and the lecturer has no written outlines on the chalkboard. Instead of opening a textbook to read the passage under consideration, he *recites* the passage from memory. He interrupts his recitation now and then to make comments on the passage or to answer his students' questions. And when he teaches the course the following term, he recites the passage again, flawlessly; he even recites some of the students' questions and his replies from the previous semester! This seems incredible, yet it was the routine method in the early Jewish academies.

The *tannaim* continued this mental preservation of Scripture commentary for almost five hundred years. During this time, they recognized two major components to their work: (1) the Law itself and legal rulings based on it (collectively called *halakah* in Hebrew) and (2) the legends, traditions, and folklore interwoven with the legal discussions (collectively called *haggadah* in Hebrew). Some teachers felt that they could reduce the *haggadah* to writing, since these teachings did not have the force of law. Apparently, written collections of *haggadah* commentary were being circulated by about A.D. 200.

By this time, the Romans had captured Jerusalem, and the Jews had scattered to the far corners of the Roman Empire. Rabbinical schools had sprung up in Babylon and northern Africa to rival the more prestigious academies in Palestine. Judah ha-Nasi and his students in Palestine orally "published" a standard *Mishna* commentary about A.D. 200, but the lecturers at the other academies began making their own compilations of the *Mishna.*

---

4. Ibid., p. 23.

This oral collection of the *Mishna* commentary and the comments on the *Mishna* became known as the *Talmud* (Hebrew, *instruction*). The academies of Palestine compiled their standard *Talmud* about A.D. 400; the academies of Babylon formed their *Talmud* about A.D. 500. Professor Goldin writes:

> Among other things, the reason the Babylonian Talmud overshadowed the Palestinian—so that in a sense it became *the* Talmud—was that in the centuries after the compilation of the Talmud, the heads of the Babylonian academies pressed hard for its adoption by various Jewish communities; and the political triumph and expansion of Islam put the Babylonian scholars at an advantage. Bagdad [sic] became a most dynamic center, attracting to its academies students from everywhere; in turn wherever they settled they brought and taught the Babylonian Talmud.[5]

So while the spreading Islamic hordes struck terror in the citizens of Roman Catholic Europe, they aided the spread of Judaism and Jewish learning—especially by carrying the commentary known as the *Talmud* throughout the Mediterranean world.

Abraham Geiger, I. Epstein, and other scholars contend that when Mohammed wrote the *Koran,* he based his teachings about the Jewish patriarchs on the *Midrash.*[6] Church fathers (e.g., Eusebius, Chrysostom, and Augustine) extracted helpful comments on Scripture from the *Midrash* and *Talmud.* Nicholas de Lyra, noted Christian commentator of the fourteenth century and one of Luther's favorites, drew many of his ideas from the *Midrash.* Even today, Christian commentators proudly refer to the biblical insights they have gained from *Judaica* (a Latin term now used to designate Jewish literature in general).

Early Christian Commentaries

In many ways, the growth of Christian Scripture commentary paralleled the growth of Jewish commentary. Church historian Jean Daniélou believes the apostolic church at Jerusalem contained several converted Jewish scribes, who made *targums* of the Old Testament "but gave it a Christian orientation."[7] The church fathers frequently commented on Old Testament Scriptures; and unlike the Jewish rabbis, they were quite willing to commit their thoughts to paper. They knew their letters could

---

5. Ibid., p. 26.

6. I. Epstein, *Midrash Rabbah,* p. xx.

7. Jean Daniélou and Henri Marrou, *The First Six Hundred Years,* trans. Vincent Cronin (New York: McGraw-Hill, 1964), p. 10.

circulate among all the churches, reaching far more of their Christian friends than they could ever instruct face to face. So we find commentary appearing in these *patristic letters** while the church was still in her infancy.

A major trend in early Christian commentaries is marked by Clement of Alexandria (ca. A.D. 200). He adopted the exegetical ideas of Philo (a Jewish scholar who had a large following in that city) by interpreting Bible events as *allegories**. In other words, Philo and Clement believed these stories were recorded to illustrate spiritual or moral truth of enduring value. They believed the events really happened, but they also felt the Bible preserved these stories to convey deeper spiritual truths. They felt it was their duty as commentators to unveil the hidden meaning behind each story.

> At times, Paul interpreted Old Testament events in an allegorical way, as Hellenistic Jewish writers often did. The best example is his interpretation of the story of Sarah and Hagar. He explained that their experience was an allegory of people who still lived under the old covenant while others lived under the new covenant of Christ (Gal. 4:21-23). . . . Hellenistic thinkers at Alexandria later developed this method of interpretation to its height.[8]

Philo and the other Jewish scholars of Alexandria had generously used allegory to interpret the Old Testament; Clement and his Christian colleagues continued the trend. Daniélou notes that "Clement used the method with discretion; in his writings the various sources are easy to disentangle. If he borrows from Philo an allegory about Sara and Abimelech, he first gives Philo's interpretation, then works out another, more christological . . . "[9]

Clement's colleagues and successors at the Christian academy of Alexandria were not so cautious, however. Radical allegory colors the work of Philo's star pupil Origen, as well as the commentaries of Justin, Irenaeus, Melito, Tertullian, and other men rooted in the Alexandrian tradition. Others used numerology, mysticism, and classical mythology in their interpretation of Scripture. A good example is Hippolytus' *Commentary on Daniel* (A.D. 203). Danker says, "They often obliterated the original intent of the [biblical] writers with a maze of fanciful exegesis both astounding and depressing to behold."[10]

A different commentary tradition began with Diodorus, Bishop of Tarsus. Before assuming the bishopric in 376, Diodorus served as a priest in

---

8. Packer, *Bible Almanac*, p. 174.
9. Daniélou and Marrou, *Six Hundred Years*, p. 129.
10. Frederick W. Danker, *Multipurpose Tools for Bible Study*, 2nd ed. (St. Louis: Concordia, 1966), p. 254.

Antioch, where another Christian academy was being formed to rival the one in Alexandria. To all intents, Diodorus functioned as head of that school. He was an outspoken *apologist** and an excellent writer. He urged his students to interpret all of Scripture—both Old and New Testaments—in the most literal way. He cautioned them to avoid looking for hidden spiritual meanings or taking every major Bible event as a symbol or "type" of something in the future.[11]

Although this literal method of Bible interpretation influenced the work of Jerome, Augustine, and other widely known writers, these men still preferred the allegorical method. Only after the Reformation did literal interpretation become the predominant method of Christian commentary on Scripture.

By the time the Babylonian *Talmud* was being circulated as the chief Jewish commentary on Scripture, two major Christian academies (Alexandria and Antioch) had developed two different methods of biblical commentary. Through *encyclical letters**, apologetic treatises, and actual books of Bible commentary, the scholars in these two schools of Bible commentary "gave the sense" of the Old Testament to their Christian friends, and applied New Testament teachings to the theological and ethical problems faced by the church as it spread into strange cultures and encountered new challenges.

Medieval and Reformation Commentaries

During the Middle Ages, Christian scholars were making great strides in commentary work. Theophylact, the Metropolitan of Bulgaria, wrote a series of brilliant commentaries on the New Testament and most of the Old during the eleventh century. Bede the Venerable and Anselm also were writing helpful commentaries at this time.

The sixteenth-century Reformation saw a flood of biblical commentators. Unlike commentators before them, the Reformers stressed a literal interpretation of Scripture. Martin Luther (1483-1546) and John Calvin (1509-1564) wrote profound, penetrating commentaries that challenged lay readers to renew their interest in the literal meaning of God's Word. While Luther wrote only on selected books of the New Testament (many feel his commentary on Galatians is his best), Calvin completed a forty-five-volume set on the entire Bible. Soon came more Protestant commentaries by Matthew Poole (1624-1679), Matthew Henry (1662-1714), John Gill (1697-1771), and a host of others.

---

11. The school of Antioch did not win the mind of Christendom on doctrinal matters, such as the divinity of Christ. But that is another story.

The seventeenth and eighteenth centuries became an age of plentiful, ponderous commentaries. When a Bible student comes across one of these venerable sets in a bookshop today, he wonders how any reader had enough patience to plow through their thousands of pages of exposition (usually in very small print). It is a tribute to our ancestors' appetite for God's Word.

What to Expect

Pastors and Sunday school teachers hold a wide range of opinion on the value of Bible commentaries. Many such people complain that commentaries are too difficult to use, too expensive, or not likely to provide new insights about a given passage. The great English pastor Charles H. Spurgeon (d. 1892) heard similar complaints. He wrote:

> It has been the fashion of late years to speak against the use of commentaries.... Usually, we have found the despisers of commentaries to be men who have no sort of acquaintance with them; in their case, it is the opposite of familiarity which has bred contempt.[12]

As Spurgeon suggests, perhaps the lingering discontent with commentaries is not so much the fault of the commentaries themselves as it is of the readers, who expect too much from a commentary. If we believe that a commentary will make plain everything that is obscure in Scripture, give us a clear view of the heavenly mysteries, or resolve every doctrinal argument that may arise, we are sure to be disappointed!

We can avoid this disappointment if we have a better idea of what a good Bible commentary should do.

First, *it should present the Scripture as clearly as possible.* Some commentators seem so preoccupied with their own pet interests (linguistics, archaeology, sociocultural backgrounds, systematic theology, or whatever) that they fail to give us a clear reading of the Word. That is essential. Commentaries sometimes provide a fresh translation of the Scriptures, along with the commentary. This may be of help as long as the commentator does not distort the translation to suit other purposes.

Second, *the commentary should explain (if possible) any confusing words or phrases in each passage.* Check a few selected passages to see whether the commentator does this. For example, does he attempt to explain what the phrase "other tongues" means in Acts 2:4, or, "They are not all Israel, which are of Israel" (Rom. 9:6), or, "the order of Melchis-

---

12. Charles H. Spurgeon, *Commenting and Commentaries* (London: The Banner of Truth Trust, 1969), p. 1.

edek" (Heb. 6:20)? The commentator may not give a final explanation of these terms, but he should offer some enlightenment.

Third, *the commentary should identify the major themes* of the book. Most of the commentator's remarks will deal with single words or phrases in the text; but if he leaves you with only that, you may not "be able to see the forest for the trees." The commentator should point out the main thrust of the Bible writer's message, so you can see how various parts of the passage contribute to the message. Look for an outline or an introductory essay (or both) discussing the major themes of the Bible book.

Fourth, *the commentary should sketch the cultural background against which the book was written.* The commentator should set the stage on which the events of the biblical narrative are enacted and review the events that prompted the writing of the book. He should describe the readers for whom the book was originally intended. All of these factors will enlarge your grasp of what you read.

Types of Commentaries

Various commentaries are described as "devotional," "exegetical," "expository," etc. These terms apply to different types of commentaries.

A *devotional commentary* is designed to give some inspiring thoughts on the Scriptures, without much detailed analysis of the text or involved theological reasoning. Some devotional commentaries come from sermons by noted pastors or radio evangelists.

A *practical commentary* is a type of devotional commentary that emphasizes the application of Scripture to daily living. The commentator may do this by asking a series of questions that probe your present spiritual condition. He may give examples of other Christians who faced problems and found answers from Scripture. Or he may use other methods to challenge you to put God's Word into practice.

A *suggestive commentary* is yet another type of devotional commentary, designed to stimulate further thought or reflection on God's Word. The commentator may mention the names of several well-known historical people who struggled with the problem being discussed in the Bible text. He may draw an analogy between a spiritual truth and some natural wonder. Or he may offer any number of "suggestive" statements to prompt your further reflection on the meaning of God's Word.

A *scholarly commentary* uses extensive research to unlock the subtle meanings of each Scripture passage. The first scholars of medieval times prided themselves on reading everything they could find on a given subject, and compiling all the pertinent information in their essays. The scholarly commentator bases his work on this approach. He quotes what other commentators have said about the text, or about a particular word, or about the person or event under study. Then he draws his own conclusions, trying to show why his view is the most reasonable.

An *expository commentary* is the most common type of scholarly commentary. This term comes from the Latin word *expositio,* which means "explanation." The expository commentator explains the message of the text, using relevant material he can garner from linguistics, theology, and ancient history. Often he will cite others who have commented on this passage, and he will try to outline the logical unfolding of the biblical writer's message.

An *exegetical commentary* is the most sophisticated type of scholarly commentary. This term comes from the Greek word *exēgeesthai,* which means "to lead out." The exegetical commentator literally "leads out" or "draws out" the meaning of each phrase or word in the original Hebrew and Greek texts. He will include plenty of word studies along the way and he may cite recent archaeological finds (scrolls, papyrus fragments, etc.) that provide a better understanding of certain words. Of course, you will find all degrees of exegesis; some studies are fairly easy for a layman with no knowledge of the Hebrew and Greek, while others are quite technical.

How to Use Commentaries

A Bible student is tempted to expect Bible commentaries to interpret the Bible for him. I must confess that we pastors are tempted even more, because we usually feel pressured to produce good Bible lessons for others, and because we usually have several commentaries within reach. It's easy to pull three or four from the shelf, compare what they say about a given passage, and massage their comments into an outline to suit our purposes. Sunday school teachers are likewise tempted.

But Bible commentaries are not intended to be crutches for hasty thinking. Ideally, they are aids to deliberate, prayerful thinking. With that end in mind, here is a suggested pattern for use. It should work with any method of Bible study. (Several Bible study methods are reviewed in Chapter 12.)

1. *Pray that God will help you understand what you read.* The psalmist prayed, "Make me to understand the way of thy precepts: so shall I talk of thy wondrous works" (Ps. 119:27). The apostle Paul told his friends in Ephesus, "Wherefore I also . . . Cease not to give thanks for you, making mention of you in my prayers; That the God of our Lord Jesus Christ, the

Father of glory, may give unto you the spirit of wisdom and revelation in the knowledge of him: The eyes of your understanding being enlightened . . . '' (Eph. 1:15-18).

God reveals Himself through the Bible. He expects you to see Him there, and He expects you to understand what you see. So it is appropriate for you to pray that He will help you understand Scripture. You can be sure that as you pray, He will give you "the spirit of wisdom and revelation" for studying His Word.

2. *Read and reread the Bible passage you plan to study.* You may miss the full impact of the passage the first time through, so review it. In fact, you may want to speed-read it the second time, to get the thematic "drift" of the passage. Ask yourself, What is the core of this Scripture passage? What is its basic message?

3. *Read the Bible passage in another version, for comparison.* In Chapter 1, I explained how to compare versions of different kinds. You may find that a second version sheds a different light on the passage. It may give the passage an altogether different meaning! (If that's the case, refer to a good exegetical commentary to see which version is giving you the most accurate rendering.)

4. *Outline the Scripture passage.* On a piece of paper, note the key thought of the passage and how the passage develops that thought step-by-step. This is especially helpful when you read poetic passages (such as Proverbs or Psalms) or complex theological passages (such as Romans or Galatians). The outline allows you to see the skeleton of the passage, and it shows how seemingly unrelated statements do supplement the theme.

5. *Reflect on what this Bible passage means for your life.* As long as you leave Bible teaching in the abstract, theoretical realm, you will get little benefit from it. But if you begin applying a passage (such as 1 John 4:11-14 or Jude 14-16) to your life, God will use the Bible study to transform you.

Notice that you still haven't consulted a Bible commentary. To this point, you have relied on what God's Holy Spirit reveals and what your own reasoning may discover in the passage.

6. *Consult a commentary for further insights.* Instead of letting the commentary provide the substance of your study, let it shape your study after you have begun. A good commentary will provide facts about Bible culture or history that may not be gathered through personal study and reflection. It will point out subtle nuances in the Hebrew or Greek text, which the English versions might not convey. It will correct any tendency toward *heterodox** or *heretical** doctrine based on one passage by referring to other Bible passages that more fully explain God's truth about the issue.

I believe that if you follow this six-step pattern, you will get the maximum benefit from a Bible commentary. The commentary will be a help instead of a hindrance to your study—a walking stick instead of a crutch.

Watch that "Slant"!

Before the Lord called me into the pastoral ministry, I was a newspaper reporter. In newspaper writing I had to carefully avoid giving a biased "slant" to an article. A reporter can slant an article by omitting some of the facts, making snide remarks, or describing the subject in derogatory terms. And the reporter may not even realize that personal bias has crept into the article. (That's one reason why we have editors!)

Bible commentaries may be slanted, too. Like a reporter, a Bible commentator may omit certain facts, or ignore or detract from other points of view because he feels his interpretation of a given passage is the only true interpretation. He slants the comments to his own way of thinking, often without realizing it.

Of course, we should expect a commentator to share his opinions with us, especially when we come to obscure passages of Scripture. But he does us a disservice if he omits contradictory facts or views in hopes of strengthening his argument. And we do ourselves a disservice if we consult only the commentaries that are slanted to suit our own views. When Charles H. Spurgeon drew up a catalogue of Bible commentaries for his students, he warned that he was including many books with which he disagreed. He said:

> Where we have admitted [to the catalogue] comments by writers of doubtful doctrine, because of their superior scholarship and the correctness of their criticisms, we have given hints which will be enough for the wise. It is sometimes very useful to know what our opponents have to say.[13]

That's good advice for any reader of commentaries! Proceed with caution, watch for the slants, yet appreciate the rich diversity of views among the commentators.

When buying a commentary for a friend, you may need to be even more cautious, because you do not want to buy one with a slant that will offend him. It is seldom wise to buy a Bible version or Bible reference book as a gift. Unless you know specifically what your friend wants, give a bookstore gift certificate.

There is no infallible set of tests for discovering the theological bias of a commentary, but what the commentator says about the following passages will likely reveal any "slant":

Arminianism*—Deut. 5:10,29; Ps. 33:13-15; Matt. 10:22; 24:10-13;

---

13. Ibid., p. 34.

Acts 10:28; Rom. 9:4 ff.; Col. 1:22,23; Heb. 3:6,14; 6:11,12.

Calvinism*—Prov. 16:4; Jer. 1:4,5; John 6:37-44; Rom. 4:4,5; 9:4 ff.; 11:5-6; 1 Cor. 15:10; 2 Thess. 2:13; 1 Pet. 1:3-5.

Unitarianism*—Deut. 6:4; 1 Kin. 8:60; John 1:1; 17:3; I Tim. 2:5; Phil. 2:5-11.

Universalism*—Is. 29:18-24; 52:13-15; 57:15-21; Matt. 18:1-4, 10-14; Luke 3:5,6; 1 Tim. 4:10.

Dispensationalism—Rom. 2:28-3:31; Eph. 1:10,11; 2:11-19; 3:2-6; Col. 1:24-27; Heb. 1:1,2; 8:8-12.

Amillennialism*—Matt. 25:31-46; Mark 13:32-37; Acts 1:6,7; 1 Cor. 15:51,52; 1 Pet. 3:3-10; Rev. 20.

Premillennialism—Is. 65:19-25; Zech. 9:9,10; 14:16,17; Heb. 8:11; Rev. 20.

Postmillennialism*—Luke 18:7,8; 1 Cor. 15:24-28; Col. 3:1-4; Eph. 1:10; Rev. 20.

Rapture and Tribulation—Matt. 24:21-31,40-44; Luke 21:35,36; 1 Thess. 4:15-17; 2 Thess. 2:3.

Higher Criticism

In addition to theological bias, the commentary writer's approach to higher criticism can also affect the content of the commentary. In the analogy of the hotel building in Chapter 1, we said that textual criticism might be called "lower criticism" because it is the entry level of serious Bible study. The further stages of serious Bible study, where we consider the *meaning* of Scripture, are called "higher criticism" (simply because we can move on to using these methods only after the Bible text has passed the inspection of lower criticism).

Bible commentators disagree about how to do this higher-critical study. A commentator may feel so strongly about certain higher-critical methods that he uses the commentary to promote those approaches. Being aware of some of the various methods of higher criticism that a Bible commentator may employ will help in weeding out any underlying emphases on the method itself.

Form criticism*—The German scholar Hermann Gunkel (1862-1932) developed this method. He observed that nearly every generation has its unique style of oral or written history-keeping. This unique style (form) can identify which generation created a piece of literature. If the record of a certain event began as an oral record and was later put into writing, the written record would still bear the marks of the oral record. Gunkel believed he could identify several "forms" in the Old Testament, several layers of tradition. So he analyzed sections such as Genesis and Psalms to determine when certain portions of them originated, and who originated them. Martin Dibelius, Rudolf Bultmann, and other scholars have used form criticism to analyze the New Testament as well.

Literary criticism (or *source criticism*)—For centuries, Christian scholars have examined the literary style, the purpose, and the implied cultural background of each book of the Bible. Origen (second century A.D.) compared the style of the Epistle to the Hebrews with the known epistles of Paul, and declared that Paul had not written Hebrews. His student Dionysius compared the Gospel of John and the Book of Revelation and concluded that John did not write both, because the two styles were so different.

Other literary critics have tried to ascertain the authorship, date, and place where each book of the Bible was written. Some feel that the Book of Genesis was written and/or edited by men from four different eras of Israel's history (the "documentary hypothesis"). Others believe that two, three, or more men wrote the Book of Isaiah. Still others believe that Matthew and Luke used Mark's Gospel as their basic source, along with other records of Jesus' life.

Obviously, the literary critic employs a variety of methods to arrive at these conclusions, and to a great extent he relies on his own opinions to interpret what he finds.

Redaction criticism*—Gerhard von Rad (1901–1971) and other Old Testament scholars pointed out that the writer of Deuteronomy was actually making a revised edition of the earlier Mosaic law of Exodus, restating some of the laws to conform with a later theological view. Martin Dibelius noticed a similar pattern in the Gospels of Matthew and Luke, which seemed to rework the history of Mark to suit other purposes. This study of how a biblical writer edits older written material is what we call redaction criticism (from the German *redakteur,* "editor").

Commentators use these methods and a host of others (such as "audience criticism" and "canon criticism") to answer basic questions about a passage of Scripture, such as who wrote it, when, why, and to whom. After a commentator has considered what the writer meant in the original setting where the Scripture passage took shape, he moves on to consider what the passage means for us today.

There is a basic difference in the way liberal and conservative writers use higher criticism.

Generally speaking, the liberal believes that the Bible is a collection of writings by men with a variety of theological views. He uses higher criticism to sort out these strands of thought and to judge which strands provide greater theological understanding. W. F. Albright, Raymond E. Brown, and Martin Dibelius are writers who take this approach.

The conservative believes that the Bible is basically the work of one Author, the Holy Spirit, who worked through a variety of human authors to produce the Scriptures. So he uses higher-critical methods to show the unity of the Bible. F. F. Bruce, C. F. Keil, and Edward J. Young are examples.

ANNOTATED BIBLIOGRAPHY

There are hundreds of Bible commentaries now available. The titles chosen for this bibliography are written from a conservative, evangelical perspective unless otherwise indicated, and I have tried to note where a commentator has a marked theological bias. I have listed only works that are currently in print (though some excellent commentaries are out of print). The latest publication data is based on *Books in Print 1981-1982,* 4 vols. (New York: R. R. Bowker, 1981) and *Current Christian Books: 1980-1981* (Colorado Springs: Christian Booksellers Association, 1979).

WHOLE BIBLE

Albright, W. F., and David Noel Freedman, eds., *The Anchor Bible,* 59 vols. projected. Garden City, N.Y.: Doubleday, 1964-

This is an ecumenical commentary, including volumes by Jewish, Roman Catholic, and Protestant scholars. Evangelical readers will not like the higher-critical approach in several volumes (e.g., the lengthy discussion of the documentary theory in E. A. Speiser's volume on Genesis). However, *The Anchor Bible* gives excellent background information about the Bible languages and recent archaeological findings that shed light on Scripture. Raymond E. Brown's two volumes on the Gospel of John and Markus Barth's on Ephesians are perhaps the best in this series. Each volume contains the commentator's own translation of the book being considered.

Black, Matthew, and H. H. Rowley, eds. *Peake's Commentary on the Bible.* New York: Thomas Nelson, 1962.

Several reviewers feel that this is the best commentary based on the Revised Standard Version. (Frankly, I prefer *The New Bible Commentary.*) *Peake's* delves into some rather thorny theological problems, so laymen may fear that it is "over their heads." But it yields rich rewards to anyone who does concentrated study. This edition contains a helpful series of Bible maps.

Brown, Raymond E., Joseph A. Fitzmeyer, and Roland E. Murphy, eds. *The Jerome Bible Commentary.* Englewood Cliffs, N.J.: Prentice-Hall, 1969.

Named in honor of the brilliant fourth-century scholar who penned the Latin Vulgate, *The Jerome Bible Commentary* is an outstanding Roman Catholic commentary. Barber points out that this commentary "supplies a remarkable contemporary interpretation which at times is at variance with accepted Catholic doctrine" (ML 46). Despite these variances, *The Jerome Bible Commentary* is sure to be a standard for Roman Catholic readers for many years to come. Most of the writers are American. No single translation is used, though the commentary often cites the Confraternity edition, which has now been replaced by the NAB.

Buttrick, George A., ed. *The Interpreter's Bible,* 12 vols. Nashville: Abingdon, 1951-1957.

On each page, this commentary offers parallel texts from the King James Version and the Revised Standard Version, with commentary alongside. This innovative idea gives the reader a good comparison of versions that use quite different manuscripts as their source, so they tend to balance one another textually. The chief disadvantage of this arrangement is that it leaves little space for the actual commentary. Many of the comments show a liberal bias, especially with regard to authorship and date of the Bible books.

Calvin, John. *Calvin's Commentaries,* 22 vols. Grand Rapids: Baker, 1979.

Though not as well known as Calvin's *Institutes of the Christian Religion,* these commentaries exhibit the same keen insight into spiritual and ethical matters. Spurgeon observes that "of all commentators I believe John Calvin to be the most candid. In his expositions he is not always what moderns would call Calvinistic; that is to say, where Scripture maintains the doctrine of *predestination* * and grace he flinches in no degree, but inasmuch as some Scriptures bear the impress of human free action and responsibility, he does not shun to expound their meaning in all fairness and integrity. He was no trimmer and pruner of texts" (CC, 4). David W. and Thomas F. Torrance have abridged Calvin's New Testament commentaries to make a twelve-volume set (Grand Rapids: William B. Eerdmans, 1979).

Carter, Charles W., Ralph Earle, and W. Ralph Thompson, eds. *The Wesleyan Bible Commentary,* 7 vols. Grand Rapids: Baker, 1979.

This is one of two major Wesleyan Bible commentaries to be published in recent years (the other being *The Beacon Bible Commentary*). Unfortunately, *The Wesleyan Bible Commentary* usually expounds the obvious meanings of the text and seldom ventures into difficult territory. The writers have presented sound interpretations of Scripture, but their preoccupation with the safest, most traditional insights is disappointing.

Clements, R. E., and Matthew Black, eds. *The New Century Commentary,* 35 vols. projected. London: Marshall, Morgan and Scott, 1970-   .[14]

This commentary is "supposedly based on the RSV, although for the most part the writers work from the original texts" (ML, 47). Generally, the commentators have taken liberal views of the authorship and dates of Bible books. There are exceptions to this, however, such as Donald Guthrie's commentary on Galatians

---

14. Published in the United States by (Grand Rapids: Eerdmans).

They also pass over some portions of Scripture found in the KJV but not in the RSV (because different manuscripts were used in translating the RSV).

Cook, F. C. *The Bible Commentary,* 10 vols. Grand Rapids: Baker, 1981.

Originally published in England in the late 1800s as *The Speaker's Commentary,* this set was designed to address higher-critical concerns from a conservative stance. It includes the work of eminent writers such as B. F. Westcott, George Rawlinson, and E. H. Plumptre—often regarded with suspicion in their day because they considered using higher-critical methods. Most Christians would now accept this work as one of real integrity. Warren W. Wiersbe praises it as "scholarly without being shallow, and . . . evangelical without being narrowly denominational."

Earle, Ralph, ed. *Adam Clarke's Commentary on the Entire Bible.* Grand Rapids: Baker, 1979.[15]

This classic Wesleyan-Arminian commentary was published in London in 1844 as six volumes. Clarke's languid, meandering style was more appropriate to the days of long reading hours, but it is a bit exasperating today. Dr. Ralph Earle, former professor at the Nazarene Theological Seminary, has deftly cut out Clarke's less relevant comments to produce this meaty volume.

Gaebelein, Frank E., ed. *The Expositor's Bible Commentary,* 12 vols. Grand Rapids: Zondervan, 1979-1981.

This commentary on the NIV utilizes much of the research that the translators did as they worked on the NIV itself. It provides good word studies and a conservative view of authorship and dates. It is a thorough and scholarly work, offering helpful linguistic insights.

Gill, John. *Expositions on the Old and New Testaments,* 6 vols. Grand Rapids: Baker, [n.d.].

This centennial reprint of Gill's classic is mainly of interest to collectors. Gill's is largely devotional, and he often uses the allegorical method of interpretation, so his comments are quite speculative. He offers little of real substance to the serious Bible student.

Guthrie, Donald, J. A. Motyer, A. M. Stibbs, and D. J. Wiseman. *The New Bible Commentary: Revised,* 3rd ed. Grand Rapids: Eerdmans, 1970.

This commentary is a bit uneven in depth; its treatment of the Gospels or the New Testament *General Epistles,* * for example, is more meticulous than its treatment of the *Major Prophets.* * But it does deal with most of the difficult words and phrases in each passage. The commentary's supplemental articles are also helpful. Most of the writers of *The New Bible Commentary* come from a Reformed Church background. This commentary is based on the RSV.

---

15. Also available as 3 volumes from (Nashville: Abingdon, 1979).

Harper, A. F., ed. *The Beacon Bible Commentary,* 10 vols. Kansas City, Mo.: Beacon Hill, 1964-1969.[16]

This Wesleyan-Arminian commentary on the KJV is not as reluctant as *The Wesleyan Bible Commentary* to tackle the difficult passages of Scripture. It often quotes earlier commentators' views on a given passage. It occasionally dips into critical studies of the Hebrew or Greek words involved, but it would have been strengthened by more frequent and more detailed word studies. The introductions are generally brief, but they do give the overall theme of each book and an outline. The commentary has a strong treatment of messianic prophecies and most Pauline Epistles but contains shallow treatment of biblical covenants and *eschatology.**

Harrison, E. F., and Charles F. Pfeiffer, eds. *The Wycliffe Bible Commentary.* Chicago: Moody, 1962.

Forty-eight evangelical American scholars contributed to this work, which is highly regarded by conservative Christians. It does not treat many passages in depth, and this is its chief weakness. But the exposition of the text is sound, so far as it goes.

Henry, Matthew. *An Exposition of the Old and New Testaments,* 6 vols. Old Tappan, N.J.: Revell, [n.d.][17]

Undoubtedly the most popular commentary among Protestant readers, Henry's work is a devotional commentary. Seldom does he offer any background on the Hebrew or Greek texts. Rather, he deals with the KJV as it is, exploring the practical implications of Scripture for daily living. Henry employs quaint illustrations from his own age (he was a pastor in Chester, England in the late 1600s), and some of these are now difficult to understand. But his wisdom and spiritual maturity are still evident. Spurgeon told his students, "Every minister ought to read Matthew Henry entirely and carefully through once at least. I should recommend you to get through it in the next twelve months after you leave college" (CC, 3).

Howley, G. C. D., F. F. Bruce, and H. L. Ellison, eds. *The New Layman's Bible Commentary.* Grand Rapids: Zondervan, 1979.

This British-based commentary project has a *neo-orthodox** slant. The writers reject Moses' authorship of the Pentateuch, and the unity of the Book of Isaiah. The scholarship is quite good and the comments are easy to grasp. But its higher-critical methods will not be acceptable to more conservative readers.

Hubbard, David A., and Glenn W. Barker, eds. *The Word Biblical Commentary,* 52 vols. projected. Waco: Word, 1982-

---

16. Also available from (Grand Rapids: Baker, 1979) and as one volume from (Kansas City, Mo.: Beacon Hill, 1979).

17. Also available as three volumes from (Grand Rapids: Baker, 1979); as one volume from (Grand Rapids: Zondervan, 1979); as a one-volume abridged edition entitled *Matthew Henry's Concise Commentary on the Whole Bible* (Chicago: Moody, 1979); and as a three-volume abridged edition, with notes by Thomas Scott and other writers from (Nashville: Thomas Nelson, 1979).

Here is the first major exegetical commentary to be produced by conservative American scholars in our generation. This *Resource Guide* is going to press before the first volumes of Word's commentary have appeared, but from advance samples it promises to be a thorough and original work. Each writer makes his own new translation of the text. A section called "Comment" gives an exegetical treatment of key Hebrew or Greek words, while another section called "Explanation" expounds the practical meaning of the passage. This series could rival the *New International Commentary* sets.

Jamieson, Robert, A. P. Fausset, and David Brown. *Unabridged Bible Commentary.* Grand Rapids: Eerdmans, 1974.[18]
This is one of the earliest English-language commentaries to grapple with the Hebrew and Greek linguistics of the Bible (first edition in 1871). Most of the insights of Jamieson, Fausset, and Brown have been supported by subsequent discoveries such as Egyptian papyri and the Dead Sea Scrolls. This commentary does not make practical application of the Scripture as well as one would like. But its comments on the text form a basic resource for the serious Bible student.

Lange, John Peter, ed. *A Commentary on the Holy Scriptures,* rev. ed., 12 vols. Grand Rapids: Zondervan, 1980.
This series presents the best conservative German scholarship of the late 1800s. Dr. Philip Schaff enlarged Lange's original work in the process of translating the work into German, and several reviewers feel the work is now too cumbersome. Yet Barber calls it "one of the best multivolume commentaries available. It is particularly helpful on the O.T.!" (ML, 46). Note its Lutheran theological position on baptism and other subjects.

Maclaren, Alexander. *Expositions of Holy Scripture,* 17 vols. Grand Rapids: Baker, 1975.
This is actually a series of expository sermons that Maclaren used to lead his congregation through the Bible. The series does not focus on key words or phrases in Scripture; rather, it deals with the major themes, devoting a chapter (a sermon) to each theme. While Maclaren's *Expositions* make enjoyable devotional reading, they provide little help for serious study. Some professors recommend that ministerial students read this series as a model of expository preaching.

McGee, J. Vernon. *Thru the Bible,* 5 vols. projected. Nashville: Thomas Nelson, 1981-
As a modern counterpart to Maclaren's *Expositions,* this commentary is superior to it in many respects. McGee does devote some attention to key Hebrew and Greek words, explaining them in terms that laymen may readily understand. He also answers many of the questions raised by modern cults and heterodox Bible teachers. At the core, Dr. McGee's *Thru the Bible* commentary is a pastoral work.

---

18. Also available as one volume from (Grand Rapids: Zondervan, 1979) and as *Jamieson Fausset and Brown Combination* (commentary and dictionary) (Grand Rapids: Zondervan, 1979).

It shows his deep concern for applying God's Word to everyday situations, a skill that he learned during his pastorates in Nashville, Dallas, and Los Angeles. This material was first aired on Dr. McGee's "Thru the Bible" Radio Network, which leads its listeners through the entire Bible with a five-year series of expository messages. Dr. McGee is a conservative evangelical.

Ogilvie, Lloyd J. *The Communicator's Commentary,* 12 vols. projected. Waco: Word, 1982-
This is the first complete commentary based on the NKJV, and it promises to be an effective bridge between the scholarly commentaries which are too technical for lay readers and the devotional commentaries which often fail to investigate the full implications of the text. Writers in this series include Earl Palmer, Myron Augsburger, and other well-known expository preachers.

OLD TESTAMENT

Gibson, John C. L. *The Daily Study Bible,* 20 vols. projected. Philadelphia: Westminster, 1982-
This series seems intended as a companion to William Barclay's New Testament commentaries by the same name. It has a noticeable liberal viewpoint, endorsing the documentary hypothesis (the idea that several different editors compiled the Pentateuch), minimizing the *typological** significance of the Old Testament, and finding immediate fulfillment to many prophecies that evangelicals consider end-time prophecies.`

Harrison, R. K., ed. *The New International Commentary on the Old Testament,* 25 vols. projected. Grand Rapids: Eerdmans, 1976-
Already winning a reputation as the most thorough Old Testament commentary produced by evangelical American scholars, the NICOT provides meaningful Hebrew word studies and sets the cultural backdrop of Old Testament events. Laymen may feel that the NICOT is too scholarly to suit their taste; however, the challenging content of the series is well worth concentrated study.

Keil, C. F., and Franz Delitzsch. *A Biblical Commentary on the Old Testament,* 10 vols. Grand Rapids: Eerdmans, 1971.
More extensive word studies than the NICOT make Keil and Delitzsch's work foreign territory to many lay readers. But ministers recognize it as *the standard* Old Testament commentary, written from a conservative viewpoint. Keil and Delitzsch's exploration of the Hebrew text is still the best, despite the new insights from archaeological digs at Qumran, Ebla, and other ancient *Semitic** libraries. Osborne and Woodward observe that, even with the passage of time, Keil and Delitzsch's commentary is "still unsurpassed for general exegetical excellence" (HSB, 121).

Unger, Merrill F. *Unger's Commentary on the Old Testament,* 2 vols. Chicago: Moody, 1981.
Unger rejects the documentary hypothesis (the idea that several different editors compiled the Pentateuch). He presents a forceful premillennial view of

Christ's return in his comments on Psalms and the prophets. Overall, his commentary is strongly conservative and evangelical, though Unger often borrows his linguistic insights from the more liberal *Anchor Bible.*

Wiseman, Donald J., ed. *The Tyndale Old Testament Commentaries,* 15 vols. Downers Grove, Ill.: InterVarsity, 1979.

Compact and inexpensive, the Tyndale series is likely to become a layman's favorite. Most of the contributors are British evangelicals. Their comments are brief, but perceptive. One bookseller states that the Tyndale series is gaining popular acceptance because the "comments are very helpful, yet not so lengthy as to tire the reader" (*Christianity Today,* Feb. 5, 1982, p. 99).

THE PENTATEUCH

Allis, Oswald T. *The Five Books of Moses,* 2nd. ed. Philadelphia: Presbyterian and Reformed, 1949.[19]

Actually, this is a treatise attacking liberal theories about the authorship and date of the first five books of the Old Testament. Allis makes his point with a chapter-by-chapter commentary on the Pentateuch, emphasizing passages that confirm the books were written by Moses. It is a fascinating study.

McGee, J. Vernon. *Thru the Bible: Genesis through Deuteronomy*, vol. 1. Nashville: Thomas Nelson, 1981.

This series of sermons from Dr. McGee's "Thru the Bible" radio broadcasts should be quite popular. McGee writes from a pastor's perspective, giving many folksy illustrations to highlight events of early Bible history. The commentary is devotional and quite suggestive, with strong emphasis on the Old Testament symbols ("types") of the tabernacle, which foreshadowed Christ's sacrificial death on the cross. It is a good commentary for the beginning Bible student.

Mackintosh, Charles Henry. *Genesis to Deuteronomy*. Neptune, N.J.: Loizeaux Brothers, 1972.

As a devotional commentary, Mackintosh's work ranks alongside Matthew Henry's. American evangelist Dwight L. Moody praised this commentary. The volume reflects Mackintosh's dispensationalism and other Plymouth Brethren doctrines.

Genesis

Griffith-Thomas, W. H. *Genesis: A Devotional Commentary.* Grand Rapids: Eerdmans, 1958.

Thomas' vivid imagination makes him a favorite commentator of many pastors. He is able to picture the original setting of Bible events in such colorful terms that the reader feels transported to that place and time, to relive the Bible experience. Barber says this commentary is "possibly the most helpful devotional exposition of Genesis available" (ML, 95).

---

19. Also available from (Grand Rapids: Baker, 1979).

Leupold, H. C. *An Exposition of Genesis,* 2 vols. Grand Rapids: Baker, 1942.

Warren W. Wiersbe, former pastor of the Moody Church in Chicago, calls this commentary "my favorite" (BLBS, 13). The author is a Lutheran who writes from an amillennial viewpoint. Even readers who disagree with his theology will be pleased by his keen insight into the significance of Genesis events.

Pink, Arthur W. *Gleanings in Genesis.* Chicago: Moody, 1966.

Pink likes to interpret Scripture in terms of allegories and "types," and perhaps he tries too hard to find the allegories. He may draw symbolic lessons from objects or events that were never intended to be symboiic, but he does breathe life into many Genesis passages that we might otherwise take for granted.

Exodus

Davis, John J. *Moses and the Gods of Egypt.* Grand Rapids: Baker, 1971.

Recently discovered papyrus documents in Egypt describe the elaborate religious system of the pharaohs. Davis uses this information to reexamine Moses' confrontation with the hardhearted Pharaoh Amenhotep II. This makes a lively and interesting study.

Pink, Arthur W. *Gleanings in Exodus.* Chicago: Moody, 1964.[20]

Pink's commentary on Exodus is a good devotional study, but his search for types and allegories is as persistent as it was in his Genesis commentary.

Bonar, Andrew A. *A Commentary on the Book of Leviticus.* Grand Rapids: Baker, 1978.

Bonar ably discusses the symbolic meaning of Israel's ceremonies, the furniture of the tabernacle, and their God-given system of ritual and civil law; however, he is not an extremist in looking for types and symbols. This is a good devotional commentary.

Kellogg, Samuel H. *The Expositor's Bible: The Book of Leviticus.* North Minneapolis: Klock and Klock, 1978.

This commentary also deals with the symbolism of the Levites' ceremonies, but not in as much detail as we find in Bonar's commentary. Instead, Kellogg gives more emphasis to the historical impact that Jewish civil laws had upon their worship.

Numbers

Jensen, Irving L. *Everyman's Bible Commentary: Numbers.* Chicago: Moody, 1971.

Jensen is a respected teacher of inductive Bible study methods, and his expertise is obvious here. He shows how to penetrate Numbers' bewildering mass of laws and statutes to find their meaning for God's relationship with man. The reader

---

20. Also available from (Grand Rapids: Baker, 1979).

can learn much about the inductive method by following Dr. Jensen through this study.

Jones, Kenneth E. *Numbers.* Grand Rapids: Baker, 1979.

This brief survey of the Book of Numbers is especially suited to devotional study. It does not examine the book with as much theological depth or as analytically as Jensen's commentary, but it is still quite useful.

Deuteronomy

Craigie, P. C. *The New International Commentary on the Old Testament: Deuteronomy.* Grand Rapids: Eerdmans, 1976.

One of the best volumes in the NICOT series, Craigie's work is first-class evangelical scholarship. He offers a perceptive review of God's covenant with Israel. He cites Jesus' frequent references to Deuteronomy as a textbook for the coming kingdom of God. In all, Craigie's commentary is an excellent treatment of the key ideas in Deuteronomy.

Wright, G. Ernest. *The Interpreter's Bible: The Book of Deuteronomy,* ed. George A. Buttrick. Nashville: Abingdon, 1953, vol. 2, pp. 309-537.

Dr. Wright has a more liberal view than the other commentaries I have mentioned. He employs liberal form criticism and literary criticism to evalute Deuteronomy, attributing various portions of the book to different writers. Evangelical readers will not accept this approach. Nevertheless, there is value in his interesting comments about the culture of Israel and how its worship rituals compared to those of its pagan neighbors.

Schultz, Samuel J. *Everyman's Bible Commentary: Deuteronomy.* Chicago: Moody, 1971.

Professor Schultz of Wheaton College has given us this brief but well-informed commentary. It reveals his knowledge of recent archaeological research and his sound exegetical method.

THE HISTORICAL BOOKS

Crockett, William D. *A Harmony of the Books of Samuel, Kings, and Chronicles.* Grand Rapids: Baker, 1951.

This classic work, first published in 1897, offers a consecutive history of Israel's and Judah's kings from the parallel accounts of the Old Testament. Crockett dispels many apparent contradictions in these accounts.

Thiele, Edwin R. *A Chronology of the Hebrew King.* Grand Rapids: Zondervan, 1977.

Here Thiele unravels the dates of the kings' coronations and deaths by showing that the historians of Israel and Judah used two different dating systems. This fascinating study contradicts most earlier attempts to fix the dates of these events. It also supports the "early date" of the Exodus, which conservative scholars insist was about 1440 B.C. This work is based on Thiele's more exhaustive study entitled,

The Mysterious Numbers of the Hebrew Kings (Grand Rapids: Eerdmans, 1965), now out of print.

Joshua

Davis, John J. *Conquest and Crisis*. Grand Rapids: Baker, 1969.

This appears to be the best conservative commentary on Joshua now available. Davis is not afraid to grapple with perplexing questions—such as the miraculous destruction of Jericho—in an objective manner. He also discusses subsequent events recorded in Judges and Ruth.

Redpath, Alan. *Victorious Christian Living*. Old Tappan, N.J.: Revell, 1955.

Redpath's devotional study complements the more serious exegesis of Davis' commentary cited above. It does not examine Joshua in a systematic fashion, but it does point out practical lessons God's people may learn from the book. Redpath borrows heavily from Maclaren's comments.

Judges-Ruth

Cundall, Arthur E., and Leon Morris. *The Tyndale Old Testament Commentaries: Judges and Ruth*. Downer's Grove, Ill: InterVarsity, 1968.

Cundall uses a liberal higher-critical approach to the history of the Judges; even so, his commentary is superb. Morris reveals new insights into Moabite culture (from current archaeological digs), that help us to understand the poignant drama of Ruth.

McGee, J. Vernon. *Ruth: The Romance of Redemption*. Nashville: Thomas Nelson, 1982.

Many reviewers consider this to be the best section of Dr. McGee's old commentary series, so this reprinting is welcome. He brings to light several aspects of Ruth's personality that would escape the notice of a casual reader, and shows how Ruth's story illustrates God's redemption of mankind.

Wood, Leon J. *The Distressing Days of the Judges*. Grand Rapids: Zondervan, 1975.

Wiersbe calls this "the finest commentary on Judges to appear in recent years" (BLBS, 14). Wood's commentary is brief, but full of pertinent facts.

1 and 2 Samuel

Davis, John J. *The Birth of a Kingdom*. Grand Rapids: Baker, 1970.

Davis uses historical records from other nations of the Near East to confirm and round out the royal histories in his Old Testament commentaries. His scholarly work brings interesting sidelights to the study of 1 and 2 Samuel.

Hertzberg, Hans Wilhelm. *The Old Testament Library: 1 and 2 Samuel*, trans. J. S. Bowden. Philadelphia: Westminster, 1965.

This commentary considers 1 and 2 Samuel from a form-critical perspective. Hertzberg compares 1 and 2 Samuel to the writings of others who were recording royal histories during that period. He helps us understand that these books are a striking departure from the usual kingly chronicles of that day. They reveal the monarch's foibles as well as his fine points.

1 and 2 Kings

Gray, John. *The Old Testament Library: 1 and 2 Kings,* 2nd ed. Philadelphia: Westminster, 1971.

Gray believes that the content of 1 and 2 Kings was compiled by several exilic and post-exilic Jewish historians, rather than the royal chroniclers themselves. He uses a literary-criticism approach to try to separate the supposed layers of tradition in these books. Evangelical readers may shun Gray's commentary on this account, but it still provides a noteworthy discussion of the kings' histories.

Whitcomb, John C., Jr. *Solomon to the Exile.* Grand Rapids: Baker, 1971.

This evangelical commentary seems rather superficial when compared with Gray's because it does not attempt to explain the apparent discrepancies between Kings and Chronicles. Yet Whitcomb does provide a clear summary of the events, and he briefly assesses the impact of each king on the history of Israel and Judah.

1 and 2 Chronicles

Myers, Jacob M. *The Anchor Bible,* ed. W. F. Albright and David Noel Freeman. *1 and 2 Chronicles,* 2 vols. Garden City, N.Y.: Doubleday, 1965.

Professor of Old Testament at the Lutheran Theological Seminary in Gettysburg, Dr. Myers brings excellent linguistic knowledge and firm conservative views to this work. He maintains that one author (possibly Ezra) wrote both books, that Israel's law and *cultus** were revealed by God rather than borrowed from other nations, and that the writer affirms the preeminent power of God to guide Israel's *theocratic** government. Myers does endorse the documentary hypothesis of the Pentateuch.

Ezra-Nehemiah-Esther

Ironside, H. A. *Notes on the Books of Ezra, Nehemiah, and Esther.* New York: Loizeaux Brothers, 1951.

Ironside does not plow very deeply into the cultural or historical material of these books, but he does draw many practical lessons from them. He has a tendency to look for allegories and types in unlikely places.

McGee, J. Vernon. *Esther: The Romance of Providence.* Nashville: Thomas Nelson, 1982.

This commentary ranks as a close second to McGee's study of Ruth. It is another colorful character study, although it fails to give much insight into the workings of the Persian Empire.

Job

Barnes, Albert. *Notes on the Old Testament, Explanatory and Practical: Job,* 2 vols. Grand Rapids: Baker, 1950.

Barnes' *Notes* have been well known for many years, and this is one of the best commentaries in the series. Spurgeon said, "The student should purchase this work at once, as it is absolutely necessary to his library" (CC, 75). Barnes capably deals with the issues of *theodicy** as raised by the Book of Job.

Gordis, Robert. *The Book of Job.* New York: Jewish Theological Society of America, 1978.

This commentary is for the more advanced student. It includes the entire text of Job in Hebrew, a new translation of the text, and an original commentary. Gordis does not lean as heavily on earlier rabbinic comments as other Jewish commentaries often do. His work is fresh and interesting, with keen word studies of the Hebrew. Dr. Gordis has served as professor of religion at Temple University and professor of Bible at the Jewish Theological Seminary.

Morgan, G. Campbell. *The Answers of Jesus to Job.* Grand Rapids: Baker, 1973.

In this series of expository sermons, Morgan shows how Jesus answered Job's cries of suffering, especially in the Sermon on the Mount. It is a fine example of scriptural preaching.

Psalms

Alexander, Joseph A., *The Psalms Translated and Explained.* Grand Rapids: Baker, 1979.

Professor Alexander of Princeton University prepared this expository study of the Psalms. He discusses some of the most difficult passages (such as the *imprecatory Psalms**) with maturity and wisdom.

Dahood, Mitchell. *The Anchor Bible: Psalms,* ed. W. F. Albright and David Noel Freedman, 3 vols. Garden City, N.Y.: Doubleday, 1965-1970.

This may be the most technical study of the Psalms now available. Father Dahood, a Roman Catholic scholar, carefully analyzes the poetic pattern of each Psalm, its unique phrasing, etc., in light of other types of ancient poetry. He finds many parallels of style between the Psalms and the Ugaritic poetry found at Ras Shamra. Some of his changes to the text, based on Ugaritic, appear speculative, and conservative scholars are not always in agreement with him.

Kidner, Derek. *The Tyndale Old Testament Commentaries: The Psalms,* 2 vols. Downers Grove, Ill: InterVarsity, 1973-1975.

For a clear evangelical commentary on the Psalms, one could hardly wish for a better set than Kidner's. He takes a simple expository approach to the Psalms, unearthing rich spiritual truths in the process. Wiersbe says his books are "a delight to use; I would not part with them" (BLBS, 15).

Perowne, J. J. Stewart. *The Book of Psalms,* 2 vols. Grand Rapids: Zondervan, 1976.

This is surely one of the best commentaries by this Anglican scholar, if a confirmed Baptist such as Spurgeon could call it "a masterpiece of extraordinary learning and critical skill, although not altogether what we would desire" (CC, 89). Perowne's introductory articles bring needed depth to the study of the Psalms, which laymen often read only on the devotional level.

Spurgeon, Charles H. *The Treasury of David,* 7 vols. Grand Rapids: Baker, 1977.[21]
This book reveals the expository genius of Charles H. Spurgeon, long-time pastor of the (Baptist) Metropolitan Tabernacle in London. Spurgeon had a gift for discerning the practical application of Scripture; he had an equally remarkable gift for eloquent speaking and writing. Both gifts make *The Treasury of David* a treasure indeed. Veteran pastor Wilbur M. Smith wrote, "This is one set of books no minister will ever sell, unless he has lost faith in the Word of God, and no longer intends to preach or teach" (PBS, 145).

Proverbs

Bridges, Charles. *The Geneva Commentary Series: Proverbs,* 2 vols. London: Banner of Truth, 1979.
Reviewers agree that Bridges' commentary is "the classic" work on Proverbs (BLBS, 15; CC, 104; ML, 106). Perhaps his greatest strength is his skill at relating the Proverbs to other parts of Scripture. Bridges shows how the practical, ethical truth of this book resurfaces again and again throughout the written Word.

Scott, R. B. Y. *The Anchor Bible: Proverbs,* ed. W. F. Albright and David Noel Freedman. Garden City, N.Y.: Doubleday, 1965.
Evangelical readers will not appreciate the parallels that Scott draws between Proverbs and pagan wisdom literature. But he does a commendable job of explicating the ethical content of this book. As with other volumes of *The Anchor Bible,* this one contains a new translation of the Scripture.

Ecclesiastes

Hubbard, David Allan. *Beyond Futility.* Grand Rapids: Eerdmans, 1976.
Dr. Hubbard (president of Fuller Theological Seminary) hears an echo of modern man's despair in this ancient book. Despair about money, fame, fickle friends, capricious health—all of which may make modern man feel that life is futile—were facing the writer of Ecclesiastes. In this stirring devotional book, Hubbard examines how "the Preacher" moves beyond futility to faith in the everlasting God.

Leupold, H. C. *An Exposition of Ecclesiastes.* Grand Rapids: Baker, 1966.
Wiersbe feels this is "probably the best" commentary on Ecclesiastes (BLBS, 16). Leupold does make a more thorough analysis of the text than Hubbard does; the approach is deductive rather than devotional. Leupold's commentary is a refreshing look at this neglected Old Testament book.

---

21. Also available as 3 volumes from (Grand Rapids: Zondervan, 1974).

Song of Solomon

Gill, John. *An Exposition of the Book of Solomon's Song.* London: W. H. Collingridge, 1854.[22]

This is not a part of Gill's commentary set on the entire Bible, yet Spurgeon calls this "the best thing Gill ever did" (CC, 113). Gill believes the Song of Solomon is an allegory of Christ's love for the church. This elaborate devotional commentary follows that thesis.

Ironside, H. A. *The Song of Solomon.* Neptune,N.J.: Loizeaux Brothers, 1933.

Ironside believes this love poem is a double allegory—first of God's love for His chosen people, then of Christ's love for His church. He draws many lessons about Christ's self-sacrifice for the church, the church's submission to Christ, and related themes. Ironside writes from a Plymouth Brethren perspective.

THE MAJOR PROPHETS

Harper, A. F., ed. *Beacon Bible Commentary: The Major Prophets.* Kansas City, Mo.: Beacon Hill, 1966.

This is an expository commentary by four writers from the Church of the Nazarene. Its discussion of prophecy is helpful, though not very deep. The writers hold an amillennial view of endtime prophecies (see pp. 658-659) and use Wesleyan-Arminian terminology (e.g., the "sanctification and call" of Isaiah, p. 22). They identify the double fulfillment of some prophecies such as the predicted birth of Immanuel (Is. 7:14); the commentator says the prophecy refers to "events then about to happen" in the Exile and also to Jesus' birth.

Scott, R.B.Y. *The Relevance of the Prophets,* rev. ed. New York: Macmillan, 1968.

In his introduction to the first edition of this book, Scott declared that he had written it for "ministers and laymen who are not afraid of serious critical study of the Bible" (p. viii). He applies form criticism and literary criticism to the prophets at a few points, but in general his book does not really treat the higher-critical issues raised as we study the Major Prophets. The real value of this book is Scott's discussion of prophecy as a religious institution, and his assessment of the prophet's impact on Israel's social order. It is a most perceptive study.

Isaiah

Jennings, F. C. *Studies in Isaiah.* New York: Loizeaux Brothers, 1935.

Here we find a good devotional commentary on Isaiah. Jennings does discuss some of the key Hebrew ideas, especially the concept of *Messiah;* however, he does not move into an intricate analysis of the text. Jennings is a respected conservative writer.

---

22. Collingridge still has this book in print.

Leupold, H. C. *An Exposition of Isaiah.* Grand Rapids: Baker, 1977.

Leupold provides another conservative commentary on Isaiah, defending the traditional view that Isaiah wrote the entire book that bears his name. Leupold interprets Isaiah's end-time messianic prophecies with an amillennial viewpoint.

Young, Edward J. *The New International Commentary on the Old Testament: Isaiah,* ed. Young and R. K. Harrison, 3 vols. Grand Rapids: Eerdmans, 1965-1972.

Dr. Young advocates the traditional view that Isaiah wrote this entire prophecy. He explicates Isaiah's messianic prophecies with reverence, and interprets the end-time predictions with an amillennial approach. Young's three-volume set seems to be the best conservative commentary on Isaiah published thus far. Young comes from a Reformed Church background.

Jeremiah-Lamentations

Bright, John. *The Anchor Bible: Jeremiah,* ed. W. F. Albright and David Noel Freedman. Garden City, N.Y.: Doubleday, 1965.

Barber calls this "a surprisingly conservative commentary in a predominantly liberal series" (ML, 111). And he's right on both counts.

Harrison, R. K. *The Tyndale Old Testament Commentaries: Jeremiah and Lamentations,* ed. D. J. Wiseman. Downers Grove, Ill: InterVarsity, 1973.

As professor of Hebrew at Wycliffe College in Toronto, Dr. Harrison has earned a reputation for solid conservative scholarship. This volume adds to that reputation. Dr. Harrison deals with the textual problems (such as the authorship of Lamentations) in a thoroughly conservative way. Wiersbe calls this a "most satisfying" commentary (BLBS, 16).

Jensen, Irving L. *Everyman's Bible Commentary: Jeremiah.* Chicago: Moody, 1966.

Very simply written, this inductive study is well-suited to the beginning Bible student. It would also make a good discussion springboard for group study.

Laetsch, Theodore F.K. *A Bible Commentary: Jeremiah.* St. Louis: Concordia, 1952.

This Lutheran writer discusses God's wrathful judgment of Judah in a way that helps us realize His pending judgment of modern society. Laetsch points out the grievous injustices in Judah that led to the nation's fall; as he does, we can see clear similarities to the injustices in modern Western society.

Ezekiel

Feinberg, Charles L. *The Prophecy of Ezekiel.* Chicago: Moody, 1969.

Feinberg interprets these end-time visions with a premillennial perspective. Barber praises it as "the best work on the subject!" (ML, 112). Dr. Feinberg was formerly a professor at Talbot Theological Seminary and now has a popular Bible-study radio program.

Taylor, John B. *The Tyndale Old Testament Commentaries: Ezekiel.* Downers Grove, Ill.: InterVarsity, 1969.
This commentary by a brilliant scholar has marked liberal biases. Yet it provides good insight into the practical lessons of Ezekiel's prophecy.

Daniel

Gaebelein, A. C. *The Prophet Daniel.* Grand Rapids: Kregel Publications, 1968.
Perhaps one of the leading premillennial, dispensational works on Daniel, Gaebelein's commentary is a favorite of many conservative pastors. Dr. Gaebelein was a close friend of Dr. C. I. Scofield, who was an early champion of dispensational prophecy. Dr. Gaebelein's commentary resounds with his own conviction that we are living in the last age before Christ returns to set up His earthly kingdom.

Leupold, H. C. *An Exposition of Daniel.* Grand Rapids: Baker, 1969.
Leupold demonstrates that the Book of Daniel is open to more than one interpretation, as he makes a strong case for Christ's amillennial return, based on Daniel. Leupold's commentary is thorough, thoughtful, and scholarly. If you do not understand or agree with the amillennial view of Christ's return, be sure to read this book.

Walvoord, John F. *Daniel: The Key to Prophetic Revelation.* Chicago: Moody, 1970.
Dr. Walvoord (President of Dallas Theological Seminary) interprets the Book of Daniel with a premillennial viewpoint. He cites many recent archaeological finds that aid our understanding of the Babylonian climate in which Daniel was writing. This evidence helps to confirm that Daniel wrote the book.

Wilson, Robert Dick. *Studies in the Book of Daniel,* 3 vols. Grand Rapids: Baker, 1979.
Even though Wilson did not have the benefit of recent archaeological discoveries around Babylon, he used what *was* known in his time to answer the scholars who claim Daniel was written after the Exile (when many of the book's prophecies would have been fulfilled). Wilson also interprets Daniel's end-time prophecies from an amillennial point of view.

THE MINOR PROPHETS*

Feinberg,Charles L. *Minor Prophets,* rev. ed. Chicago: Moody, 1976.
As a converted Jew, Dr. Feinberg brings a sensitive heart to this discussion of God's judgment on ancient Israel. He emphasizes the need for repentance, not only by the Old Testament Jews, but by every person who tries to be spiritually

self-sufficient. This is a revised edition of Dr. Feinberg's five-volume series entitled, *Major Messages of the Minor Prophets,* which originally was published by the American Board of Missions to the Jews. He interprets end-time prophecies with a premillennial perspective.

Gaebelein, Frank E. *The Four Minor Prophets.* Chicago: Moody, 1977.

This excellent devotional commentary is best for beginning students of the Minor Prophets. Dr. Gaebelein considers four of the twelve Minor Prophets—Obadiah, Jonah, Habakkuk, and Haggai. He makes a strong case for the premillennial return of Christ.

Hailey, Homer. *The Minor Prophets.* Grand Rapids: Baker, 1972.

Hailey's new paraphrase of the Scripture makes this commentary unique. His commentary on each prophet is brief but very practical.

Harper, A. F., ed. *Beacon Bible Commentary: The Minor Prophets.* Kansas City, Mo: Beacon Hill, 1966.

This scholarly commentary outlines the major themes of each prophet, drawing upon the insights of classic commentators such as Clarke, Fausset, and Keil and Delitzsch. At times, the commentary is little more than a paraphrase of the KJV, but fortunately that is not true overall. The comments are simple, explanatory, and easy to understand. (One wishes the writers had given us more Hebrew word studies here, since the Minor Prophets contain some of the most novel expressions in Hebrew poetry.)

Keil, K. F. *Biblical Commentary on the Old Testament: The Twelve Minor Prophets,* ed. K. F. Keil and Franz Delitzsch. Grand Rapids: Eerdmans, 1950.

Several reviewers feel this is Keil's best commentary in his ten-volume series. His detailed explanation of the linguistics may discourage the lay reader, but Keil does draw some challenging spiritual lessons from the Minor Prophets that no one should overlook.

Pusey, Edward B. *The Minor Prophets,* 2 vols. Grand Rapids: Baker, 1979.

This is a classic amillennial commentary. Spurgeon felt Pusey was "far too much swayed by patristic and medieval commentators" in this work (CC, 131). But that makes his work all the more valuable for readers who wish to see how various church leaders have viewed the prophets over the span of church history.

Hosea

Mays, James L. *The Old Testament Library: Hosea,* ed. G. Ernest Wright, et al. Philadelphia: Westminster, 1969.

Barber feels this is "one of the better works" in the OTL series (ML, 115). Dr. Mays examines the theory that two different writers composed this book, and he uses literary criticism to discern various strands of authorship in the book. Yet the overall thrust of Mays' commentary is not on dissecting its authorship, but on explaining the relevance of Hosea's message for today. His work is very worthwhile for that reason, regardless of his conclusions about authorship.

Morgan, G. Campbell. *Hosea.* Grand Rapids: Baker, 1974.

This is an excellent amillennial commentary on Hosea's prophecy. It is a devotional commentary, and Morgan is considered one of the best devotional writers of this century.

Joel

I am not aware of a good single-volume commentary on this prophet. See Dr. Feinberg's work on the Minor Prophets.

Amos

Cripps, Richard S. *A Critical and Exegetical Commentary on the Book of Amos,* rev. ed. North Minneapolis: Klock and Klock, 1981.

One wishes the revisers of this commentary had done more to update the 1929 edition. The excavations in Israel since 1948 have shed much new light on the eighth-century B.C. monarchy; Cripps cites none of that information. Even so, his practical comments on the text are helpful. See especially his discussion of the "Day of the Lord."

Obadiah

I am not aware of a good single-volume commentary on this prophet. See Dr. Feinberg's work on the Minor Prophets.

Jonah

Banks, William L. *Everyman's Bible Commentary: Jonah.* Chicago: Moody, 1968.

This devotional commentary also offers a serious treatment of the text for more scholarly students. Barber notes that Banks "admirably blends historical data with Hebrew word studies" (ML, 116).

Fairbairn, Patrick. *Jonah.* Grand Rapids: Baker, n.d.

Fairbairn is well known for his studies in typology; but that figures less into this commentary than in his other works. Here Fairbairn seems more intent on analyzing the personality of the prophet, rather than showing the "types" that Jonah's story presents for us.

Martin, Hugh. *The Geneva Commentary Series: Jonah.* London: Banner of Truth Trust, 1978.

This thorough commentary by a Scottish Presbyterian leader has plenty of good meat for us. Spurgeon called it "a first-class exposition of Jonah . . . . No one who has it will need any other" (CC, 137).

Micah

I am not aware of a good single-volume commentary on this prophet. See Dr. Feinberg's work on the Minor Prophets.

Nahum

Maier, Walter A. *The Thornapple Commentaries: Nahum,* ed. George V. Schick. Grand Rapids : Baker, 1980.

Dr. Maier (d. 1950) was a noted Lutheran radio evangelist. In this commentary, he defends the traditional authorship of Nahum and makes many applications of the prophet's hopeful message to the needs of readers today. It is one of the most thorough commentaries on Nahum now available.

Habakkuk, Zephaniah, and Haggai

I am not aware of good single-volume commentaries on these prophets. See Dr. Feinberg's work on the Minor Prophets.

Zechariah

Baron, David. *Kregel Reprint Library: The Visions and Prophecies of Zechariah,* 3rd ed. Grand Rapids: Kregel Publications, 1972.

Wiersbe calls Baron's work *"The* commentary on this book" (BLBS, 17). Baron is a converted Jew with a keen interest in messianic prophecy; he finds plenty to discuss in Zechariah! He offers a premillennial perspective on the predictions of Christ's return.

Leupold, H. C. *An Exposition of Zechariah.* Grand Rapids: Baker, 1965.

Leupold confirms his reputation as an amillennial writer with this fine commentary. He is reasonable, articulate, and not too erudite. This commentary is excellent.

Unger, Merrill F. *Zechariah.* Grand Rapids: Zondervan, 1963.

Although Unger examines the more technical, linguistic curiosities of Zechariah as well as the "types" of the Restoration Temple, he does not lose sight of the prophet's overall message. Unger shows how Zechariah fixed the people's hopes on the coming Messiah and tried to prepare them spiritually for the Messiah's advent. The people scoffed at what Zechariah had to say, but his prophecy became pregnant with meaning when Christ did appear. His prophecy was cited by the early Christians and by Jesus Himself. Unger gives a premillennial view of Christ's return.

Malachi

Moore, Thomas V. *The Geneva Commentary Series: Haggai-Malachi.* London: Banner of Truth Trust, 1974.

This commentary contains Moore's own translation of these prophets and his cogent comments on their significance. Spurgeon praised it as "a capital book" (CC, 139). Moore writes from a Reformed perspective.

Morgan, G. Campbell. *The Morgan Library: Malachi's Message for Today.* Grand Rapids: Baker, 1972.

Morgan writes in a popular, devotional vein. This work will stir the interest of a beginning student in the Minor Prophets, as it avoids bewildering excursions into the technical aspects of the Hebrew. Morgan serves up plenty of current, practical applications from Malachi's prophecy.

APOCRYPHA

Bartlett, John R. *The Cambridge Bible Commentary: The First and Second Books of the Maccabees.* Cambridge: Cambridge Univ. Press, 1973.

Using the text of the NEB, Bartlett leads us through these important books of intertestamental history. His introductory articles are weak (especially the section entitled, "The Historical Value of I Maccabees"). But Bartlett redeems himself somewhat by weaving historical footnotes from Josephus and other sources throughout his commentary, giving broader background to the work.

Charles, R. H., ed. *The Apocrypha and Pseudepigrapha of the Old Testament in English,* 2 vols. Oxford: Clarendon, 1963.

This is the most exhaustive critical edition of the Apocrypha that could be found. The book introductions and critical notes are extremely detailed; the comments are brief but exegetically sound. Charles' work will probably be the chief English-language source for study of the Apocrypha for years to come.

Snaith, John G. *The Cambridge Bible Commentary: Ecclesiasticus.* Cambridge: Cambridge Univ. Press, 1974.

Snaith draws out the practical implications of this apocryphal book for Old Testament Jewish ethics. His comments often refer to other Jewish literature for corroboration and further insight into ancient Jewish standards. The commentary is simple, but informative.

NEW TESTAMENT

Bruce, F. F., ed. *The New International Commentary on the New Testament,* 18 vols. projected. Grand Rapids: Eerdmans, 1960-

The editors at Eerdmans explain that this is a series "serving the interests of both pastor and scholar" (BRW, 27). It is a monumental project. The introductory articles themselves read like major research essays, yet the introductions and commentaries are easy for the educated layman to understand. They explore the richness of the Greek language and generally provide a conservative solution to textual problems. The entire set is excellent.

Barclay, William. *The Daily Study Bible,* 18 vols. Philadelphia: Westminster, 1975-1976.

The compact size of each volume makes this set handy for classroom or travel use. Barclay gives his own translation of each passage, followed by his commentary (which is largely devotional). Barclay thinks along neo-orthodox lines, yet all evangelicals can profit from his comments.

Falwell, Jerry, Edward E. Hindson, and Woodrow Kroll, eds. *Liberty Bible Commentary on the New Testament.* Nashville: Thomas Nelson, 1978.

Compiled by staff and associates of Liberty Baptist College, this commentary intends to take a fundamentalist approach to the New Testament. However, it does not differ significantly from the interpretation of other evangelical writers. Based on the KJV, the *Liberty Bible Commentary* gives very brief comments on the Scripture. It usually restates the content in simpler words and points out the obvious implications of the text.

Hendriksen, William. *New Testament Commentary.* Grand Rapids: Baker, 1953-

A conservative writer of great clarity, Dr. Hendriksen provides a simple commentary that holds true to the evangelical tradition. "He always sees the practical side of God's truth," Wiersbe writes (BLBS, 19). He favors amillennialism.

Howley, G.C.D. *The New Layman's Bible Commentary.* Grand Rapids: Zondervan, 1979.

Howley comments on the RSV, explicating many of the textual problems that the RSV translators tried to resolve. He shows a neo-orthodox bias in some areas (e.g., the authorship of certain N.T. Epistles), but his valuable spiritual teaching commends him to even the most conservative readers.

Lenski, Richard C.H. *An Interpretation of the New Testament,* 12 vols. Minneapolis: Augsburg, 1933–1946.

This is one of the few recent commentaries written from an Arminian, amillennial vantage point. Lenski analyzes the Greek text carefully, but not pedantically. He argues against premillennialism, but in favor of infant baptism and *consubstantiation.* *

Tasker, R.V.G. *The Tyndale New Testament Commentaries,* 20 vols. Grand Rapids: Eerdmans, 1957–1971.

Quickly becoming a favorite of pastors, this set does not plow as deeply into Greek syntax and idioms as does the *New International Commentary—N.T.* It is also less expensive, since it is in paperback. The British writers who predominate the staff of this project sometimes show a neo-orthodox bias, but not so strongly as to mar the prestige of this work for conservative evangelical readers.

THE GOSPELS

Ryle, J. C. *Expository Thoughts on the Gospels,* 4 vols. Grand Rapids: Baker, 1977.

Originally written for family Bible study, this devotional commentary remains a classic. Bishop Ryle was a deeply spiritual man; his writings flow from a loving heart. They are especially good for the beginning Bible student.

Scroggie, W. Graham. *A Guide to the Gospels.* Old Tappan, N.J.: Revell, 1975.

Scroggie plumbs the theological depths of the Gospels. His work is well-suited to a serious, thoughtful reader who wishes to know as much as possible about the person and work of Christ. Barber observes that Scroggie's commentary is "worth an entire shelf of books on the same subject" (ML, 139).

Matthew

Barclay, William. *The Beatitudes and the Lord's Prayer for Everyman.* New York: Harper and Row, 1975.

Here Barclay deals with two "summit" passages of Matthew in much more detail than was possible in his *Daily Study Bible.* This is a good devotional study for the beginner.

Barclay, William. *The Daily Study Bible: Matthew,* rev. ed., 2 vols. Philadelphia: Westminster, 1975.

As with other volumes in this series, Dr. Barclay offers a portion of the Scripture for daily reading along with two or three pages of commentary. His comments are largely devotional and suggestive, although they give evidence of careful study of the Greek text. Many laymen enjoy this series, and his two volumes on Matthew make an appropriate introduction to the set.

Tasker, R.V.G., ed. *Tyndale New Testament Commentaries: Matthew.* Grand Rapids: Eerdmans, 1961.

This commentary on the KJV brings in many insights from recent higher-critical studies (such as Tasker's comment that Matthew 13:1 may refer to Matthew's own house). Dr. Tasker provides a surprising amount of information about New Testament Jewish customs and family life in this little volume. Conservative readers will not like his frequent rejection of KJV readings in favor of some other version, but his comments are well tempered and valuable.

Mark

Swete, H. B. *Kregel Reprint Library: Mark.* Grand Rapids: Kregel, 1978.

Reviewers recommend this more than any other commentary on Mark. Swete has a reputation for clear, perceptive analysis of Scripture, and this volume confirms it. Be sure to consult this classic, even though Swete did not have the benefit of some ancient fragments of Mark that archaeologists have uncovered since his time.

Taylor, Vincent. *The Thornapple Commentaries: Mark.* Grand Rapids: Baker, 1981.

Taylor employs a great deal of textual criticism in this commentary. While the linguistic details may bewilder a new Bible student, a more experienced reader will appreciate them. Taylor's approach tends to be neo-orthodox, and he questions the authenticity of certain passages. But his Greek word studies alone are worth the time invested in this book.

Luke

Gideon, Virtus E. *A Study Guide Commentary: Luke.* Grand Rapids: Zondervan, 1967.

This volume from Zondervan's popular series makes an excellent text for study groups. Dr. Gideon of Southwestern Baptist Theological Seminary offers a good evangelical tour of Luke's gospel with discussion questions at the end of each chapter. However, he provides little insight into the Greek text.

Godet, Frédéric L. *Kregel Reprint Library: A Commentary on the Gospel of St. Luke,* trans. E. W. Shalders and M. D. Cusin, 2 vols. Grand Rapids: Kregel, 1981.

Godet probes the meaning of virtually every phrase in Luke's gospel. His commentary is an invaluable resource for studying any portion of Luke, and you are apt to return to it again and again. Barber says it "deserves a place on the shelf of every pastor" (ML, 147).

Marshall, I. Howard. *Contemporary Evangelical Perspective Series: Luke, Historian and Theologian.* Grand Rapids: Zondervan, 1971.[23]

This is an excellent overview of the life of Christ as recorded by Luke. Dr. Marshall often refers to the other Gospels to fill in the gaps in Luke's account, giving us a fuller description of Jesus' ministry. While Marshall's commentary is fairly detailed, it is not too technical for the layman.

John

Brown, Raymond E. *The Anchor Bible: The Gospel According to John,* ed. W. F. Albright and David Noel Freedman, 2 vols. Garden City, N.Y.: Doubleday, 1966–1970.

Dr. Brown is a leading Roman Catholic scholar of the New Testament, and this commentary is a masterpiece of research. He deals with John's profound theological passages (such as John 1) in a most provocative way, and discerns many characteristics of Jesus that other commentators fail to mention. This is one of the best volumes in *The Anchor Bible* series.

Morris, Leon. *The New International Commentary on the New Testament: The Gospel According to John.* Grand Rapids: Eerdmans, 1970.

This is the best conservative commentary on John to be published in recent years. Morris unlocks fascinating secrets from the Greek text—shades of meaning one would miss by reading even the best English version. This is a superb treatment.

Pink, Arthur W. *An Exposition of the Gospel of John.* Grand Rapids: Zondervan, 1975.

For an easy-to-understand, devotional commentary on John, Pink's is the best choice. His comments are simple but not superficial; perceptive but not radical. This commentary would be superb for a deductive study of John's Gospel, be-

---

23. The more advanced student will be interested in Dr. Marshall's volume, *The New International Greek Testament Commentary: The Gospel of Luke* (Grand Rapids: Eerdmans, 1978). It is a commentary on the Greek text itself, using the Nestle edition.

cause it surveys the major themes of the book without detailed word studies or cultural comments.

Acts of the Apostles

Bruce, F. F. *The New International Commentary on the New Testament: Acts.* Grand Rapids: Eerdmans, 1954.

Dr. Bruce is a recognized authority on the life of the apostle Paul, and his extensive study of Paul's life makes this volume especially good. He explores each event with scholarly thoroughness, but he remains sensitive to the practical concerns of the reader. Of all the commentaries on Acts, Barber calls this "perhaps the best expository work for the pastor" (ML, 152).

Jensen, Irving L. *Acts: An Independent Study.* Chicago: Moody, 1973.

Dr. Jensen, who is professor of Bible at the conservative Bryan College in Dayton, Tennessee, is a leading proponent of inductive Bible study. This study of Acts is his best by far. It is an excellent laboratory for learning the inductive method of Bible study.

Romans

Barnhouse, Donald Grey. *An Exposition of Bible Doctrine, Taking the Epistle to the Romans as a Point of Departure,* 4 vols. Grand Rapids: Eerdmans, 1952–1964.

This series of expository sermons by a famed Presbyterian is sure to inspire anyone who reads it. While Dr. Barnhouse focuses on the contemporary significance of Romans, he does not lose sight of the gradual development of the church's understanding of this book. The commentary is actually an informal study of historical theology, and a first-rate study at that.

Hodge, Charles. *A Commentary on the Epistle to the Romans,* rev. ed. Grand Rapids: Eerdmans, 1950.

Hodge's thorough commentary is acclaimed as one of the best evangelical studies of Romans. Dr. Hodge was a leader of the evangelical minority at Princeton Seminary in the mid-1800s. His writings are strongly Calvinistic, but even non-Calvinists will value his analytical treatment of Romans.

Käsemann, Ernst. *Commentary on Romans,* trans. Geoffrey W. Bromiley. Grand Rapids: Eerdmans, 1978.

Käsemann is a conservative German scholar, and he handles the Epistle of Romans with respect for its normative influence upon the early church. This commentary will be well received in America as pastors become better acquainted with it.

Lloyd-Jones, D. Martyn. *Romans: An Exposition,* 6 vols. projected. Grand Rapids: Zondervan, 1971-

In these volumes, Dr. Lloyd-Jones explores the doctrines of atonement and justification with faithful fervor. Because of his purpose, this is not a commentary on the entire Epistle of Romans; it passes over Romans 1-3 and 8-16. Even so, it is an excellent devotional and doctrinal study.

Luther, Martin. *Commentary on the Epistle to the Romans,* trans. J. Theodore Mueller. Grand Rapids: Kregel, 1976.

This commentary is excerpted from the notes Luther used in his historic series of lectures at Wittenberg University in 1512-1513. It was during this lecture series that God revealed to Luther the full impact of the statement, "The just shall live by faith" (Rom. 1:17). Ironically, Luther has little to say about that passage here; he provides a much fuller discussion of justification in his commentary on Galatians 3:11ff. But this commentary on Romans still holds real historical interest.

Moule, Handley C.G. *The Expositor's Bible: Romans.* Fort Washington, Pa.: Christian Literature Crusade, 1979.

Another devotional commentary, Moule's work is more compact and more expository than Barnhouse's. It does not lead us into an involved study of linguistics, however. It is probably best for a Bible student who does not know Greek very well.

1 Corinthians

Godet, Frédéric L. *Kregel Reprint Library: A Commentary on the First Epistle of St. Paul to the Corinthians,* trans. A. Cousins. Grand Rapids: Kregel, 1977.

This reprint of Godet's commentary, first published in 1886, restores a treasure to the hands of modern Bible students. Godet gives us very thoughtful comments on the text. He skillfully analyzes the doctrinal terms of 1 Corinthians, and he offers some of the best background information on the cultural and moral climate of Corinth, even without the benefit of recent archaeological digs in that area.

Morgan, G. Campbell. *The Corinthian Letters of Paul.* Westwood, N.J.: Revell, 1946.

Morgan's sermon series on Corinthians makes a good devotional study. He was one of the best expository preachers of the first half of this century, and his application of 1 Corinthians to the moral problems of our times should not be missed.

Morris, Leon. *The Tyndale New Testament Commentaries: First Corinthians,* ed. R.V.G. Tasker. Grand Rapids: Eerdmans, 1958.

Reviewers agree that this is one of the best volumes of the TNTC. Morris perceives the basic themes of Paul's letter to the Corinthians, and he describes those themes clearly and simply. Morris' treatment of 1 Corinthians 12-14, concerning spiritual gifts, is especially helpful.

Nelson, Wilbur E. *Believe and Behave.* Nashville: Thomas Nelson, 1979.

This series of Dr. Nelson's teaching programs from "The Morning Chapel Hour" radio program forms a good devotional commentary on 1 Corinthians.

Dr. Nelson applies 1 Corinthians to the moral and spiritual problems of modern Christians, making this a most practical study. This is the first commentary based on the New King James Version.

2 Corinthians

Hodge, Charles. *The Thornapple Commentaries: An Exposition of the Second Epistle to the Corinthians.* Grand Rapids: Baker, 1980.

Hodge probes 2 Corinthians at more depth than most modern commentators do. He explicates the doctrinal themes of 2 Corinthians, and correlates them to Paul's teachings in other epistles. As noted earlier, Hodge's works are strongly Calvinistic.

Hughes, Philip E. *The New International Commentary on the New Testament: Paul's Second Epistle to the Corinthians.* Grand Rapids: Eerdmans, 1962.

Barber believes this commentary "may well be regarded as the finest conservative exposition of this epistle!" (ML, 166). I would agree, at least as far as modern commentaries are concerned. Hughes applies excellent Greek scholarship to the letter, and gives us a thorough analysis of the doctrinal terms Paul uses. This commentary is the most academic of the ones listed in this section.

Nelson, Wilbur E. *The Confident Christian.* Nashville: Thomas Nelson, 1981.

Like Nelson's volume on 1 Corinthians, this commentary is a very practical review of the epistle. It is also based on the New King James Version.

Galatians

Lightfoot, J. B. *The Epistles of St. Paul,* 3 vols. Winona Lake, Ind.: BMH Books, 1981.[24]

Lightfoot applies rigorous literary criticism to Paul's letters. He was one of the first to question the traditional view that Paul wrote this epistle on his *first* missionary journey, just after he returned from Galatia; Lightfoot believed it was written on Paul's *third* journey, and most modern commentators agree with him on this point.

Luther, Martin. *Commentary on St. Paul's Epistle to the Galatians.* Grand Rapids: Baker, 1979.[25]

John Bunyan said, "I prefer this book of Martin Luther's (except the Bible) before all the books I have ever seen, as most fit for a wounded conscience" (CC, 176). Indeed, Luther's commentary on Galatians brings us the full flower of his teaching on justification. This reformer's doctrine of salvation through faith alone was firmly rooted in Paul's epistles to the Romans and the Galatians; so this commentary gives us an intimate view of the Bible study that shaped Luther's life work.

---

24. Currently available as one volume from (Grand Rapids: Zondervan, 1979).
25. Also available from (Greenwood, S.C.: Attic, 1978) and as *Commentary on Galatians* (Grand Rapids: Kregel, 1979).

Ridderbos, Herman N. *The New International Commentary on the New Testament: Galatians,* trans. Henry Zylstra. Grand Rapids: Eerdmans, 1953.

Using the ASV, this Dutch Reformed scholar has produced a commentary of great clarity and thoughtfulness. Ridderbos displays his familiarity with the Greek text only when necessary; one never feels he is trying merely to impress the reader.

Ephesians

Eadie, John. *A Commentary on the Epistle to the Ephesians.* Grand Rapids: Zondervan, 1975.

Wiersbe calls this his "standard commentary" on Ephesians (BLBS, 24), and it's easy to see why. Eadie summarizes the best of the classical commentaries on this epistle (e.g., Calvin and Henry), then reexamines each passage in the light of his own study. Eadie has a good grasp of New Testament Greek, but he does not overwhelm us with it.

Kent, Homer A., Jr. *Everyman's Bible Commentary: Ephesians.* Chicago: Moody, 1971.

This study of the nature and function of the early church is vital to any Christian. Kent's exposition of the text is first-rate, and sheds much revealing light on New Testament church life. This would make an excellent basis for a discussion-group study.

Moule, Handley C.G. *Ephesians,* 2nd ed. Fort Washington, Pa.: Christian Literature Crusade, 1975. [26]

Here is a good devotional commentary. Like Kent's work, it focuses on the nature of the church. Moule's style of writing is a bit harder to follow than Kent's, but his deeper theological insights complement the other book.

Philippians

Lightfoot, J. B. *St. Paul's Epistle to the Philippians.* Grand Rapids: Zondervan, 1957.

We should expect an impeccable piece of New Testament Greek scholarship from Lightfoot, and he does not disappoint us in this regard. His commentary contains a revised Greek text of the entire epistle, with textual notes in which Lightfoot dissects the meaning of every significant Greek word and phrase. This commentary is too sophisticated for most laymen, but pastors and other advanced students will love it.

Martin, Ralph P. *The Tyndale New Testament Commentaries: Philippians.* Grand Rapids: Eerdmans, 1960.[27]

While not as technical as Lightfoot's work, this commentary gives good insight

---

26. Also available as *Studies in Ephesians* (Grand Rapids: Kregel, 1977).
27. Also available from (Greenwood, S.C.: Attic Press, 1977).

into the Greek text of Philippians. Martin makes plenty of devotional comments as well. He points out the encouragement this letter still gives to Christians who are sorely tested by life's problems, as Paul was.

Colossians-Philemon

Lightfoot, J. B. *St. Paul's Epistles to the Colossians and Philemon.* Grand Rapids: Zondervan, 1957.

Deep, scholarly analysis of the Greek text is the hallmark of Lightfoot's work. His background articles on the culture of the times and the teachings of various Jewish and Christian sects are also quite good.

Moule, Handley C.G. *Colossian and Philemon Studies.* North Minneapolis: Klock and Klock, 1981.

Moule's exegesis of the Greek text is not as thorough as Lightfoot's, nor are his theological tendencies as liberal. Evangelical readers will prefer this volume.

Bruce, F. F., and E. K. Simpson. *The New International Commentary on the New Testament: Ephesians and Colossians,* ed. Ned B. Stonehouse. Grand Rapids: Eerdmans, 1958.

This is the best recent commentary on Colossians, written from an evangelical perspective. Bruce helps us appreciate the compassionate personality of Paul and his fatherly love for the "babes in Christ" who were being swayed by false teachers.

1 and 2 Thessalonians

Hiebert, D. Edmond. *The Thessalonian Epistles.* Chicago: Moody, 1971.

Hiebert provides a premillennial perspective on these two letters, which evangelical readers will appreciate. His analysis of the Greek may be too technical for beginning Bible students, but he makes some striking applications of Paul's message to the situation of Christians today.

Morris, Leon L. *The New International Commentary on the New Testament: Thessalonians,* ed. R.V.G. Tasker. Grand Rapids: Eerdmans, 1959.

Danker believes this commentary is solely "for popular consumption" (MTBS, 270), and it is easier to read than the other commentaries noted. But Morris should not be dismissed too easily. His comments are penetrating and practical, and this commentary will be of great help to the beginning Bible student.

THE PASTORAL EPISTLES

Dibelius, Martin, and Hans Conzelmann. *Hermeneia: The Pastoral Epistles,* ed. Helmut Koester. Philadelphia: Fortress, 1972.

The Hermeneia series was produced by leading liberal Bible scholars, mostly from Europe. This volume is one of the best in the series. Dibelius and Conzelmann draw upon the apostolic fathers, Hellenistic philosophers, and rabbinic sources to paint the cultural background of the *Pastoral Epistles**. They give a moderate interpretation of controversial passages (e.g., 1 Tim. 2:12 on women's roles in the church; 1 Tim. 5:17ff. on the duties of presbyters, and 2 Tim. 3:16 on the purpose of Scripture).

Hendriksen, William. *Thessalonians, Timothy, and Titus.* Grand Rapids: Baker, 1979.

This excellent study interprets Paul's words about the return of Christ in an amillennial fashion, so some evangelical readers may be wary of reading it. But Hendrikson offers many insights from the early church fathers and from recent archaeological discoveries at Thessalonica—insights not found in older or more devotional commentaries.

Kent, Homer A., Jr. *The Pastoral Epistles.* Chicago: Moody, 1958.

This simple commentary is a good evangelical counterpart to the Hermeneia volume. Kent defends Paul's authorship of the Pastoral Epistles and provides a good review of the apostle's major themes in these letters.

1 and 2 Timothy

Hiebert, D. Edmond. *Everyman's Bible Commentary: I and II Timothy,* 2 vols. Chicago: Moody, 1957–1958.

Here is a fascinating devotional commentary—a bit more technical than most, but full of inspiring ideas. Young ministers will appreciate these volumes because Hiebert makes Paul's advice to a young pastor relevant for today. Lay leaders will benefit by reading them, too.

Titus-Philemon

Hiebert, D. Edmond. *Everyman's Bible Commentary: Titus and Philemon.* Chicago: Moody, 1957.

This volume is not as thorough as Hiebert's treatment of 1 and 2 Timothy, but it seems to be the best available on these two short epistles. New commentaries are needed in this area.

THE GENERAL EPISTLES

Bowman, John Wick. *The Layman's Bible Commentary: Hebrews, James, 1 and 2 Peter.* Atlanta: John Knox, 1962.

This simplified commentary by Professor Bowman of San Francisco Theological Seminary is too sketchy to be of much value to pastors or teachers, but it does introduce the beginning student to these often-neglected New Testament letters. Professor Bowman shows a liberal bent as he speculates on the authorship of these letters.

Hiebert, D. Edmond. *An Introduction to the Non-Pauline Epistles and Revelation.* Chicago: Moody, 1977.

This conservative treatment of the General Epistles is good for beginners. Hiebert fills in more of the historical background than Bowman does, and he maintains traditional views of the authorship and dates of these letters.

Reicke, Bo. *The Anchor Bible: The Epistles of James, Peter, and Jude,* ed. W. F. Albright and David Noel Freedman, vol. 37. Garden City, N.Y.: Doubleday, 1964.

Reicke's fourteen-page general introduction to these epistles is excellent. Although he questions the authorship of 1 and 2 Peter and raises other higher-critical questions that will bother evangelical readers, he capably outlines the cultural and historical background of all four epistles. Throughout the commentary, Reicke tells how the early church tried to present the gospel of Christ in the hostile environment of the Roman and Greek territories; he identifies a raft of ethical problems that this presented for the early Christians.

Hebrews

Brown, John. *The Geneva Commentary Series: An Exposition of the Epistle of the Apostle Paul to the Hebrews,* ed. David Smith, 2 vols. London: Banner of Truth Trust, 1976.

Bible students were very happy to see the Banner of Truth reprint this classic of 1862. Brown rambles more than modern commentators do, but he uncovers some real gems of spiritual truth along the way. His discussion of the Hebrew tabernacle is especially good.

Bruce, F. F. *The New International Commentary on the New Testament: Hebrews,* ed. R.V.G. Tasker. Grand Rapids: Eerdmans, 1964.

Here is another exceptional volume in the NICNT series. Dr. Bruce explains the complex symbolism of Hebrews in a most enlightening way, and shows how Christ's death and resurrection climaxed the old sacrificial system. Bruce's commentary also illumines the Old Testament books of Leviticus and Deuteronomy as he discusses God's purpose for the Hebrew sacrificial system. This is good, meaty reading.

Hughes, Philip Edgcumbe. *A Commentary on the Epistle to the Hebrews.* Grand Rapids: Eerdmans, 1977.

Wiersbe is ecstatic about this book. He says it is "essential for your library; I cannot recommend it too much!" (BLBS, 25). Others may not be so enthused, especially if they disagree with Hughes' literal interpretation of Old Testament "types." Even so, this commentary ranks with Bruce's as one of the clearest evangelical expositions of Hebrews published in recent years.

Owen, John. *An Exposition of the Epistle to the Hebrews,* 7 vols. Grand Rapids: Baker, [n.d.][28]

The noted Scottish theologian Thomas Chalmers called this commentary "a work of gigantic strength as well as gigantic size" (CC, 188). Owen traces the most minute detail of symbolism from this book back to the Old Testament, and attempts to explain the spiritual significance of it. You will find plenty of good in-

---

28. Also available as an abridged one-volume edition entitled, *Hebrews: The Epistle of Warning* (Grand Rapids: Kregel, 1973).

sights here, but you must sift through heaps of speculation to get at them. Kregel's one-volume abridgment helps.

James

Johnstone, Robert. *Lectures on the Epistle of James.* North Minneapolis: Klock and Klock, 1977.[29]

Although the title says "lectures," this commentary runs in the devotional vein. It is a good introduction to James for a beginning Bible student.

Mayor, Joseph B. *The Epistle of Saint James.* North Minneapolis: Klock and Klock, 1977.[30]

Here is an in-depth study of James, complete with the Greek text and a full array of textual notes. Mayor's interpretation is solidly conservative, but he does not apply the teaching of James to modern life as often or as meaningfully as Johnstone does. This commentary is best for the advanced student who would like to peruse the Greek, phrase by phrase.

1 and 2 Peter

Green, E.M.B. *The Tyndale New Testament Commentaries: Epistles of II Peter and Jude,* ed. R.V.G. Tasker. Grand Rapids: Eerdmans, 1968.

This commentary by a conservative Anglican writer capably answers many of the questions that critics have raised about the authorship of these epistles. Green also goes beyond such scholarly matters to apply the truth of these epistles to modern problems. The result is an excellent commentary.

Leighton, Robert. *Kregel Reprint Library: A Practical Commentary on the First Epistle General of St. Peter,* 2 vols. Grand Rapids: Kregel, 1972.

This classic commentary on 1 Peter deserves notice from every reviewer. Leighton was Archbishop of Glasgow in the mid-1600s and his work reflects the quiet, meditative approach to Bible study that was common in that era. Leighton's comments are largely devotional and practical.

Stibbs, A. M. *The Tyndale New Testament Commentaries: I Peter,* ed. R.V.G. Tasker. Grand Rapids: Eerdmans, 1959.

Stibbs' thorough exposition makes a good introduction to Green's volume. Stibbs is also a conservative Anglican writer; he respects the traditions concerning this epistle's authorship and date, but is willing to examine these matters in light of recent literary criticism. Stibbs draws out many practical lessons for Christians who live under persecution, and stresses 1 Peter's hopeful message of the imminent return of Christ.

---

29. Also available as part of the Geneva Commentary Series from (London: Banner of Truth Trust, 1977).
30. Also available from (Grand Rapids: Baker, 1978).

1, 2, and 3 John

Boice, James M. *The Epistles of John: An Expositional Commentary.* Grand Rapids: Zondervan, 1980.

Dr. Boice has distinguished himself as a radio preacher and as pastor of a large Presbyterian church in Philadelphia. This series of messages comes from his preaching ministry; they deal with the ethical and spiritual concerns of a Christian's everyday life. Dr. Boice grapples with 1 John's exhortation to live "above sin," and provides some helpful insights about what this means for us.

Westcott, B. F. *The Epistles of Saint John.* Grand Rapids: Eerdmans, 1966.

Westcott reproduces the entire Greek text of these epistles with critical notes and an excellent exposition of their messages. Reviewers agree that this is a classic; however, pastors and advanced Bible students will appreciate it far more than most laymen.

Jude

Coder, S. Maxwell. *Everyman's Bible Commentary: Jude, The Acts of the Apostates.* Chicago: Moody, 1967.

Here is a brief commentary on a brief epistle. Coder points out that the first-century danger of apostasy is just as real today. His comments are concise, practical, and well worth reading.

Revelation

Because there are as many interpretations of the Book of Revelation as there are interpreters, I am listing more titles than for most other books of the Bible.

Colclasure, Chuck. *The Overcomers.* Nashville: Thomas Nelson, 1981.

Mr. Colclasure is a Presbyterian writer, a graduate of Westminster Theological Seminary who supports the amillennial view of Christ's return. His brief devotional commentary highlights Revelation's message of hope for battle-worn Christians who are about to see their Vindicator return for them. It is an excellent beginner's guide to the amillennial view of Revelation.

Hendriksen, William. *More Than Conquerors.* Grand Rapids: Baker, 1979.

Wiersbe lauds this as "the best amillennial treatment I have ever found" (BLBS, 26). Hendriksen has certainly treated Revelation with more thoroughness and depth than Colclasure. This commentary was first published in 1939, and has become something of a modern classic.

Mounce, Robert. *The New International Commentary on the New Testament: Revelation,* ed. R.V.G. Tasker. Grand Rapids: Eerdmans, 1977.

This thorough, conservative commentary avoids many of the exaggerated ideas that may be drawn from the symbols of Revelation. Mounce considers the premillennial and amillennial interpretations of Revelation 20:1–10, and decides that the text indicates a premillennial return of Christ. Mounce believes that only the martyrs of the final tribulation era will reign in the millennium, and he feels that the millennium may not be a literal, earthly reign (p. 359).

Newell, William R. *The Book of the Revelation.* Chicago: Moody, 1979.

This premillennial interpretation, first published in 1935, is now considered one of the best conservative commentaries on Revelation. Newell propounds the premillennial, pretribulational return of Christ in a well-reasoned but emphatic way. This study is good for beginning students who wish to understand the premillennial view of the end time.

Walvoord, John F. *The Revelation of Jesus Christ.* Chicago: Moody, 1966.

Walvoord strongly expounds the premillennial return of Christ. As president of Dallas Theological Seminary, he is an influential leader in conservative circles. He articulates the approach that most modern evangelicals take to Revelation, i.e., that it predicts literal events which will occur in history and that the symbols and "signs" of Revelation can help us ascertain when Christ's return is near.

7.
Bible Dictionaries, Encyclopedias, and Handbooks

The reference book section of most Christian bookstores now offer a delightful variety of Bible dictionaries and encyclopedias. Many have full-color photographs of Holy Land sites. Some contain up-to-date information on archaeologists' work, which give interesting insights into the Bible. Some are popularly written; others are academic. One writer recently noted that "more Bible dictionaries and encyclopedias have appeared in the last two and one-half centuries than all other biblical aids put together."[1] There is an enticing abundance of Bible knowledge.

Yet these books are not a recent innovation; they go back much farther than two or three centuries. The first Bible dictionary was compiled in the fourth century A.D. by Bishop Eusebius of Caesarea (d. A.D. 339). Eusebius was a consummate scholar; however, scholarly interest was not his only reason for compiling a Bible dictionary. Emperor Constantine had asked him to supervise the restoration of many churches and Christian shrines in Palestine that were destroyed during the persecutions of Emperor Diocletian. To raise money for that project, Eusebius needed to stimulate interest among the wealthy Christian families of the empire. In modern parlance, he needed a good public-relations campaign. Besides that, Eusebius saw hundreds of Christian pilgrims coming to his province each year in search of Bible sites. They needed reliable information—a travel guide!

So around A.D. 330, Eusebius compiled a dictionary of about six hundred Palestinian places. The book did not include all of the places mentioned in the Bible (as Jerome discovered when he tried to translate the dictionary into Latin). Yet it did include other points of interest in the area, correlated to the Bible. Eusebius gave the location of each Bible site, quoted the Scriptures pertaining to it, and offered a few comments to stimulate interest. A modern biographer says:

---

1. Charles T. Fritsch, quoted in *Recommending and Selling Biblical Reference Works* (Grand Rapids: Eerdmans, 1980), p. 18.

The information Eusebius gives about the character of the present inhabitants of certain villages, and about the existence of Roman garrisons in others, can have no archaeological interest, and no topological significance. . . . It suggests rather that with pilgrims in mind Eusebius was trying to sound reassuring and encouraging.[2]

He seems to have achieved that goal, for the stream of pilgrims swelled to a flood. Emperor Constantine and his mother Helena were among them, and they granted Eusebius large sums of money to erect churches at the supposed site of the Holy Sepulchre in Jerusalem, at the Grotto of the Nativity in Bethlehem, on the Mount of Olives, and elsewhere.[3]

Eusebius' dictionary (called the *Onomasticon*) also stimulated interest in excavating the sites of biblical events. Eusebius himself sponsored some of these early "digs," unscientific and inconclusive though they were.

Eusebius aroused in Christians a desire to learn about the Holy Land, and that desire has never abated. In fact, that curiosity is greater today than it has ever been, and gives rise to the continuing flood of Bible dictionaries, encyclopedias, and handbooks.

Filling in the Gaps

Perhaps the greatest value of these books is the way they fill in the gaps of our Bible knowledge. For example, the Scriptures may mention a city in passing, with no details about the military or commercial importance of the city (such as Carchemish and Pergamos). Or the Scriptures may mention a powerful king, general, or other secular leader without explaining his impact upon secular history (such as Cyrenius and Tiberius). Perhaps a religious custom, doctrine, or concept is mentioned in the Bible with little explanation of how it originated (such as baptism, ordination, or praying for the dead). A Bible dictionary or encyclopedia will explain such things, at least as far as Bible scholars can explain them.

These books are a valuable supplement to a good Bible commentary, which is more concerned about the Scripture text itself.

Suppose you were studying the Book of Hosea. A good Bible commentary would provide background information about the political climate of Hosea's day, the impending collapse of the nation, the impact of Hosea's stern preaching, and so on. As it leads you through this book, the commentary may note some interesting facts—such as the Hebrew divorce decree (Hos. 2:2) or the price of a slave bride (Hos. 3:2). But if you wanted to learn more about Jezreel, the ancient city for which Hosea named his first

2. D. S. Wallace-Hodrill, *Eusebius of Caesarea* (Westminster, Md.: The Canterbury Press, 1961), p. 205.
3. Ibid., pp. 20,21.

son, you would look up "Jezreel" in a Bible encyclopedia or dictionary, and find information like this:

JEZREEL (jĕz´ rĕ-ĕl, jĕz´ rĕl, Heb. *yizre'el, God soweth*).
1. A city on the border of the territory of Issachar (Josh. 19:18), not far from Mount Gilboa. The Israelites made their camp near it before the battle of Gilboa (I Sam. 29:1), its people remaining faithful to the house of Saul. Abner set Ishbosheth over it among other places (II Sam. 2:9). Ahab built a palace there (I Kings 21:1), and his son Joram also lived there (II Kings 8:29). Naboth was a Jezreelite, and he was stoned outside the city for refusing to give up his vineyard to Ahab (I Kings 21). Jehu ordered that the heads of Ahab's 70 sons be placed in heaps at the gate of Jezreel (II Kings 10:1–11). . . .[4]

With this information, you can imagine how Hosea's neighbors must have felt when he named his firstborn for that city; either the prophet had terribly poor taste or God had directed him to choose this name for the boy to warn them of coming tragedy (cf. Hos. 1:4,5).

Perhaps you are puzzled by Paul's exhortation in 1 Thessalonians 4:26: "Greet all the brethren with a holy kiss." So you turn to "Kiss" in a Bible dictionary and find an explanation like this:

Kiss. Kissing the lips by way of affectionate salutation was customary among near relatives of both sexes. . . . Between individuals of the same sex, and in a limited degree between those of different sexes, the kiss on the cheek as a mark of respect or an act of salutation has at all times been customary in the East, and can hardly be said to be extinct even in Europe. In the Christian Church the kiss of charity was practiced not only as a friendly salutation, but as an act symbolical of love and Christian brotherhood. Rom. 16:16; 1 Cor. 16:20; 2 Cor. 13:12; 1 Thess. 5:26; 1 Peter 5:14. . . .[5]

This explains a foreign custom that seemed quite natural for the early Christians, though it might seem strange to modern Americans. A Bible commentary may give a brief explanation but for much detail and for thorough Scripture cross-referencing, you must turn to a Bible dictionary.

Or suppose you read the passage in Paul's letters where he says, "I will . . . that women adorn themselves in modest apparel, with shamefacedness and sobriety; not with braided hair, or gold, or pearls, or costly array" (1 Tim. 2:9), and you wonder how stylish women did dress in Paul's time. The Bible commentary is not apt to elaborate at this point; a concordance will give little help, because words like *make-up* or *jewelry* do not

---

4. Merrill C. Tenney, ed., *The Zondervan Pictorial Bible Dictionary* (Grand Rapids: Zondervan, 1967), p. 432.
5. William Smith, *Smith's Dictionary of the Bible*, rev. F. N. and M. A. Peloubet (Nashville: Thomas Nelson, 1979), p. 338.

appear in Scripture. So you turn to a Bible encyclopedia (which contains Bible topics but also topics not specifically mentioned in Scripture), and read under "Make-Up":

> From earliest times women have used beauty aids. In ancient Palestine, Egypt and Mesopotamia women put dark eyeshadow around their eyes. At first this was to protect their eyes against the strong sunshine. But it soon became a matter of fashion. The women used their fingers, spatulas made of wood or bronze, or fine brushes to put on their eyeshadow. And they had polished metal mirrors in which to study the effect![6]

This sort of fascinating information comes from ancient literature and from modern archaeological digs, which have uncovered actual cosmetics and cosmetic mirrors. This particular article continues for about half a page, and the editors tell us that more details may be found under the encyclopedic headings of "Clothes-Making," "Daily Life," and "Dress." These three random examples suggest ways you might use a Bible dictionary or encyclopedia to fill in the gaps of your Bible knowledge.

What to Expect

Dictionaries and encyclopedias are not just different names for the same thing. Each of these study aids has unique features.

A *dictionary* is a list of important words or phrases. It explains their various meanings, their rootage in other words, and often their pronunciation. A Bible dictionary endeavors to list all the important words in the Bible, such as the proper names of people and places, terms for religious rites and customs, doctrinal terms, and so on. It focuses on the Bible itself. It does not attempt to tell you about terms related to the Bible—such as the names of modern towns in Bible lands, post-biblical documents like the Dead Sea Scrolls, or technical procedures of Bible criticism. When the Bible itself does not mention such things, the Bible dictionary does not describe them. It is a repertory of *Bible* words and phrases.

An *encyclopedia,* on the other hand, is not limited to Bible words and phrases. It discusses anything the editors feel might help in understanding the Bible. A secular encyclopedia covers the whole gamut of human learning—literature, history, philosophy, religion, biology, physics, and all the rest. A Bible encyclopedia touches all sorts of topics related to the Bible—archaeology, military history, astrology and astronomy, ancient etiquette, and so on—even though the Bible does not explicitly refer to these subjects. A Bible encyclopedia also discusses many key topics from the Bible

---

6. Pat Alexander, ed., *Eerdmans' Concise Bible Encyclopedia* (Grand Rapids: Eerdmans, 1980), p. 162.

itself, such as important people and places. For example, here is a selected list of topics from the supplementary volume of *The Interpreter's Dictionary of the Bible*[7] (which is actually an encyclopedia):

Lachish	Lex Talionis
La'ir	Libnah (city)
Laodicea	Lists, Ethical
Latin Versions	Literary Criticism
Law in the OT	Literature, The Bible As
Lectionary Cycle, Rabbinic	Literature, Early Christian
Letter	Liturgical Materials, NT
Leviticus	Lord

As you can see, the encyclopedia contains some interesting topics that you would not find in a simple dictionary of Bible words. For this reason, a Bible dictionary and a Bible encyclopedia should be used together; they supplement one another.

In either type of book, you should first expect to find *a clear definition* of each subject. If the writer is not sure of the meaning, he should tell what is known of the subject instead of tossing out some ambiguous statement. Here is an example of a responsible treatment that concedes that much still is not known:

> **Unicorn,** the rendering of the Authorized Version of the Hebrew *reêm,* a word which occurs seven times in the Old Testament as the name of some large wild animal. The *rĕêm* of the Hebrew Bible, however, has nothing at all to do with the one-horned animal of the Greek and Roman writers, as is evident from Deut. 33:17. . . . Considering that the *reêm* is spoken of as a two-horned animal of great strength and ferocity, that it was evidently well-known and often seen by the Jews, that it is mentioned as an animal fit for sacrificial purposes, and that it is frequently associated with bulls and oxen, we think there can be no doubt that some species of wild ox is intended. . . .[8]

While we do not conclusively know the meaning of some Bible terms such as *unicorn, behemoth,* or *leviathan,* a Bible dictionary or encyclopedia should clearly describe the meaning of terms that are known, such as *cubit, Rephaim,* or *satrap.* Most English Bible versions do not translate or explain these words, so a dictionary or encyclopedia is necessary to understand what they mean.

Second, you should expect this type of book to give *a variety of Bible references to the term* (if the Bible mentions it more than once). Here is an

---

7. Keith Crim, ed., *The Interpreter's Dictionary of the Bible,* suppl. vol. (Nashville: Abingdon, 1976).

8. Smith, *Dictionary of the Bible,* pp. 720,721.

example of a place name that occurs again and again in Bible history; but its occurrence might be overlooked without the dictionary's list of Scripture references:

> MEDEBA (*mêdᵉbā,* possibly 'water of quiet'). A plain and city of Reuben (Jos. xiii. 9, 16) on the right side of the Arnon. An old Moabite town taken from Moab by Sihon (Nu. xxi. 21-30), it was used by the Syrian allies of Ammon as a camping-site after their defeat at the hand of Joab (1 Ch. xix. 6-15). . . . It also figured in the history of the intertestamental era (1 Macc. ix. 36 ff. as 'Medaba'; Jos., *Ant.* i. 2.4), before being captured by Hyrcanus after a long seige (Jos., *Ant.* xiii. 9.1).[9]

The foregoing example also illustrates the third important quality of a good Bible dictionary or encyclopedia: It should provide *relevant information from ancient literature other than the Bible.* The abbreviations "Jos., *Ant.*" in this example refer to Josephus' *Antiquities,* an important first-century A.D. history of the Jewish people. Other articles might mention the writings of Pliny, Marcus Aurelius, or other ancient authorities who shed light on Bible topics. This is a valuable feature.

Fourth, you should expect a good Bible dictionary or encyclopedia to convey *the latest findings of archaeologists, linguists, and other Bible scholars.* Publishers may issue periodic revisions of the book or bring out a supplemental volume to give their readers up-to-date information. A good case in point is the supplementary volume of *The Interpreter's Dictionary of the Bible.* Issued fourteen years after the first volumes came off the press, the supplement provides further information about topics such as the Hyksos of Egypt and the Gnostic "Gospels" of Nag Hammadi, based on recent findings.

Most Bible dictionaries and encyclopedias will attempt to describe the locations of Bible sites. (Shades of Eusebius!) Since the writers must rely on local tradition or archaeological finds to pinpoint a site, and since archaeologists keep uncovering new data, those map pins have to be moved. Writers of the older Bible dictionaries, such as Smith's, could only guess where cities such as Ekron (Josh. 25:45,46) and Hazor (Josh. 11:1; 1 Kin. 9:15) might be located; however, excavations in this century have confirmed their locations.

Fifth, you should expect a good Bible dictionary or encyclopedia to mention *any alternate names or spellings of a given subject.* Often a place-name was changed when foreign conquerors captured the site (e.g., Baal-Gad became "Paneas" under the Greeks and "Caesarea Philippi" under the Romans). Pagan deities were given various names (e.g., Nabu/Nebo or Merodach/Marduk). And older English versions such as the KJV give

---

9. J. D. Douglas, ed., *The New Bible Dictionary* (Grand Rapids: Eerdmans, 1962), p. 801.

archaic English names to objects that we know by other names today. Your Bible dictionary or encyclopedia should give these alternate terms.

Finally, you should expect the book to have *an efficient system of cross-references to related topics.* You will find the cross-references as "See" or "See Also" notes, usually at the end of an article. A Bible dictionary article on "Philistines," for example, might end by saying, "See also *Caphtor, Joshua, Samson,* and *Saul.*" This directs you to further information about the Philistines under those headings.

How to Use these Aids

If you know the alphabet, you will be able to use a Bible dictionary or encyclopedia. Finding things is just that simple—follow the alphabet to the topic you have in mind.

After you have owned one of these books for a while, you will be pleased to realize how many ways you can use it. Here are some examples:

—to find more detailed information about a Bible person or place
—to define the meaning of an obscure Bible term
—to follow the history of an ancient culture
—to research the origins of a Christian or Jewish doctrine
—to compare lifestyles in Bible times with modern lifestyles
—to visualize (with maps and other illustrations) what you are reading in the Bible
—to analyze a Bible book as literature (history, poetry, *apocalyptic literature*,* etc.)

And the list might go on. No wonder so many pastors and Sunday school teachers like to take these books to their Bible classes! As Warren Wiersbe says, "An educated person is not one who knows all the answers, but one who knows where to find them" (BLBS, 8). The answers to many Bible questions can be found in short order in a Bible dictionary or encyclopedia.

Bible Handbooks

Unlike Bible dictionaries or encyclopedias, which list articles in alphabetical order, the Bible *handbook* lists articles chronologically or according to the order of the books of the Bible (Genesis to Revelation). The Bible handbook is a late arrival on the publishing scene; the first of its kind was *Halley's Bible Handbook,* published in 1924. *Halley's* is still the most popular reference book of this type.

Some Bible handbooks give a synopsis of each Bible book along with related items about such things as archaeological finds. (*Eerdmans' Handbook to the Bible* is an example.) Others emphasize the historical background to each book and provide only a minimal outline of the Scripture itself. (*Halley's* is an example.)

Although Bible handbooks are occasionally advertised as "encyclope-dias,"[10] the Bible handbook is usually less thorough than the Bible dic-tionary or encyclopedia can be, simply because of space limitations. A cer-tain amount of the text (sometimes the bulk) must go into rehearsing the Bible narrative itself, so the writer can highlight only a few interesting facts from the archaeologists' or linguists' store of knowledge. Some lay readers enjoy using a Bible handbook because it only covers the highlights of biblical research.

ANNOTATED BIBLIOGRAPHY

This list includes only works that deal with the full range of bibli-cal knowledge, so it excludes some interesting supplemental works like *Baker's Dictionary of Theology,* edited by Everett F. Harrison, and Eerd-man's fine *Theological Dictionary of the Old Testament* and *Theological Dictionary of the New Testament.* As in the previous chapters, I have omitted books that are out of print.

BIBLE DICTIONARIES

Davis, John D. *Davis Dictionary of the Bible.* Grand Rapids: Baker, 1979.[11]

This is one of the classics in the field, having remained in popular demand since its first printing in 1924. *The Davis Dictionary* lacks the most recent archaeologi-cal data, but its basic information is still sound. Davis writes from a conservative theological perspective.

Douglas, J. D., ed. *The New Bible Dictionary.* Grand Rapids: Eerdmans, 1975.

Produced by the Tyndale Fellowship for Biblical Research (a group of evangeli-cal British scholars), this dictionary offers some of the most current archaeologi-cal and linguistic data about the Bible. Most articles have bibliographies, giving sources for more detailed information on those subjects. This is an exceptional work. Several articles are neo-orthodox in tone (e.g., "Biblical Criticism," "In-terpretation," and "Isaiah, Book of").

Hastings, James, ed. *Dictionary of the Bible,* rev. F. C. Grant and H. H. Rowley. New York: Charles Scribner's Sons, 1963.

Hastings achieved an interesting blend of conservative and liberal scholarship on the staff of this project. Discoveries since this dictionary was first published (1898–1904) have left it outdated in some respects; the revisers did not fully solve

10. Examples are *Eerdmans' Family Encyclopedia of the Bible* and *Nelson's Bible Ency-clopedia for the Family.*

11. Also available from (Old Tappan, N.J.: Revell, 1979) and (Nashville: Broadman, 1924).

that problem. But Hastings' dictionary still offers a good dialogue of liberal/conservative views on Bible topics. Some of its articles (e.g., "Faith," "Predestination," "Sermon on the Mount") are the best you will find anywhere. Hastings' work includes terms from the Apocrypha.

Miller, Madeleine S., and J. Lane Miller, *Harper's Bible Dictionary*. New York: Harper and Row, 1973.

Written with a liberal perspective, this dictionary gives useful background on the home life of Bible times, the geography and climate of Palestine, and other subjects of popular interest. Although brief on Bible history and theology, it might be used to supplement Unger's or Zondervan's (see Tenney) dictionaries, which are strong in those areas.

Smith, William. *Smith's Bible Dictionary*, rev. F. N. Peloubet and M. A. Peloubet. Nashville: Thomas Nelson, 1979.[12]

Though one of the oldest Bible dictionaries, Smith's remains one of the most popular. Its articles are brief and informative, with a minimum of speculation. In fact, Barber thinks many of its articles are "unquestionably superior to similar articles in modern dictionaries" (ML, 44). The Peloubet revision takes account of important archaeological finds in the late 1800s, which most other editions of Smith's do not.

Tenney, Merrill C., ed. *The Zondervan Pictorial Bible Dictionary*. Grand Rapids: Zondervan, 1969.

Tenney's articles are concise, meaty, and reliable. This is a good volume for quick reference. It has numerous illustrations, though many are of inferior quality. The bibliographies are of varying usefulness, and many major articles (e.g., "Resurrection of Jesus Christ") have no bibliography at all.

The Tyndale Illustrated Bible Dictionary, 3 vols. Wheaton: Tyndale, 1980.

Undoubtedly the most beautiful Bible dictionary, with hundreds of color illustrations, this set was originally produced in Great Britain by a team of conservative Bible scholars. (Some "Briticisms" remain in the text, but not enough to confuse American readers.) The articles are designed for lay readers; they are simply written and perceptive, but they are not too deep. This set makes an excellent but expensive gift.

Unger, Merrill F. *Unger's Bible Dictionary*. Chicago: Moody, 1966.

Dr. Unger has revised *Barnes' Bible Encyclopedia,* an excellent work published in 1913, to provide a more detailed discussion of key theological concepts and more up-to-date information on Bible sites. Many of Unger's articles (e.g., "Elec-

---

12. Also available from (Nashville: A. J. Holman, 1979); (Old Tappan, N.J.: Spire Books, 1979); (New York: Jove, 1967); and (Grand Rapids: Zondervan, 1979). *The New Smith's Bible Dictionary* (Garden City, N.Y.: Doubleday, 1979) is a complete revision of Smith's dictionary. It applies literary criticism to many of the Bible texts that Smith left untouched. Unfortunately, it shortens or deletes some of Smith's good doctrinal entries.

tion" and "Sanctification") compare the doctrines of various Christian communions more succinctly than any other articles I have found. The photographs are good and the sixteen color maps are superb, but the black-and-white maps are poor. With all things considered, this dictionary is perhaps the best.

BIBLE ENCYCLOPEDIAS

Alexander, Pat, ed. *Eerdmans' Concise Bible Encyclopedia.* Grand Rapids: Eerdmans, 1981.

This book reworks the material of the immensely popular Bible handbook *Eerdmans Family Encyclopedia of the Bible* into alphabetical order. The articles are quite brief, Scripture references are sparse, and there are no bibliographies. The slim paperback format makes it easy to carry, but does not justify the price.

Bromiley, Geoffrey W., ed. *The International Standard Bible Encyclopedia,* rev. ed., 4 vols. projected. Grand Rapids: Eerdmans, 1979–

Here is a notable achievement by leading evangelical Bible scholars. The revised ISBE is even better than its well-acclaimed predecessor (published in 1939). The clearly outlined articles make its information easy to find, yet one can see the academic excellence and scholarly depth of every article. The bibliographies are quite good, though they often rely on out-of-print materials. The new ISBE should rival the *Interpreter's Dictionary* for thoroughness and usefulness.

Bruce, F. F., ed. *Nelson's Bible Encyclopedia for the Family.* Nashville: Thomas Nelson, 1982.

Designed especially for young readers, this encyclopedia has hundreds of full-color illustrations and a popular text. Twenty major topics include "Clothes, Jewelry and Cosmetics," "Travel and Communication," "Sport and Leisure," and a host of other subjects to fascinate any Bible reader. This should become one of the best-selling Bible encyclopedias, stimulating more interest in Bible study, especially among teenagers and new Christians.

Buttrick, George A. and Keith Crim, eds. *The Interpreter's Dictionary of the Bible,* 5 vols. Nashville: Abingdon, 1962, 1976.

An immense undertaking, this is surely the most exhaustive Bible encyclopedia of recent years. Nearly three hundred Christian and Jewish scholars collaborated on the IDB. Their work has a liberal viewpoint, and is thoroughly documented with journal articles and monographs of scholarly weight. The IDB puts a wealth of modern biblical research in the hands of any pastor or layman; it is an invaluable resource.

Pfeiffer, Charles F. *The Biblical World.* Grand Rapids: Baker, 1966.

Pfeiffer's book is especially good in covering the cultures of Egypt, Assyria, Babylon, and Rome—empires that encroached on the biblical world. It provides interesting quotations from the documents of these nations to illustrate biblical customs and laws.

Pfeiffer, Charles F., Howard F. Vos, and John Rae, eds. *Wycliffe Bible Encyclopedia,* 2 vols. Chicago: Moody, 1975.

This popularized treatment of Bible topics is not as thorough as other Bible encyclopedias. The writers are evangelical conservatives and their work generally reveals this position. However, they part company with other conservatives to approve source-critical methods of interpretation.

Schaff, Philip A., and J. J. Herzog, eds. *The New Schaff-Herzog Encyclopedia of Religious Knowledge,* rev. Lefferts A. Loetscher, 15 vols. Grand Rapids: Baker, 1949-1955.

This set covers not only Bible subjects but church history, world religions, Christian missions, biographies of religious leaders, and a host of other topics concerning religion in general. A layman may feel this is more encyclopedia than he will ever need, but it is excellent for libraries and readers who have wide-ranging interests.

BIBLE HANDBOOKS

Alexander, David and Patricia. *Eerdmans' Handbook to the Bible.* Grand Rapids: Eerdmans, 1973.

This colorful book summarizes Bible history in an entertaining and informative way, with related articles about recent archaeological finds concerning these events. The full-color photography is stunning and the maps are quite detailed. But the text of the book tries to straddle the work of a Bible history and a Bible handbook, and comes off doing neither very well.

Halley, Henry. *Halley's Bible Handbook,* rev. ed. Grand Rapids: Zondervan, 1976.

Halley's book is the classic in this field, and this revised edition goes a long way toward updating its archaeological data. Halley cites many archaeological finds that confirm the authenticity of Bible history. He holds a conservative view of the authorship and dating of Bible books, and makes a good case for this view. This revision is also better than the original in terms of illustrations; the photographs and drawings are clearer and more meaningful than in Halley's original.

Packer, J. I., Merrill C. Tenney, and William White, Jr., eds. *The Bible Almanac.* Nashville: Thomas Nelson, 1980.

Having served as a project coordinator for this book, I may be accused of prejudice; but I believe *The Bible Almanac* is the best Bible handbook now available. Its forty-six articles (organized by subject in rough chronological order) discuss every major aspect of Bible culture and history; they are written in a conservative, evangelical tone. The book contains over five hundred illustrations, many of which have never been published before. And its detailed index is superior to any I have seen in competing works.

Unger, Merrill F. *Unger's Bible Handbook.* Chicago: Moody, 1966.

Barber calls this "the best work of its kind from the conservative point of view" (ML, 47), even ranking it ahead of Halley's Bible Handbook. Unger's book is truly superior in its handling of theological topics. But it does not measure up to Halley's in providing archaeological material of popular interest, nor does the style of writing have the popular appeal of *The Bible Almanac.*

Willmington, H. L. *Willmington's Guide to the Bible.* Wheaton: Tyndale, 1981.

Dr. Willmington summarizes the content of each book of the Bible and draws out the chief spiritual lessons to be learned from it. His archaeological information is not very deep or current. There are no illustrations. The book is designed to be a teaching resource rather than a personal study resource. The author's fundamentalist teachings are very evident at points.

8.
Bible Atlases

Atlas was the mythical Greek god who was condemned to carry the world on his shoulders. So it was a stroke of advertising genius when seventeenth-century map publisher Gerard Mercator printed a sketch of this god on the frontispiece of his map collection, with the title: *Atlas, or a Geographical Description of the World.*

That was in 1636. Few people today remember the name Mercator, but the name of Atlas is applied to almost every popular collection of maps.

A reliable Bible atlas is a prized possession of the Bible student. It helps him visualize where biblical events took place. It demonstrates how far the Israelites traveled in their wilderness wanderings, or Jesus on His Galilean preaching tour, or Paul on his missionary exploits. A Bible atlas with relief markings (lines or shadings that show the contours of the land) conveys some idea of the land features, such as the rugged terrain where Amos lived or the arid desert lowlands around the Dead Sea.

The better Bible atlases contain a *gazetteer,** which lists significant towns, rivers, and other features with code numbers to help you locate them on the maps. A gazetteer will usually provide the pronunciation of place names. These features save you a great deal of time.

A few atlases have articles about the geography and climate of Palestine, perhaps with rainfall and temperature charts to give you some idea of how the climate of the Holy Land compares to your own. Some have historical summaries that review the major events of Bible history in a given region. And the more recent atlases have photographs showing how Bible sites look today. (Who would have thought that a Muslim mosque would now stand on the site of the temple in Jerusalem?)

After that introduction you may be eager to look at some Bible atlases, but keep in mind that we do not know exactly where many Bible sites were. And even when we do know the locations (thanks to the archaeologists' findings) the mapmakers may not show the information accurately. Most Bible maps are drawn by map specialists who are accustomed to working with modern geographical data. They redraw political boundaries, change the names of a few cities or countries, or show minute geographical changes caused by earthquakes and the like; but most of the map features remain the same.[1] For the most part, the mapmaker is dealing with familiar territory. But when he draws a map of the biblical world he must locate cities and trade routes that disappeared centuries ago. The only means of checking the work is to consult some other bewildered artist's Bible map. Even when the map is drawn, the mapmaker must let the archaeologists and Bible scholars judge its accuracy, because no one else can. (He could put Pittsburgh on the wrong side of the Susquehannah River and millions of people would notice it. But if he put Beth-shan on the wrong side of the Jordan, few would notice and fewer would correct him.)

A noted authority on Bible geography, Denis Baly, says this problem is much more common than we realize. While reviewing a well-known current Bible atlas, he groans that its accuracy is ". . . deplorable. It has Petra in three different places, none of them the right one, Ctesiphon in two places, and so on. It even has the Dead Sea misplaced on one map."[2] Even with this warning about the problems of mapmakers, let me still urge you to have a Bible atlas. In spite of some possible inaccuracies, it will give you a better understanding of the Bible narrative than using your imagination.

What to Expect

You should expect any good Bible atlas to include *maps from various eras of biblical history*. One basic map for the Old Testament and one for the New (with minor rescrambling of boundaries and place names) are not enough. The atlas should show the spread of early civilizations across the "Fertile Crescent" of Mesopotamia before the time of Abraham. It should show the route of the Israelites' wilderness journey from Egypt to Canaan. It might even show the stages of their conquest of Canaan, but it should certainly show the tribal divisions of the land after the conquest. The atlas should show how the land was divided by the rival nations of Israel and Judah after King Solomon.

You should expect New Testament maps to show the Roman provinces of Jesus' day, Jesus' travels in Judea, and Paul's missionary journeys. The omission of any of these maps will hinder your study of the Bible.

You should expect a good Bible atlas to *name the rivers, mountains, and other major geographical features*. This should go without saying, but I

---

1. I am oversimplifying the mapmaker's work in order to make a point. A professional map-maker—a *cartographer*—will describe the task of revising a map as much more complicated than this.

2. Denis Baly, "What to Look for in a Biblical Atlas," *The Biblical Archaeologist* (Winter 1982), p. 61. He is describing the *Rand McNally Bible Atlas,* by E.G.H. Kraeling (New York: Rand McNally, 1956).

have been surprised to find several Bible atlases that do not name such features (except for a few major ones like the Mediterranean Sea or the Jordan River).

You should expect the atlas to *identify cities that figure significantly in Bible history.* There are many degrees of detail in this regard from one atlas to another. Some name only the major cities such as Jerusalem, Bethel, and Tyre, but omit the smaller (but important) towns such as Gilgal, Emmaus, and Sidon. Also look for names of Roman provinces on any New Testament map of the Mediterranean world; with these identified, you will know what the Book of Acts means when it refers to areas such as Dalmatia, Achaia, or Pamphilia.

Any Bible atlas should have *a gazetteer of the places and features shown on its maps.* As I have already explained this index and pronunciation guide is a great help in locating a Bible city or some other site.

The best Bible atlases will *show geographical contours in relief.* They use colors, shadings, or fine contour lines to show the surface features of a map area. Some atlases use different colors to identify *political* boundaries rather than geographical features. This can be confusing in the selection and use of an atlas, so look closely to see which you have.

Another feature of the best atlases will be *a delineation of major trade routes.* This quickly shows that Palestine was an important crossroads in the ancient world and a military prize that often attracted surrounding nations such as Egypt and Assyria.

Finally, the best atlases will *include charts and/or maps of rainfall.* Remember that Palestine is largely an arid region, where people depend on regular rains or snows for their survival. When the people of Bible times failed to get adequate rains for several seasons, they had severe famine. Baly writes, "In view of the tremendous importance of rainfall in the life of the Israelites and surrounding peoples it is surprising how little attention is given in biblical atlases to climate."[3] Fortunately, the newest atlases provide this information.

How to Use a Bible Atlas

Advice about the use of a Bible atlas is difficult to give because each book is laid out in its own way. Perhaps these suggestions will be of some help:

1. *Remember that the city or feature you are trying to locate may have an alternate name.* In Chapter 7, I pointed out that a good Bible dictionary or encyclopedia should give this information. For example, you may not

---

3. Ibid., p. 62.

be able to locate "Zion" on a Bible map, but the Bible dictionary will explain that "Zion" is another name for Jerusalem.

Using an atlas with a Bible dictionary or encyclopedia will also help locate some lesser-known places that may not be shown on a Bible map at all. A good example would be the Mount Salmon (or Zalmon) mentioned in Psalm 68:14. I know of no Bible atlas that shows it, but *Smith's Bible Dictionary* suggests that in light of another reference in Judges 9:48 it must be "a hill near Shechem."[4] Any Bible atlas should show where Shechem is.

2. *Beware of duplicate names.* For example, the Old Testament describes two cities named "Bethel" and at least three cities named "Gibeah." Consult a Bible dictionary or encyclopedia to learn about such duplicate names and where to locate the particular city you are trying to find.

3. *Be sure to consult the proper map for the period of history you are studying.* This seems elementary, but it may require some thought and effort. Finding Tekoa, Amos' home town, requires using a map of Palestine *after* the Israelite conquest. In order to find Caesarea you must consult a New Testament map of Palestine—and know which Caesarea you want to locate, because there were two. The Bible dictionary or encyclopedia will tell when the city was established, and the map *legend** will tell what period is covered by the map.

4. *Compare the scale of a Bible map to that of a map of an area you know, to get an idea of relative sizes and distances.* Many Bible readers assume that Palestine is much larger than it really is. After all, so many significant events have occurred there, and the country is displayed on a full-page map, as we are accustomed to seeing the United States displayed. But Palestine is actually about the size of New Hampshire. "From Dan to Beersheba" (Judg. 20:1) was about half the distance from New York to Washington, D.C.

5. *Keep a supply of tracing paper in your atlas.* A Bible map compresses many eras of history onto one page. A map of Palestine in Old Testament times, for example, must show the cities built during more than 2000 years. A piece of tracing paper can be used to "lift off" the key cities you are studying, or to trace the travels of a Bible character without the distraction of other irrelevant details.

Study Bibles, reference Bibles, and other reference books often have good sets of Bible maps in them. (The map and gazetteer in *The New Oxford Annotated Bible* are the best I've seen.) But such compact map sets can seldom offer the detail and depth of information that a full-fledged Bible atlas contains. It is worth having to aid your study.

---

4. William Smith, *Smith's Bible Dictionary,* rev. F. N. and M. A. Peloubet (Nashville: Thomas Nelson, 1979), p. 581.

ANNOTATED BIBLIOGRAPHY

While an *atlas* has traditionally been a collection of maps with some accompanying text and charts, this list also includes *geographies*, which are studies of the geography of Palestine (often with some supplementary maps). These books are so closely related to atlases that it seemed fitting to list them here.

ATLASES

Aharoni, Yohanan, and Michael Avi-Yonah. *The Macmillan Bible Atlas*, rev. ed. New York: Macmillan, 1977.

Providing a different map for every major event of Bible history (264 maps in all), *The Macmillan Bible Atlas* is one of the most interesting to read straight through. It is not as colorful as some; the map captions are sometimes difficult to read; and it does not show as many of the small Bible cities as one would like. But it does offer the best sequential review of Bible history that I have found in a Bible atlas.

Blaiklock, E. M., ed. *The Zondervan Pictorial Bible Atlas*. Grand Rapids: Zondervan, 1972.

This atlas describes the history of the Jews from patriarchal times through the New Testament era, and shows how the geography of Palestine affected their destiny in many ways. Though it is called an atlas, this book more appropriately belongs under the "Geographies" section because its bulk is devoted to the narration of Israel's history and geography. However, it has thirty-two pages of full-color maps and an excellent gazetteer. The two-color printing throughout the rest of the book gives it less eye appeal than the full-color atlases have. But its data is reliable, and it is detailed enough to help serious Bible students.

Gardner, Joseph L. *Reader's Digest Atlas of the Bible*. Pleasantville, N.Y.: Reader's Digest Association, 1981.

A detailed narrative of Bible history in simple *Reader's Digest* style is the greatest strength of this Bible atlas. Like Macmillan's atlas, this one is easy to read straight through (though it does not illustrate as many events). Striking color photos of archaeological objects and informative articles about current "digs" are other appealing features of this atlas. The maps are colorful and show excellent relief. (The best is the beautiful four-page map, "Biblical Sites in the Holy Land," with a thirty-page gazetteer.) This volume is good for studying history as well as studying geography because of the excellent narrative text.

Pfeiffer, Charles F. *Baker's Bible Atlas*, rev. ed. Grand Rapids: Baker, 1973.

The gazetteer in this volume is excellent and up-to-date. It identifies biblical sites by their modern names as well as their biblical names, which helps in following news of current archaeological finds in these areas. The maps are fairly detailed, though they are not as colorful as some in other atlases.

Wright, G. Ernest, and Floyd V. Filson. *The Westminster Historical Atlas to the Bible.* Philadelphia: Westminster, 1956.

This atlas seems to offer the best combination of features—informative text, colorful and detailed maps (95 in all), and a good gazetteer. Wright and Filson assign dates to some Bible events (such as the Exodus) that conservative readers will question. But their narrative of Bible history is clear and generally dependable.

GEOGRAPHIES

Aharoni, Yohanan. *The Land of the Bible,* trans. A. F. Rainey. Philadelphia: Westminster, 1980.

Aharoni is one of the foremost Israeli scholars of today; this book and his *Macmillan Bible Atlas* reflect his firsthand knowledge of Palestine. Aharoni describes key events of the intertestamental period, such as the Maccabean Revolt, which will be of special interest to students of the Apocrypha. He scarcely refers to New Testament events, however.

Baly, Denis A. *The Geography of the Bible,* rev. ed. New York: Harper and Brothers, 1978.

Baly's work is a standard textbook at many Christian colleges. The illustrations are not as clear or colorful as those found in other atlases or geographies, but this is more than offset by Baly's superior knowledge of Palestinian geography. He describes not only *topography** but also the botany, meteorology, and other aspects of the Holy Land closely tied to its geography.

National Geographic Society, *Everyday Life in Bible Times.* Washington D.C.: National Geographic Society, 1967.

The exquisite full-color illustrations make this a treasure for any Bible student. The maps are first-rate (although they try to show both modern and ancient placenames, which is confusing). The color photographs of modern Israel, showing how the Israelis have continued many biblical customs, give this book tremendous popular appeal.

Smith, George Adam. *The Historical Geography of the Holy Land.* London: Collins, 1974.[5]

This is the standard classic in the field of Bible geography. First published in 1894, Smith's volume has been revised and updated many times to keep abreast of more recent data about the Holy Land. Smith spent many years in Palestine while it was under Turkish control. His book is a good narrative of the land itself, but it is oblivious to the most recent developments (such as the modern Israelis' land reclamation projects).

---

5. Also available from (Grand Rapids: Kregel).

9.
Bible Surveys
and Introductions

When a college student takes an introductory course in Bible, the basic text is sure to be a Bible survey or introduction. Surprisingly, however, very few laymen know that these books are available or think to use them in Bible study.

A Bible *survey** is what its name implies: a simple "walking tour" through the Bible, citing the points of interest and showing how various parts of the Scripture are related to one another. The Bible *introduction** attempts to show the significance of the Bible as a whole. It unfolds the redemptive theme of Scripture and shows how various Bible events illustrate that theme. The survey summarizes Scripture; the introduction analyzes Scripture. The survey is for beginning students; the introduction is for more advanced students.

More advanced Bible students shun surveys because they rehearse the obvious. But they will give you a clear overview of Bible history and (in the better books) a good overview of major Bible doctrines. So they have real value to the beginning student, preparing him for more in-depth Bible study.

Not a Casual Exercise

The simplicity of most of these books leads some laymen to think they can read straight through them, as they might read a Bible handbook. But that's not true. Though simple in format, a Bible survey or introduction is packed with meaty information.

Let's consider two examples. Here is a brief quotation from Samuel J. Schultz's book, *The Old Testament Speaks,* in the chapter entitled "Fading Hopes of Davidic Kings:"

> Zedekiah was under constant pressure to join the Egyptians in a rebellion against Babylon. When Psammetichus II succeeded Necho (594) Edom, Moab, Ammon, and Phoenicia joined Egypt in an anti-Babylonian coalition, creating a crisis in Judah. With a wooden yoke around his neck Jeremiah dramatically announced that Nebuchadnezzar was God's servant to whom the nations should willingly submit. Zedekiah was assured that sub-

mission to the Babylonian king would avert the destruchus of Jerusalem (Jer. 27).[1]

Now here is an excerpt from Edward J. Young's book, *An Introduction to the Old Testament*:

> . . . [Jeremiah] 27, although dated (verse 1) in the beginning of the reign of Jehoiakim, belongs, as its context shows, to the reign of Zedekiah. The chapter shows how the prophet thwarted the designs of five neighbouring peoples, Edom, Moab, Ammon, Tyre, Zidon (verse 2), to induce the Judean king to unite with them in a rebellion against Babylon. Jeremiah further spoke to Zedekiah about the folly of such action (verses 12–22).[2]

Dr. Schultz's book is a Bible *survey*; Dr. Young's is a Bible *introduction*. In comparing their treatment of the same Scripture passage, we see Dr. Schultz summarizes the impact of the event itself upon the prophetic career of Jeremiah, upon the politics of Zedekiah, and upon the survival of Judah as a nation. But Dr. Young analyzes the record of the event in the Book of Jeremiah and shows how that record builds Jeremiah's overall theme.

These treatments entice the inquisitive reader to a more thorough study of Zedekiah and his rebellion against Babylon. The reader might look up the word *yoke* in an exhaustive concordance and find the exact Scripture passage where Jeremiah's yoke prophecy is recorded (Jer. 27:1–14). Or he might turn to an article on Zedekiah in a Bible dictionary and read more about the king's life, as in this excerpt from *Smith's Bible Dictionary*:

> It is evident that Zedekiah was a man not so much bad at heart as weak in will. It is evident from Jer. 27 and 28 that the earlier portion of Zedekiah's reign was marked by an agitation throughout the whole of Syria against the Babylonian yoke. Jerusalem seems to have taken the lead, since in the fourth year of Zedekiah's reign we find ambassadors from all the neighboring kingdoms—Tyre, Sidon, Edom, and Moab—at his court to consult as to the steps to be taken. The first act of rebellion of which any record survives was the formation of an alliance with Egypt. . . .[3]

The inquisitive reader may also consult articles on Necho, Egypt, or Jeremiah in a Bible dictionary, or check on Psammetichus II in a Bible handbook or encyclopedia, or read a good expository commentary on

---

1. Samuel J. Schultz, *The Old Testament Speaks,* 3rd ed. (New York: Harper and Row, 1980), p. 227.
2. Edward J. Young, *An Introduction to the Old Testament,* rev. ed. (Grand Rapids: Eerdmans, 1964), p. 237.
3. William Smith, *Smith's Bible Dictionary,* ed. F. N. and M. A. Peloubet (Nashville: Thomas Nelson, 1979), p. 760.

Jeremiah 27 for further background information. The survey or introduction is simply the first step in using all of these research avenues to better understand the Scripture itself.

Higher Criticism

As with commentaries, questions about higher criticism occur in the use of Bible surveys or introductions. In fact, some authors of these books take the opportunity to discuss higher-critical problems, citing passages of Scripture that illustrate their views. A good example is Charles A. Briggs' *General Introduction to the Holy Scriptures.* Briggs was an early liberal leader in source criticism, and he explores this theme throughout his book.

Donald Guthrie's *New Testament Introduction* is a more recent example, and it demonstrates that conservative scholars must employ various methods of higher criticism, too (though not to the extent that more liberal scholars do). Foremost among the recent Bible introductions that make liberal use of source criticism and form criticism are Robert and Feuillet's *Introduction to the Old Testament*; Sellin and Fohrer's *Introduction to the Old Testament*; and the *Introduction to the New Testament* by Feine, Behm, and Kümmel. (Sellin and Fohrer's volume also employs literary criticism, more so than the others.)

Being aware of the methods writers use to analyze Scripture and to discuss Bible history can often explain why experts disagree. This awareness helps us evaluate a particular writer's view more carefully.

How to Use these Aids

Bible surveys and introductions come in so many different formats that it is impossible to give a simple set of guidelines for using them. You may be alerted to the special features of each book in the preface. Here are some general tips that might help you:

1. *Keep a concordance and Bible dictionary close at hand.* The example from Jeremiah 27 shows how these other reference books might supplement your reading. The Bible survey or introduction paints the broad outlines; the other reference books will help sketch in the details.

2. *Use a current Bible encyclopedia to update the archaeological data.* Many old surveys and introductions are still in print because the publisher assumes they are still up-to-date. But new archaeological finds may alter what the writer has said about the military, political, or cultural background of a given event. If the publication date of the book is more than ten years old, be sure to check a more recent Bible encyclopedia for new insights.

3. *Use the index.* Lay readers often ignore an index, but it can guide you through these books. For example, Merrill C. Tenney defines and describes the Greek philosophy of Epicureanism in the opening chapter of his *New Testament Survey.*[4] A quick glance at the index tells you that he discusses it again—this time in the full context of Paul's speech on Mars' Hill—on page 286 of that volume. Since a Bible survey or introduction generally proceeds through the Bible book by book, you may need to use the index to track down all the references to a given subject that interests you.

ANNOTATED BIBLIOGRAPHY

In this list I have included several Bible histories because they serve basically the same function as Bible surveys. The writers have a variety of theological views, to offer you a wider choice.

INTRODUCTIONS AND SURVEYS

Anderson, Bernhard W. *Understanding the Old Testament,* 3rd ed. Englewood Cliffs, N.J.: Prentice-Hall, 1975.

Anderson's popular introduction examines the major theological themes of the Old Testament such as covenant-making and vicarious sacrifice. The text is easy to understand; the illustrations are crisp. Along the way, Anderson explains the documentary hypothesis of the Pentateuch, form criticism of the Psalms, and other higher-critical concerns. He has a rather liberal perspective.

Archer, Gleason L. *A Survey of Old Testament Introduction,* rev. ed. Chicago: Moody, 1973.

Dr. Archer is a young professor at Trinity Evangelical Divinity School who has already won a wide reputation as a conservative Old Testament scholar. Barber applauds this introduction as "a definitive study which takes its place among the front rank of works in the field . . ." (ML, 81).

Childs, Brevard. *Introduction to the Old Testament as Scripture.* Philadelphia, Pa.: Fortress, 1979.

Using a higher-critical method now popular in Europe, called *canon criticism,** Professor Childs attempts to show how Jews of the intertestamental era selected the writings that we now consider to be Scripture. He seeks to demonstrate that the Old Testament is a product of the Judeo-Christian tradition as much as it is a source of that tradition.

Feine, Paul, Johannes Behm, and Werner Georg Kümmel, *Introduction to the New Testament,* trans. A. J. Mattill, Jr., rev. ed. Nashville: Abingdon, 1979.

---

4. Merrill C. Tenney, *New Testament Survey* (Grand Rapids: Eerdmans, 1961), pp. 76-78.

This introduction shows what higher-critical methods can uncover in the New Testament. The authors are leading German champions of higher-critical Bible study. Their book is sophisticated and often bewildering (especially in their discussion of the Gospels); it is meant for the advanced Bible student.

Gundry, Robert H., *A Survey of the New Testament,* rev. ed. Grand Rapids: Zondervan, 1982.

Dr. Gundry's survey has been a standard textbook in evangelical colleges since its first publication in 1970. Outline headings printed in the margin help the reader find Dr. Gundry's comments on every significant New Testament passage. His outlines are well worth the price of the entire *Survey.*

Guthrie, Donald. *New Testament Introduction,* rev. ed. Downers Grove, Ill.: InterVarsity, 1971.

Wiersbe terms this Bible survey "essential" (BLBS, 17). Guthrie makes a solid case for the conservative view of scriptural inspiration as he reviews the seeming discrepancies in the Gospels and other matters that trouble first-time readers of the New Testament.

Harrison, Everett F. *Introduction to the New Testament.* Grand Rapids: Eerdmans, 1971.

Here is another excellent conservative survey of the New Testament. Harrison does not resolve the Synoptic problem as clearly as Guthrie, and he seems to avoid some difficult issues that other survey writers have tackled. But his treatment is clear and easy to follow.

Schultz, Samuel J. *The Old Testament Speaks,* 3rd ed. New York: Harper and Row, 1980.

The most simply written Old Testament survey I have found, Dr. Schultz's book is nevertheless full of useful information about the military, political, and religious influences of nations that affected ancient Israel. His book shows a good acquaintance with the newly discovered historical records of Assyria, Babylon, and other ancient cultures.

Tenney, Merrill C. *New Testament Survey,* rev. ed. Grand Rapids: Eerdmans, 1969.

This was the basic textbook for the introductory course in New Testament when I was a college student, and many conservative schools still use it. Dr. Tenney provides a clear narration of New Testament events, but he also sketches in interesting background details, such as the Greek and Roman philosophies of that day, the Jewish sects and political parties, and so on. The maps and other illustrations are quite good.

Unger, Merrill F., *Introductory Guide to the Old Testament.* Grand Rapids: Zondervan, 1951.

Surely one of the best conservative introductions, Dr. Unger's book mounts a strong defense of the Old Testament text. Unger explains why we should still consider Moses to be the writer of the Pentateuch, Isaiah the writer of the entire Book of Isaiah, Daniel the writer of the Book of Daniel, and so on. However, one wishes the publisher would update this book with information from more recent archaeological finds.

Young, Edward J. *An Introduction to the Old Testament,* rev. ed. Grand Rapids: Eerdmans, 1960.

Young's survey is a good counterpart to Anderson's, as far as matters of higher criticism are concerned. Dr. Young addresses students who are more advanced than Anderson's audience. But his narrative of Old Testament history is still easy for beginners to follow, and he shows how a conservative scholar deals with the higher-critical problems that we find in the Old Testament.

HISTORIES

Bright, John. *A History of Israel,* 3rd ed. Philadelphia: Westminster, 1981.

A former professor at Union Theological Seminary, Richmond, Bright recounts Israel's history with scholarly depth and flair. He gives a liberal slant to critical matters (e.g., he identifies two authors of Isaiah). But his comparison of Israel's religion to the religions of her neighbors is still unsurpassed.

Bruce, F. F. *New Testament History.* Garden City, N.Y.: Doubleday, 1977.

Dr. Bruce covers the history recorded in New Testament Scripture as well as the attendant history recorded in secular sources such as Josephus. This book will be prized by beginning New Testament students because it digests so much vital information for them. More advanced students will appreciate Bruce's conservative handling of the dates of Jesus' ministry, the significance of the Book of Revelation, and other sensitive issues.

Harrison, R.K., *Old Testament Times.* Grand Rapids: Eerdmans, 1970.

Harrison describes the great cultures surrounding the ancient nation of Israel, drawing upon fairly recent discoveries (such as the Lachish Letters, the Dead Sea Scrolls, and the excavations at Hazor) to provide an interesting backdrop to Old Testament studies. The photographs are superb.

Pfeiffer, Charles F. *Old Testament History.* Grand Rapids: Baker, 1973.

Pfeiffer's chronology has a liberal slant; for example, he favors a "late date" for the Exodus (about 1250 B.C.). But conservative readers will enjoy his articulate description of Israel's rise and progress, even though they may not agree with all the dates assigned to Bible events.

Tenney, Merrill C. *New Testament Times.* Grand Rapids: Eerdmans, 1965.

This book is not to be confused with Dr. Tenney's equally good *New Testament Survey.* While the other book summarizes the content of the New Testament as literature, this book reviews New Testament *events* in the broader context of history. This book is not as well known as Tenney's *Survey,* but it deserves to be.

Wood, Leon J., *A Survey of Israel's History*. Grand Rapids: Zondervan, 1970.
    Here is a good, conservative study of Old Testament history. Although it is not as detailed as Bright's book, and it passes over many interesting events, Wood's book is still helpful. It's excellent for the beginner.

10.
Language Study Aids

If you live near a Bible museum, seminary, or library that houses actual Bible manuscripts in Hebrew and Greek, take the opportunity to look at some of them. When you first see the long rows of blocky Hebrew letters or the wispy, cursive lines of Greek script, you realize what a difficult task Bible translators have. Before they can figure out the meaning of these words, they must figure out what the words are, because the characters are so different from our own English alphabet. Most of us muse over these manuscripts, breathe a prayer of thanks for Bible translators, and go on our way.

But perhaps you are someone who would like to know enough about biblical Hebrew or Greek to glimpse the subtle shades of meaning that English translations cannot express. Perhaps you are a minister, and you would like to translate the Scriptures from the original language to gain insights for sermon texts.

This chapter surveys the various books that have been written as study aids for those who want to learn the languages of the Bible. I am not going to teach you Hebrew or Greek. But I am going to introduce you to a set of reference books that can unlock the Bible languages.

Word Studies

This is one of the easiest language study tools to use.[1] In fact, its use requires no knowledge of Hebrew or Greek at all. The *word study** lists the most significant Hebrew or Greek words of the Bible with definitions, examples of usage, and a bit of linguistic background to show how the words are related.

You will find Bible word studies organized in one of these ways:

1. Alphabetically, according to the Hebrew or Greek alphabet. Gerhard Kittel's *Theological Dictionary of the New Testament* uses this pattern. You can find entries easily if you know the Greek alphabet, or you can refer to an index that gives the English translation of each word.

2. Alphabetically, according to a transliteration of the Hebrew or Greek. A transliteration converts the Hebrew or Greek pronunciation into English letters; it *does not translate* the word into an English word. (Figure

---

1. The only thing that might be easier is an analytical concordance. See Chapter 5.

15 shows the difference between a transliteration and a translation.) An example of a word study organized by transliteration is R. Laird Harris' *Theological Wordbook of the Old Testament.* Again, you can locate words most easily if you are already acquainted with Hebrew; if not, you must use the index (coded to the word list in Strong's *Exhaustive Concordance*).

3. Alphabetically, according to English translations of the Hebrew or Greek. This type of book is designed for a reader with no knowledge of the languages. *Vine's Expository Dictionary of the New Testament* and *Nelson's Expository Dictionary of Old Testament Words* follow this pattern. If you wish to study the Greek terms for *love,* for example, you can find the information under "L" in Vine's. If you are not acquainted with Greek but hear someone mention the Greek word *phileo,* you can find that word in the index of the same book; it will refer you to the article on *kiss* and *love.*

Figure 15—Transliteration vs. Translation

Many Bible students are confused by these two similar-sounding words, *transliteration* and *translation.* They are used frequently in literature about Bible languages. A *transliteration* expresses the pronunciation of a foreign word in the letters of our own alphabet, so that we can pronounce the word. A *translation* expresses the meaning of that word in English. Some language-study aids give us both a transliteration and a translation of each Hebrew or Greek word. Here are some examples:

Hebrew Word	Transliteration	Translation
מוּת	mûth	to die, kill
סָלַח	sàlach	to forgive
שִׂנְאָה	sina'āh	hatred
קֹדֶשׁ	qòdesh	holiness; holy thing; sanctuary

Greek Word	Transliteration	Translation
'απογράφω	apographò	to enroll
θεμέλιος	themélios	foundation
καρδία	kardía	heart
ἑρμηνεύω	hermēneuō	to interpret

Sources: Merrill F. Unger and William White, Jr., eds., *Nelson's Expository Dictionary of the Old Testament* (Nashville: Thomas Nelson, 1980). W. E. Vine, ed., *An Expository Dictionary of New Testament Words* (Nashville: Thomas Nelson, n.d.).

Lexicons

The more advanced Bible student who knows something about Hebrew or Greek will prefer a lexicon, which contains more thorough word studies. Some lexicons (such as Arndt and Gingrich's Greek lexicon or Brown, Driver, and Briggs' Hebrew lexicon) contain all the words of the Bible text. But most lexicons are selective; they cover only the most common or most significant Bible words.

Using a lexicon is facilitated by knowing the Hebrew or Greek alphabet because the lexicon is usually arranged that way. But recently a few publishers have issued lexicons that are arranged by the code numbers from Strong's *Exhaustive Concordance;*[2] thus, you can look up an English word in Strong's and find the proper code, then follow the numerical list in one of these lexicons until you find the Greek or Hebrew word.

The *lexicon* analyzes the Greek or Hebrew word in much more depth than a regular word study. Compare these two treatments of the Greek word for *lampstand (luchnia)*. First, the article in Vine's word study:

LAMPSTAND
LUCHNIA (λυχνία) is mistranslated "candlestick" in every occurrence in the A.V. and in certain places in the R.V.; the R.V. has "stand" in Matt. 5:15; Mark 4:21; Luke 8:16; 11:33; "candlestick" in Heb. 9:12; Rev. 1:12, 13, 20 (twice); 2:1, 5; 11:4; the R.V. marg., gives "lampstands" in the passages in Rev., but not in Heb. 9:2.[3]

Now look at the article about this same word in Arndt and Gingrich's lexicon (many of the abbreviations refer to places where this word appears in nonbiblical Greek literature):

λυχνία, ας, ἡ ... (Hero Alex. I p. 264, 20; Plut; Dio 9, 2; Ps.-Lucian, Asin. 40; Artem. 1, 74; inscr.; pap. since PEleph. 5, 7 [284/3 BC]; LXX, Philo; Jos [s. λύχνος, beg.]; cf. Phryn. p. 313f L.) *lampstand* upon which lamps were placed or hung (s. λύχνος, beg.); not a candlestick. Τιθέναι 'επὶ τὴν λ. ('επὶ λυχνίας) put on the *(lamp)stand* Mt 5:15; Mk 4:21; Lk 8:16; 11:33. Of the seven-branched lampstand (Ex 25:31 ff; Jos., Ant. 14, 72) Hb 9:2. In Rv the seven churches of Asia appear as seven lampstands Rv 1:12 f, 20a, b; 2:1. Cf. also κινήσω τὴν λ. σου ἐκ τοῦ τόπου αὐτῆς *I will remove your lampstand from its place,* i.e., remove you fr. the circle of the

---

2. Examples are *Gesenius' Hebrew-Chaldee Lexicon to the Old Testament* and *Thayer's Greek-English Lexicon of the New Testament,* both published by Baker Book House.
3. W. E. Vine, *An Expository Dictionary of New Testament Words* (Nashville: Thomas Nelson, 1978), p. 638.

churches 2:5. Rv also likens the two witnesses of Christ to two lampstands 11.4 (cf. Zech 4:11).[4]

You can see that the lexicon contains more technical information that is of interest to the language specialist. It also discusses the Bible's use of this word in more detail than the word study does; for this reason, the lay reader can profit by using a lexicon even if he does not plan to learn the language itself.

Interlinears

Another language study aid requiring some knowledge of biblical languages is the *interlinear Bible,* which gives the full text of the Hebrew or Greek with a literal translation of each word between the lines. Some would say that an interlinear is easier to use than a lexicon. I disagree, because I think the interlinear's literal translation of the text may be more confusing than helpful. Baker Book House has introduced an interlinear New Testament with a novel twist: an interlinear word code tied to the Greek dictionary in Strong's *Exhaustive Concordance.*[5] This feature should make the interlinears easier to use, especially if Greek script befuddles you.

Grammars and Critical Editions

Although the primary goal here is to help lay readers with limited technical knowledge, let me suggest these three tools for those who are serious about learning the biblical languages: a *grammar,* a *critical edition* of the (Hebrew) Old Testament or (Greek) New Testament, and a *lexicon.*

The *grammar** teaches the basic rules of the language and introduces its vocabulary. A traditional grammar will follow the deductive approach, teaching the basic rules of syntax and providing translation exercises that demonstrate those rules. It asks the student to master basic skills of the language before translating Bible passages themselves.[6] More recently, grammars have used an inductive approach; that is, they invite you to "dive into" translating actual Bible passages and teach you the syntax and vocabulary along the way.[7]

---

4. William F. Arndt and F. Wilbur Gingrich, *A Greek-English Lexicon of the New Testament,* 4th ed. (Chicago: Univ. of Chicago Press, 1957), p. 484.

5. *The Interlinear Greek-English New Testament.* See the bibliography in this chapter.

6. Machen's *New Testament Greek for Beginners* uses the deductive approach. See the bibliography.

7. Paine's *Beginning Greek* uses the inductive approach. See the bibliography.

The *critical edition,* as explained in the chapter on "Bible Versions," gives the most authentic text of the Hebrew or Greek testament (in the opinion of the editors who compiled it). Use a critical edition for translating Scripture. Also be sure to consult the footnotes, which show alternate readings from manuscripts that the editors felt were less reliable.

Critical editions fall into two major groups, according to the procedure that the editors used in compiling them. First are the editions that seek to preserve the "Received Text" (Latin, *Textus Receptus*) of the Bible—that is, the one that the textual critics of the Middle Ages "received" from the past. Usually, these critics chose to follow what the majority of the existing manuscripts said, and this majority reading or "Majority Text" became their *Textus Receptus.* Luther, the KJV translators, and a few conservative modern translators today prefer to use the *Textus Receptus* or the "Majority Text."[8]

The second group of critical editions seek to recover the "Neutral Text," that is, what modern critics determine the text would have been, without the corruptions by later copyists. To find this "Neutral Text" they use the techniques of textual criticism developed by B. F. Westcott and F.J.A. Hort.[9] So we might say these critical editions are of "the West-cott-Hort type."

Westcott and Hort's methods are too complex to describe here, but their general tendency was to give more weight to the oldest manuscripts. They especially preferred two Greek manuscripts known as the Codex Sinaiticus and the Codex Vaticanus, which date from the fourth century A.D. When both of these manuscripts disagreed with the traditional *Textus Receptus,* Westcott and Hort tended to reject the *Textus Receptus.* So their Greek critical edition differed somewhat from the *Textus Receptus.*

Other twentieth-century critical editions, such as the Nestle text and the United Bible Society text, have done the same. Most modern Bible versions are translated from a critical edition of the Westcott-Hort type.[10] De-

---

8. Traditionally, the *Textus Receptus* of the Hebrew Old Testament has been the Masoretic Text edited by Aaron ben Moshe ben Asher (tenth century A.D.), while the *Textus Receptus* of the Greek New Testament has been Erasmus' critical edition published in 1512. But the editors' method of compiling the *Textus Receptus* calls for following the majority of the manuscripts; so conservative scholars are still making "Majority Text" critical editions, as more manuscripts are found. An example of these new "Majority Text" editions is *The Greek New Testament According to the Majority Text,* edited by Arthur L. Farstad and Zane C. Hodges. (See the bibliography.)

9. This applies primarily to the Greek New Testament. Generally scholars still follow the *Textus Receptus* of the Hebrew Old Testament, because even recent manuscript discoveries (such as the Dead Sea Scrolls) seldom disagree with it.

10. For a good comparison of the *Textus Receptus* and the Westcott-Hort type of critical editions, see Lewis Foster, *Selecting a Translation of the Bible* (Cincinnati: Standard, 1978), pp. 38–40.

ciding which approach to textual criticism you favor—to preserve the "Received Text" or to recover the "Neutral Text"—will determine which Greek critical edition you use.

I have already explained the purpose of a lexicon. A related book that may be of interest is Bruce M. Metzger's *Lexical Aids for Students of New Testament Greek,* rev. ed. (Princeton: Theological Book Agency, 1970). This little paperback is designed to teach the vocabulary of *koine* Greek by (1) listing the words in descending order of frequency, with English definitions and examples of how we have borrowed the Greek word in our own language, and (2) listing each word according to its root word, showing how the Greeks derived specialized words from common, frequently used words. Thus you can begin memorizing the Greek words that occur most often in the New Testament and work your way down to the less frequent words. After a while, the meaning of a strange word is apparent because you recognize its root. So you lean less and less upon your lexicon and more and more upon your growing knowledge of the Greek vocabulary. A similar aid for learning Hebrew is George M. Landes' *A Student's Vocabulary of Biblical Hebrew* (New York: Charles Scribner's Sons, 1961).

Hebrew and Greek Concordances

Concordances to the Hebrew and Greek Testaments list every occurrence of a word in the original-language text. Obviously, one of these concordances will not help to look up a verse that you vaguely recall! But they will provide other occurrences of a Hebrew or Greek word that interests you.

For example, let's say you were reading your Greek New Testament and came across the tongue-twisting word *anthrōpareskos* ("men-pleasers"). To see where else that word is used, you could consult a word study such as Vine's *Expository Dictionary.* But a faster and more reliable way would be to look it up in a Greek concordance (under "a" if you're using one alphabetized by the Greek words, under "m" if you're using one alphabetized by the English translations).

ANNOTATED BIBLIOGRAPHY

WORD STUDIES—HEBREW

Archer, Gleason, R. Laird Harris, and Bruce Waltke. *Theological Wordbook of the Old Testament,* 2 vols. Chicago: Moody, 1980.

This set lists about six thousand Hebrew words used in the Old Testament, making it the most complete Hebrew word study now available. It explains the theological significance of these words, and aptly illustrates their development in Israel's religious thought. The chief disadvantage for the lay reader is that the set is arranged by Hebrew transliterations. If you don't know Hebrew, you must trace a word through Strong's *Exhaustive Concordance* to Strong's number-coded "Hebrew and Chaldee Dictionary," to the index in the *Theological Wordbook,* and then to the word entry.

Girdlestone, R. B., *Synonyms of the Old Testament.* Grand Rapids: Eerdmans, 1978.

Girdlestone discusses twenty-two chief doctrinal concepts of the Old Testament that are of interest to Christian readers. His chapters on "The Names of God" and "Justification" are especially rich. This is a reprint of Girdlestone's second edition, published in 1897.

Unger, Merrill F., and William White, Jr., eds. *Nelson's Expository Dictionary of the Old Testament.* Nashville: Thomas Nelson, 1980.

This book is designed for the lay reader who knows nothing of biblical Hebrew; it is arranged according to English (KJV) translations of Hebrew words. It contains over five hundred of the most common Hebrew terms, plus their derivatives. The *Expository Dictionary* is written in a simple, informative style to match W. E. Vine's classic *Expository Dictionary of New Testament Words.* Unfortunately, it does not have a Hebrew index and is not coded to Strong's "Hebrew and Chaldee Dictionary"; such features would have made it more useful to the advanced student. But the book is ideal for the lay reader who knows nothing of Hebrew.

Vine, W. E. *Vine's Expository Dictionary of Old Testament Words,* ed. F. F. Bruce. Old Tappan, N.J.: Revell, 1978.

Vine was compiling this book as a companion volume to his New Testament word study when death cut short his work. Dr. Bruce attempted to finish it, but the results are disappointing. It covers only about two hundred words, and the choice is uneven; many crucial terms are left out. The book is arranged according to English (KJV) translations of the Hebrew words.

WORD STUDIES—GREEK

Brown, Colin, ed. *New International Dictionary of New Testament Theology,* 3 vols. Grand Rapids: Zondervan, 1976–1978.

Originally published in Germany, this work discusses 340 key theological topics of the New Testament. Arranged alphabetically in English, it discusses these concepts in much more depth than any other New Testament word study. It is certain to become a classic in this field.

Deissmann, Adolf. *Light from the Ancient East,* trans. Lionel R.M. Strachan. Grand Rapids: Baker, 1978.

First published in 1927, this book revealed what Deissmann had gathered from his study of Egyptian papyrus manuscripts in *koine* Greek. His work clarified the meaning of many Greek words that scholars had thought were unique to the New

Testament; Deissmann found they were also used in Greek business records and personal correspondence of that day.

Kittel, Gerhard. *Theological Dictionary of the New Testament,* trans. and ed. Geoffrey W. Bromiley, 10 vols. Grand Rapids: Eerdmans, 1964–1976.

Regarded as the standard work in this field, Kittel's is a mainstay of any pastor's library and holds a rich treasure for serious lay readers. One reviewer calls it "the major achievement of New Testament scholarship in this century" (HBS, 119), and I would not dispute that. Note that Kittel's theology has a neo-orthodox viewpoint. The work is arranged by the Greek alphabet.

Robertson, A. T. *Word Pictures in the New Testament,* 6 vols. Nashville: Broadman, 1943.

This work is an old favorite (first published in 1930–1933). It does not cover as many words as Kittel's, nor does it discuss them in as much depth. However, Robertson tries to be theologically precise, and he provides some interesting sidelights on New Testament themes that we tend to take for granted.

Vincent, Marvin R. *Word Studies in the New Testament,* 4 vols. Grand Rapids: Eerdmans, 1957.

Vincent explores the more devotional aspects of major New Testament themes, such as *redemption.* Ramsey, Barber, and other reviewers feel this work needs to be revised. (It was first published in 1897, before Deissmann's papyri studies were known.) However, many pastors still recommend it.

Vine, W. E. *Expository Dictionary of New Testament Words.* Westwood, N.J.: Revell, 1956.[11]

Perhaps the best one-volume word study on the Greek New Testament, Vine's *Expository Dictionary* gives crisp definitions and synonyms for most New Testament words. It is based on the KJV and RV, but also helps in understanding the most modern versions. A Greek index (using transliterated words) refers to the various English translations of any given Greek word. It is arranged alphabetically, according to the English translations.

LEXICONS—HEBREW

Armstrong, Kelly, Douglas Busby, and Cyril Carr. *A Reader's Hebrew-English Lexicon of the Old Testament,* 4 vols. projected. Grand Rapids: Zondervan, 1980–

Designed as a counterpart to Kubo's Greek lexicon, this work refers you to Brown-Driver-Briggs' Hebrew lexicon for further information. It indicates each Hebrew word's frequency in the Old Testament, as well as defining its meaning. This may be the most exhaustive word-frequency study of the Hebrew Old Testament attempted in recent years.

---

11. Also available from (Nashville: Thomas Nelson, 1978).

Brown, Francis, S. R. Driver, and Charles A. Briggs. *A Hebrew and English Lexicon of the Old Testament,* rev. ed. Oxford: Clarendon, 1972.

Based on William Gesenius' lexicon, published in German, this book is the standard Hebrew-English lexicon. It is loosely arranged in a Hebrew alphabetical order; that is, the principal words are in Hebrew alphabetical order, with related derivatives grouped around them. So Brown-Driver-Briggs is best for the student who is acquainted with Hebrew.

Gesenius, William. *Hebrew and Chaldee Lexicon,* trans. S. P. Tregelles. Grand Rapids: Eerdmans, 1949.

Tregelles was the first to translate Gesenius' lexicon into English, and this reprint of his work is a true classic. Gesenius follows a strict Hebrew alphabetical order, which separates many related Hebrew words. Brown-Driver-Briggs updated and expanded this work at many points. While some of the discussions of synonyms are still worthwhile, the value of this particular book is largely historical. (See Francis Brown, above.)

Gesenius, William. *Gesenius' Hebrew-Chaldee Lexicon to the Old Testament,* trans. S. P. Tregelles. Grand Rapids: Baker, 1979.

The editors at Baker have reorganized Gesenius' lexicon to make it more accessible to the layman. Using the first English translation of this work (published in 1847), they have rearranged the words to follow the numerical sequence of the "Hebrew and Chaldee Dictionary" in *Strong's Exhaustive Concordance.* So if you do not know Hebrew, you can look up the English word in Strong's concordance, find the numerical code for that word, and use that code to locate the appropriate article in this lexicon. One drawback is that the lexicon itself is over one hundred years old, and does not contain the insights of modern linguistic research, as does Brown-Driver-Briggs. Also, it does not cover all the Hebrew words that BDB covers.

Holladay, Willaim L., ed. *A Concise Hebrew and Aramaic Lexicon of the Old Testament.* Grand Rapids: Eerdmans, 1971.

Though much less thorough than BDB—both in terms of the words covered and the detail of the discussion—Holladay's lexicon is a useful reference for the beginner. It is much less expensive than BDB, and it does cover the most significant Old Testament words.

LEXICONS—GREEK

Arndt, W. F. and F. W. Gingrich. *A Greek-English Lexicon of the New Testament,* 2nd ed., rev. Frederick W. Danker. Chicago: Univ. of Chicago Press, 1979.

This translation of Walter Bauer's classic German lexicon contains the insights of recent papyrus studies and other advances in New Testament linguistics. It is the standard Greek-English lexicon, just as BDB is the standard Hebrew-English work. No serious New Testament student would fail to have it. The lexicon is loosely arranged according to the Greek alphabet, and includes words from classic, nonbiblical Greek literature.

Hickie, W. J. *Greek-English Lexicon to the New Testament*. Grand Rapids: Baker, 1977.

Published in handy paperback form, this lexicon is an inexpensive aid to any Greek student. It covers a surprising number of New Testament words, considering its size. Its definitions are brief and sometimes too limited; its Scripture references are useful, though not complete. Overall, Hickie's lexicon serves the purpose of a handy traveler's lexicon. For more thorough Greek word studies, see Arndt and Gingrich.

Kubo, Sakae. *A Reader's Greek-English Lexicon of the New Testament*. Grand Rapids: Zondervan, 1975.

Kubo analyzes every chapter of the Greek New Testament. In each chapter, he identifies the Greek words that appear five times or more in the New Testament; in each verse, he identifies the Greek words that appear fifty times or more. He lists rare Greek words by each Bible book in which they appear. So you can tell at a glance which words are common (and which are not so common) in New Testament usage. Kubo's definitions are quite brief, but he gives enough information to serve as a basis for a more detailed study in Arndt and Gingrich.

Liddell, H. G., and Robert Scott. *Greek-English Lexicon,* rev. Henry Stuart Jones. Oxford: Oxford Univ. Press, 1966. With a *Supplement* by E. A. Barber (1968).

Many Bible students prefer Liddell and Scott's lexicon to Arndt and Gingrich's, but this nineteenth-century work is out-of-date in many respects. The *Supplement* remedied some of the problems by bringing in the results of recent papyri finds, but Arndt and Gingrich is still more reliable.

Moulton, J. H., and George Milligan. *The Vocabulary of the Greek New Testament*. Grand Rapids: Eerdmans, 1949.

This lexicon shows how Greek New Testament words were commonly used in the everyday writings of first-century Greeks. Moulton and Milligan quote numerous examples from early business documents and letters to show what *koine* Greek words meant. However, they do not cover all the words of the New Testament, nor do they give as much theological background as other lexicons.

Souter, Alexander. *A Pocket Lexicon to the Greek New Testament*. Oxford: Clarendon, 1916.

Like Hickie's lexicon, this is a small and inexpensive list of common Greek New Testament vocabulary. Souter's definitions are concise and often more accurate than Hickie's, but he gives few Scripture references. This lexicon was a companion to Souter's own critical edition of the Greek New Testament (which may now be out of print).

Thayer, J. H. *Thayer's Greek-English Lexicon of the New Testament.* Grand Rapids : Baker, 1977.[12]

Here is another stalwart nineteenth-century work that a publisher has refurbished for the layman. The editors at Baker have rearranged Thayer's fourth edition (published in 1901) to follow the numerical sequence of the word code in Strong's *Exhaustive Concordance.* A person who does not know Greek can look up the English word in Strong's, find the code number, and follow it to the appropriate article in this edition of Thayer's. The discussions of synonyms are very good. However, note the 1901 date of the lexicon material itself; this was before the most important papyri studies were released, so the lexicon is not as up-to-date as it should be.

INTERLINEARS—HEBREW

Kohlenberger, John, III, ed. *The NIV Interlinear Hebrew-English Old Testament,* 4 vols. projected. Grand Rapids: Zondervan, 1979–

This interlinear gives the NIV Old Testament in one column (with footnotes) and in the facing column gives the Hebrew text (Kittel's *Biblia Hebraica*) with an interlinear English translation by Kohlenberger. The interlinear translation follows the NIV as closely as possible, and Kohlenberger gives Hebrew variants in footnotes. This is an excellent study tool for laymen and pastors.

INTERLINEARS—GREEK

Friberg, Barbara, and Timothy. *Analytical Greek New Testament.* Grand Rapids: Baker, 1982.

While they do not give an interlinear *translation* of the Greek text, the Fribergs do give an interlinear grammatical *analysis* of each word. That is, they use a set of symbols to show the form and function of each word in the text. A lexicon is still required to translate the word, but the Fribergs' interlinear analysis makes the translating work much easier. They use the United Bible Societies text by Aland, Black, and Metzger.

Marshall, Alfred. *The Interlinear Greek-English New Testament.* Grand Rapids: Zondervan, 1958.

This book presents the Nestle text of the Greek New Testament with Marshall's word-for-word translation between the lines. It is simple to use and gives a good idea of how the translator has to rework the literal translation into a meaningful English sentence.

White, Donald R., ed. *Interlinear Greek-English New Testament.* Grand Rapids: Baker, 1981.

White uses the *Textus Receptus* Greek New Testament published by Stephanus in 1550, and supplies a literal translation and the numerical code of each word (ac-

---

12. Also available in Thayer's original (Greek alphabetical) format from (Nashville: Broadman, 1978).

cording to the Greek dictionary in Strong's *Exhaustive Concordance*) between the lines. George R. Berry's Greek-English lexicon and Strong's Greek dictionary are printed at the back of this book for easy reference.

INTERLINEARS—ENGLISH

Winter, Ralph D. and Roberta H. *The Word Study New Testament.* Pasadena: William Carey Library, 1978.[13]

Instead of presenting a Greek text with English between the lines, this volume offers an English version (the KJV) with Strong's Greek word codes between the lines. You can also use the Winters' *Word Study Concordance* to find the Greek word, its meaning, and its other occurrences in the New Testament.

GRAMMARS—HEBREW

Greenberg, Moshe, *Introduction to Hebrew.* Englewood Cliffs: Prentice-Hall, 1965.

This simple manual for beginning students of Hebrew starts with the basic vocabulary and translation exercises, then leads into translation of actual Bible passages from Genesis. Greenberg has an interesting introductory article on "The Hebrew Language." I also appreciated his appendix article, "Orientation in the Hebrew Bible" (which helps English readers to locate passages in the Hebrew Bible, with its somewhat different canon order).

Lambdin, Thomas O. *Introduction to Biblical Hebrew.* New York: Scribner's, 1971.

Dr. Lambdin of Harvard uses the deductive method (rules of syntax first, Bible translation later) in this useful textbook. It is frustrating to wait till the last half of the book to begin translating Scripture, but Lambdin's approach is logical, orderly, and sound.

LaSor, William S. *Handbook of Biblical Hebrew,* 3 vols. Grand Rapids: Eerdmans, 1978.

LaSor introduces the student to translating Scripture early in this massive work. And his sideline comments about Hebrew culture and history help to hold your interest through this exhaustive (and otherwise exhausting) introduction to Hebrew.

GRAMMARS—GREEK

Blass, Friederich and Albert Debrunner. *A Greek Grammar of the New Testament and Other Early Christian Literature,* trans. R. W. Funk. Chicago: Univ. of Chicago Press, 1961.

Barber calls this "the finest grammar for advanced students of New Testament Greek" (ML, 123). Certainly it offers a more thorough treatment of Greek syntax and vocabulary than any other introductory grammar. Nearly all other Greek

---

13. Also available from (Wheaton: Tyndale, 1978).

textbooks make reference to it. Blass and Debrunner follow the traditional deductive method.

LaSor, William S. *Handbook of New Testament Greek,* 2 vols. Grand Rapids: Eerdmans, 1973.

LaSor's grammar is not as technically complicated as Blass and Debrunner's, so the beginner may feel more at ease with this work. LaSor also gives some practical experience in translating Scripture as the student proceeds, although the deductive approach is used.

Machen, J. Gresham. *New Testament Greek for Beginners.* New York: Macmillan, 1923.

This is the most simple Greek grammar now available, and for that reason many reviewers feel it is still the best. Dr. Machen was a noted professor of New Testament at Princeton who left that school to help in founding Westminster Theological Seminary, an evangelical Presbyterian stronghold in Philadelphia. He had an ardent desire to see ministerial students become intimately familiar with the Greek New Testament. His grammar bypasses many of the more academic aspects of Greek study and aims at giving the student a practical reading skill in Greek. Dr. Machen's approach is largely deductive; he has composed his own nonbiblical Greek sentences for the exercises.

Paine, Stephen W. *Beginning Greek.* New York: Oxford Univ. Press, 1961.

Paine uses the inductive method to teach both *koine* Greek and (in the latter portion of the book) classical Greek. He gives the student translation exercises from the Gospel of John (whose vocabulary and syntax are quite simple). Then he gradually moves backward in history to translate passages from Xenophon. The passages in John are quoted from the Nestle text.

CRITICAL EDITIONS—OLD TESTAMENT

Kittel, Rudolph. *Biblia Hebraica,* 3rd ed. New York: American Bible Society, 1937.

Kittel's critical edition has long been the standard Hebrew text *(Textus Receptus)* of the Old Testament. It preserves the traditional Masoretic Text of ben Asher (tenth century A.D.), as it has come down to us in the Leningrad Manuscript (eleventh century A.D.) with variant readings from the ben Chayyim edition (sixteenth century A.D.) of the *Textus Receptus.* The latest edition of Kittel is K. Elliger and W. Rudolph, *Biblia Hebraica Stuttgartensia,* New York: American Bible Society, 1967-77.

Rahlfs, Alfred. *Septuaginta,* 2 vols. Stuttgart: Privilegierte Wurttembergische Bibelanstalt, 1935.

This is the standard critical edition of the Greek version of the Old Testament, which is believed to have been made in Alexandria in the third century B.C. Translators compare this Greek text with the Hebrew text when the Hebrew seems uncertain or obscure. The Septuagint (Greek meaning "seventy") was so named because seventy scholars were said to have made this translation. Scholarly writers refer to it with the Roman numerals for seventy, LXX.

CRITICAL EDITIONS—NEW TESTAMENT

Aland, Kurt, Matthew Black, and Bruce M. Metzger. *The Greek New Testament,* 3rd ed. New York: United Bible Societies, 1975.

The United Bible Societies commissioned this work to be used as the standard Greek text for their translating programs. Aland, Black, and Metzger compared the Westcott-Hort critical edition with others, and with newer manuscript discoveries. They used Westcott and Hort's basic principles to select the readings that seemed most reliable, making this edition a veritable revision of the Westcott-Hort critical edition. The editors furnish a detailed *critical apparatus**—footnotes showing variants and identifying the Greek manuscripts that the editors favored. This text was used for translating the TEV and was one of the texts used for the NIV.

Farstad, Arthur L. and Zane C. Hodges. *The Greek New Testament According to the Majority Text.* Nashville: Thomas Nelson, 1982.

Farstad and Hodges were involved in the creation of the NKJV, and this critical edition grew out of work with that version. They have attempted to compile a new edition of the "Majority Text." The publisher states that this work "marks the first time in this century that the Greek New Testament has been produced using the bulk of extant manuscripts rather than the small body of Egyptian manuscripts that form the basis of current Greek texts."[14] They furnish two sets of critical apparatus. One set gives variants among the Majority Text manuscripts themselves; the other set shows where Codex Vaticanus, Codex Sinaiticus, and early papyrus manuscripts disagree with the Majority Text.

Nestle, Eberhard, ed. *Novum Testamentum Graece,* 26th ed., rev. Kurt Aland. New York: United Bible Societies, 1979.

Nestle tried to revise Westcott and Hort's work, comparing it with other critical editions by Count von Tischendorf and R. H. Weymouth. He gave special preference to Codex Vaticanus (also called Codex B). Aland has included more variants from other manuscripts and reversed Nestle's decisions at some points, in light of more recent manuscript finds. An earlier edition of this work was used for translating the NASB New Testament and was one of the texts used in translating the NIV.

CONCORDANCES—HEBREW

Mandelkern, Solomon. *Veteris Testamenti Concordantiae Hebraicae atque Chaldaicae,* rev. ed. Tel Aviv: Schocken, 1967.

Mandelkern's concordance gives a more detailed analysis of the Hebrew words

---

14. *Thomas Nelson Spring Books 1982* (Nashville: Thomas Nelson, 1982), p. 5.

than any other. But its use requires a previous knowledge of Hebrew, because it is arranged in Hebrew alphabetical order and its contents are primarily in Hebrew.

Wigram, G. V. *The Englishman's Hebrew and Chaldee Concordance of the Old Testament.* Grand Rapids: Zondervan, 1970.

This Hebrew concordance is written in English, with the numerical codes from Strong's *Exhaustive Concordance.* It is designed for readers who do not know Hebrew very well. Wigram quotes the KJV, but this concordance can be used with other translations without much trouble.

CONCORDANCES—GREEK

Moulton, W. F., and A. S. Geden. *Concordance to the Greek New Testament.* Grand Rapids: Kregel, 1979.

Moulton and Geden used the Westcott-Hort critical edition of 1881 as the text for this concordance. Their work is quite thorough and is considered the classic guide to the Greek New Testament. Moulton and Geden also note the use of any given Greek word in the Septuagint and the Apocrypha.

Wigram, G. V. *The Englishman's Greek Concordance of the New Testament.* Grand Rapids: Zondervan, 1970.

Like Wigram's Hebrew concordance, this work is written in English, is arranged alphabetically according to English translations of the Greek, and uses the numerical code of Strong's *Exhaustive Concordance.* It is easy to use, even for those not familiar with Greek.

11.
Miscellaneous
Resources

The purpose of this *Resource Guide* is to introduce a broad range of Bible study resources, but some very valuable resources do not fit any of the categories we have examined so far. This brief chapter has been reserved for a novel assortment of such Bible reference books. If you have not found the type of study aid you were hoping for in the first ten chapters, you may very well find it here.

Analyses and Outlines

The books in this category give a simple review of the Bible story. They rehearse Bible history, beginning with God's creation of all things in Genesis and climaxing with God's final redemption of His chosen people in the Book of Revelation. Some of these books also discuss the progressive development of man's relationship with God—the various covenants of mercy, dispensations of God's will, and so on. Some (such as deDietrich) furnish an actual outline of Scripture.

These books are useful in deductive Bible study to get a bird's-eye view of a certain Bible book or of the Bible as a whole, before analyzing its various parts. You may also turn to a book like this for a quick review of certain biblical events, doctrines, or ideas as you prepare a Sunday school lesson or Bible study. (In this case, it's best to have a book with a good index.)

Harmonies

In the late 1800s, as German scholars began pointing out the *Synoptic problem,** several editors compiled Gospel harmonies—that is, they laid out in parallel columns any related passages from the three Synoptic Gospels. This allowed readers to compare how Matthew, Mark, and Luke recorded the same incident or teaching; it permitted anyone to test the higher critics' theories of how the Synoptics had been written.

A flurry of gospel harmonies came from the presses around the turn of the century, but only a few have survived. The best harmonies are the ones with good *critical apparatus** (such as footnotes showing alternate English readings and variant Greek readings). A few ambitious researchers have compiled harmonies of the Synoptics *and* the Gospel of John, harmonies of the events in Paul's life, and so on. But the Synoptic harmonies are still the most striking and informative.

Use a gospel harmony for two basic purposes: (1) to study the Synoptic problem—testing theories such as the current one, that Matthew and Luke drew material from Mark and that all three drew material from another source called "Q", or (2) to fill in any information that is missing from a particular Gospel account, by seeing how the other Gospel writers record that event.

Chronologies

Ever since Bishop Ussher attempted to lay out a chronology of the Bible (see Chapter 2), Bible students have retraced his steps through the Bible records. They have tried to fix the exact calendar dates of momentous events such as the Exodus from Egypt or the crucifixion of Christ. Some scholars have published weighty monographs on this subject; others have penned colorful studies for more popular consumption. But the fact remains that we cannot absolutely fix the dates of Bible events in terms of our modern calendar.

Are the Old Testament genealogies complete? Do they overlap? Do they soar into *hyperbole** at some points? Some noble attempts have been made to solve the riddle of Bible chronology, and they are listed at the end of this chapter.

Character Studies

One fascinating form of deductive Bible study is the character study, in which you garner relevant Scripture passages about a Bible character in order to learn all you can about that figure's personality, thoughts, and activities. This can be very informative. For example, did you know that Moses had more than one wife? Or that Peter was married? Or that Jesus fed four thousand *and* five thousand people on two separate occasions? Studying the life of a Bible character will uncover many such little-known facts.

Several authors have already done the research for you; they have compiled books on the lives of Jesus, Peter, Paul, and other prominent biblical people. Perhaps the best-known writer of character studies is Herbert Lockyer, whose popular Bible character series[1] has included *All the Men*

---

1. I have not listed each of these in the bibliography, since the titles are self-explanatory. All of the Lockyer volumes are available from (Grand Rapids: Zondervan).

of the Bible (1958), *All the Kings and Queens of the Bible* (1961), *All the Women of the Bible* (1979), *All the Children of the Bible* (1979), and *All the Apostles of the Bible* (1979).

Archaeological Studies

Archaeologists keep digging up so much information about the world of the Bible that publishers can scarcely keep the reference books up to date! But there are a number of books about biblical archaeology itself —its purpose, its methods, and its important discoveries. By reading the better archaeological studies, you may be able to use other Bible reference books with more discretion. You may become more alert to statements in those resources that *are* out of date and to information about recent developments in this field.

Early twentieth-century archaeologists W. F. Albright, James B. Pritchard, and G. Ernest Wright wrote some classic books on this subject. They are not included in the bibliography because their work is dated, but you may wish to consult them for some interesting background on the methods archaeologists have used, and for their speculations about early finds in the Holy Land.[2]

ANNOTATED BIBLIOGRAPHY

ANALYSES AND OUTLINES

Baxter, J. Sidlow. *Explore the Book,* 6 vols. Grand Rapids: Zondervan, 1960.

Baxter's popular style makes this series of Bible summaries useful to anyone who wants to avoid technical theological jargon or textual problems. Baxter is conservative, evangelical, and devotional in his approach to Scripture. He has a real gift for singling out the main theological theme of each book and expressing it in simple language.

Mears, Henrietta C. *What the Bible Is All About.* Glendale, Calif.: Regal, 1979.

This synopsis of Bible doctrine from an evangelical point of view will be especially helpful to beginning Bible students. The author shows how Scripture presents great spiritual truths—such as man's redemption from sin—in both Old and New Testaments. She develops well the concept of *progressive revelation.**

---

2. W. F. Albright, *Archaeology and the Religion of Israel* (Baltimore: Johns Hopkins Press, 1946). W. F. Albright, *From the Stone Age to Christianity* (Baltimore: Johns Hopkins Press, 1946). James B. Pritchard, ed., *The Ancient Near East in Pictures* (Princeton: Princeton Univ. Press, 1955). James B. Pritchard, *Ancient Near Eastern Texts* (Princeton: Princeton Univ. Press, 1955). William M. Ramsay, *The Bearing of Recent Discovery on the Trustworthiness of the New Testament,* 2nd ed. (London: Hodder and Stoughton, 1915). G. Ernest Wright, *Biblical Archaeology,* rev. ed. (Philadelphia: Westminster, 1962).

Scroggie, W. Graham. *The Unfolding Drama of Redemption.* Grand Rapids: Zondervan, 1979.

This conservative British writer focuses on man's redemption as the principal theme of Scripture, and shows how every book of the Bible develops that theme. It is a fascinating study.

HARMONIES

Goodwin, Frank J. *A Harmony of the Life of St. Paul.* Grand Rapids: Baker, 1951.

Goodwin puts the narrative of Paul's life from the Book of Acts in parallel with statements from Paul's epistles to give us a more complete, sequential review of the apostle's life. This book can be a real aid in studying the New Testament, where Paul is such a significant character.

Pentecost, J. Dwight. *A Harmony of the Words and Works of Jesus Christ.* Grand Rapids: Zondervan, 1982.

Dr. Pentecost of Dallas Theological Seminary provides a convenient outline of the major events and teachings from Jesus' life. For each segment of the outline he reproduces the appropriate passages from all four Gospels, which he quotes from the NIV. This book is a companion volume to his book *The Words and Works of Jesus Christ,* also published by Zondervan.

Robertson, A. T. *A Harmony of the Gospels.* New York: Harper and Brothers, 1932.

Robertson places all four gospel accounts of Jesus' life in parallel columns. This has become the classic gospel harmony for seminary students, even though Robertson does not provide as much critical apparatus (variants, alternate translations, etc.) as Throckmorton does.

Throckmorton, Burton H., Jr. *Gospel Parallels,* rev. ed. Nashville: Thomas Nelson, 1979.

Throckmorton's parallel differs from Robertson's in two important ways: (1) It is based on the RSV, while Robertson uses the KJV, and (2) it has a detailed critical apparatus to help the serious Bible student, while Robertson does not. This revised edition incorporates the latest changes in the RSV text.

CHRONOLOGIES

Hoehner, Harold. *Chronological Aspects of the Life of Christ.* Grand Rapids: Zondervan, 1979.

Calendar dates cannot be assigned to the events of Jesus' life with absolute certainty, but Hoehner discusses the scholars' "best guess" about the date of Jesus' birth, His crucifixion, and other crucial happenings. He cites interesting quotations from Roman and Jewish histories that help us calculate these dates. It is an engaging discussion, even though not everyone will agree with the conclusions.

House, H. Wayne. *Chronological and Background Charts of the New Testament.* Grand Rapids: Zondervan, 1982.

This "mixed bag" of resources will help in understanding many areas of New Testament study. Mr. House's book charts a chronology of Jesus' life, a chronology of Palestine, and a chronology of the Roman Empire. But it also has charts and tables of Bible weights and measures, the transmission of the New Testament text, and a variety of other things concerning the New Testament. Pastors and Sunday school teachers will make frequent use of this resource in their teaching.

Jewett, Robert. *A Chronology of Paul's Life.* Philadelphia: Fortress, 1979.

Here is an interesting attempt to chart the events of Paul's life and to fix calendar dates for them according to Jewett's higher-critical evaluation of Paul's epistles. Conservative readers will dispute the dates that he gives to some of Paul's writings, but in the main, Jewett's study is acceptable and beneficial.

Walton, John. *Chronological Charts of the Old Testament.* Grand Rapids: Zondervan, 1979.

Walton charts Old Testament events in a conservative manner. He upholds the "early date" of the Exodus, Jericho's defeat by Joshua, and other points that liberal scholars would debate. This book is a good resource for Bible teachers.

CHARACTER STUDIES

Bruce, F. F. *Paul: Apostle of the Heart Set Free.* Grand Rapids: Eerdmans, 1977.

This character study is Dr. Bruce's best-known work, and should be the most enduring. Bruce draws on his rich knowledge of New Testament culture to give us a vivid portrait of the apostle. Again and again, the author points out Paul's theological genius and fervent personal devotion to Jesus Christ. This book will burn itself into your memory.

Deen, Edith. *All of the Women of the Bible.* New York: Harper and Row, 1955.

Only a woman could have written such a sensitive portrayal of Bible women. Mrs. Deen helps us perceive the attitudes and thinking of each woman. This devotional character study is a good resource for group discussion.

Edersheim, Alfred. *The Life and Times of Jesus the Messiah,* abridged ed. Grand Rapids: Eerdmans, 1971.

Most reviewers agree that this is the best character study of Jesus published to date. Edersheim grasps the deep theological importance of God's incarnation in Christ, and comes as close as one can to expressing it. Wiersbe says this abridged edition is not as good as the original two-volume set (BLBS, 19-20), but it is certainly worth reading.

LaSor, William S. *Great Personalities of the Bible.* Westwood, N.J.: Revell, 1965.

Here you will find biographical sketches of thirty-six Bible characters—

eighteen from the Old Testament and eighteen from the New. LaSor's treatment is not as detailed as it might be; he gives little factual background and dwells on the inspirational aspects of each person. But this is still a useful and recommended study, because he includes several characters that are often overlooked in such a book.

Ramsay, William M. *St. Paul the Traveller and the Roman Citizen.* Grand Rapids: Baker, 1979.
First published in the 1890s, this little volume shows Ramsay's familiarity with the Holy Land. (You will recall that he was cited as one of the leading biblical archaeologists from the turn of the century.) Wiersbe says this character study of Paul is "a standard work of such stature that it needs no recommendation from me" (BLBS, 23).

Whyte, Alexander. *Bible Characters.* Grand Rapids: Zondervan, 1968.
This work was published as six volumes in 1898-1902. Zondervan has done us a great service by reprinting it as one volume; this makes it more convenient and less expensive. Whyte has a colorful way of recreating Bible characters. Though he did not have access to the discoveries of archaeologists in this century, Whyte did have a brilliant imagination and a marvelous gift for narrative writing. This book is a joy to read.

ARCHAEOLOGICAL STUDIES

Cornfeld, Gaalyah. *Archaeology of the Bible, Book by Book.* New York: Harper and Row, 1978.
Cornfeld is a modern Israeli writer and photographer. His firsthand knowledge of the Holy Land serves us well in this book. His articles about the intertestamental period are especially good. However, Cornfeld's treatment of the New Testament is noticeably weak, and he does not affirm Jesus Christ to be the Son of God. The photography is also disappointing; many photos are fuzzy or poorly composed.

Kitchen, Kenneth A. *The Bible in Its World.* Downers Grove, Ill.: InterVarsity, 1977.
Of all the books on archaeology, Osborne and Woodward feel this is "the best evangelical introduction to date" (HBS, 115). However, Kitchen deals with only the most general aspects of the topic; he whets our appetite for knowledge but gives us only hors d'oeuvres of fact. One wishes he had expanded this book to describe the work archaeologists have done at a greater number of Bible-related sites, and in more detail.

Unger, Merrill F. *Archaeology and the Old Testament.* Grand Rapids: Zondervan, 1954. *Archaeology and the New Testament.* Grand Rapids: Zondervan, 1962.
In my opinion, these two books are the best layman's studies of biblical ar-

chaeology written from a conservative point of view. Dr. Unger provides a wealth of factual information about the techniques used by archaeologists and the bearing their finds have had on biblical study. But he also stimulates our interest with anecdotes or "human interest" stories that help us feel the excitement (and at times the frustration) of archaeological work. These books are top-notch reading.

Wiseman, Donald J. and Edwin M. Yamauchi. *Archaeology and the Bible*. Grand Rapids: Zondervan, 1979.

Wiseman and Yamauchi do not have the flair for popular writing that Unger has, but their book is very informative. It includes more recent archaeological discoveries than Unger had available to him. So in many respects, Wiseman and Yamauchi update Unger's work. The illustrations in this book are exceptionally good.

12.
Basic Bible Study Methods

Two complaints a pastor commonly hears are related to Bible study. The first comes from new Christians who have not been able to start any meaningful Bible study of their own. They say, "I don't know how to get started," or "It all confuses me," or "My mind wanders." The second type of complaint comes from people who have been Christians for a while, people who once enjoyed their personal Bible study but now have stopped. They say, "I don't get anything out of the Bible anymore; it just seems like a lot of words," or "I can't find anything there to help me with the problems I'm up against."

These people turn to inspirational books or magazines in hope of finding the guidance they need. Or they shuttle from one church to another, trying to find a minister who can serve up the spiritual food they lack by not studying the Bible themselves. If a Christian continues this way, his spirit will starve and he will be ill-prepared for the troubles he is sure to encounter in life.

In this *Resource Guide* I have described a wide variety of Bible versions and Bible reference books; I have suggested how you can use these tools to your greatest benefit. But the best Bible-resource library in the world will not help you if you fail to study. Meaningful Bible study begins with you—with your own desire to study the Bible and savor "the depths of the riches both of the wisdom and knowledge of God!" (Rom. 11:33, NKJV).

There's the key to the problem—*desire*. If you are truly hungry for the Word of God, nothing can keep you from studying it. If you are not hungry for the Word, pray that the Lord will renew your hunger. And stimulate that desire by giving yourself a diet of Bible study that is steady and satisfying.

Steady Bible study is important. Some people read the Bible only when they "feel spiritual"; others read it only when they "need a lift." But read the Bible regularly—if possible every day—and you will find God speaking to you regardless of your mood. That's exciting! And it will tantalize you to read His Word even more.

Satisfying Bible study (by that I mean Bible study that meets your spiritual needs) will do the same. The more you have your questions answered, your dilemmas resolved, or your conflicts quieted through Bible study, the more you'll want to dig into this Book! The Holy Spirit does these things.

He has the special ministry of revealing the truth of Scripture to us (see John 16:13,14), just as Jesus revealed the truth of Scripture to His disciples (see Luke 24:25-27,32). He brings us satisfying Bible study as we engage in steady Bible study.

Of course, we can obstruct the Spirit's work or facilitate it by the way we study. Proper Bible study methods are important. So in the next few pages, I will describe three basic methods of Bible study—the devotional method, the deductive (or synthetic) method, and the inductive (or analytical) method. There are many other methods, but these will lay a good foundation for any other type of Bible study you choose to do.[1]

The Devotional Method

When you hear a friend speak of having "daily devotions" or a "devotional study time," what image comes to your mind? You probably picture someone sitting alone with an open Bible, reading a passage of Scripture and then spending a few moments in prayer. The word *devotion* has a deeper meaning that may not be apparent from this image.

As I explained in Chapter 1, *devotion* is a private act of worship. Our English word *devotion* comes from the Latin *devovere,* which means "to vow completely." So a time of "devotions" is a time in which we give ourselves completely to the Lord. We dismiss all thoughts about job, family, finances, or whatever else may have occupied our minds, and give our minds to Him. We release all anxiety, apprehension, resentment, or any other feeling that is alien to Christ, and give our emotions to Him.

We give even our bodies to Him. There are times when we must devote the body to some other task while we devote the mind to him, but in the time of devotions we give the body to Him as well. We may kneel in prayer or sit in a relaxed position or raise our hands—whatever best expresses our full surrender to the Lord.[2] (Conversely, it is hard to "have devotions" while jogging, hanging onto a subway strap, or washing the dishes because your mind is monitoring these activities of the body.)

The significance of this personal surrender becomes even clearer when we consider the corresponding Old Testament word *cherem* ("devote" or "devoted"). When an Israelite chose an animal for sacrifice to the Lord, that animal was considered *cherem* ("a devoted thing"); the Law forbade

---

1. Howard F. Vos describes sixteen different methods in his fascinating book, *Effective Bible Study* (Grand Rapids: Zondervan, 1956).

2. In Bible times people often threw themselves headlong on the ground when they knew they were in God's presence (cf. Gen. 17:3; Lev. 9:24; Josh. 5:14; Matt. 17:6; and Luke 5:12).

him from taking back the animal or using it for some other purpose (see Lev. 27:28,29). When he brought oil, wine, or grain to the temple as an offering, the goods were considered *cherem*, and he could not take them back or divert them for his own uses (see Num. 18:11-14). Anything devoted to God was *abandoned* to God; it was surrendered to God without any reservations or conditions. So when we engage in "devotions" according to the biblical pattern, we surrender our entire selves to Him—body, mind, and all.

This contradicts the notion that "devotional Bible study" is a casual, halfhearted affair. It requires no less effort than any other type of Bible study. In fact, it demands our complete attention.

Second, returning to our English word *devotion*, notice that it implies a "vow" or promise to God. In other words, you promise God that you will worship Him at a given time (perhaps each day); and if you promise to study His Word as part of that worship time, the promise makes it a devotional Bible study. You study God's Word to fulfill your promise to Him.

Many Christians fail to continue devotional Bible study because they miss this point. They feel they need to know more of God's Word, so they promise themselves that they will study the Bible every day, every week, or whenever. In other words, they make a *resolution*. Now we all know what usually happens to resolutions: When we run into problems we bargain with ourselves and change the agreement. When we make good progress we congratulate ourselves by allowing "just one" indulgence; and before we know it the resolution falls by the wayside. So it goes with those noble resolutions to study the Bible every day. It's too easy to excuse ourselves from self-imposed training.

But true devotional Bible study is not a resolve with ourselves; it is a vow to God. We don't do it to make ourselves more knowledgeable or more serene or more spiritual. We do it to worship God. So we do not govern the study by our feelings (e.g., "I'll not study the Bible today; I'm feeling blue"). Nor do we govern it by the change or lack of change we see in our lives (e.g., "I'll not study the Bible today; I'm not getting anything from it"). We continue our study because we have promised the Lord we will do it.

The Bible encourages us to make such promises to Him. "Make vows to the Lord your God, and pay them," the Psalmist says (Ps. 76:11 NKJV). But we are also warned to take our vows seriously. "It is better not to vow than to vow and not pay" the Preacher says (Eccl. 5:5 NKJV). And the writer of Proverbs advises that "it is a snare for a man to devote rashly something as holy, and afterward to reconsider his vows" (Prov. 20:25 NKJV).

So we see that devotional Bible study is not a casual or capricious thing if we follow the true sense of the word *devotion*. Should we like to read the

Bible now and then whenever the mood strikes us, to get some emotional "lift," then we might call it "occasional Bible reading." But we could hardly call it "study." And by no means should we call it "devotional Bible study."

So devotional Bible study (1) entails a complete surrender of ourselves, (2) fulfills a promise that we voluntarily make to God, and (3) honors or exalts the Lord.

Other Bible study methods are primarily for our own enrichment. They help us learn the content of the Word; they challenge us to grow according to the Word; they correct us in light of the Word. Such methods of study edify us. And as we are edified, God is glorified. But devotional Bible study reverses those priorities: Its primary purpose is to help us exalt or honor God. It induces a climate of worship; it gives shape and direction to our worship; it helps us respond to God and glorify Him. And as He is glorified, we are edified. With this purpose in mind, let me suggest these steps for devotional Bible study.[3]

1. *Find a place of solitude.* A writer of scientific articles recently observed that "solitude, not loneliness, is a writer's best friend."[4] The same is true of a Christian at devotional time. *Solitude*—that is, being remote or secluded from other people—is the best environment for your devotional study.

Many Christians feel frustrated because they think they must be completely cut off from the rest of the world for their devotional time. But that is seldom possible. The children are sleeping in the next room; the paperboy is wheeling past the window; rush-hour traffic rumbles in the background.

You probably will not have the aloneness that a monk in his monastery cell might have, but you can have *solitude.* You can retreat temporarily from human contact and conversation to become more aware of God's presence. Even in the midst of David's tumultuous battles and victories, he sensed the Lord saying, "Be still, and know that I am God" (Ps. 46:10). David could not be alone, but he could be in solitude. So can you.

Go to a quiet room and close the door behind you. Turn off the radio, the TV, or any other voices from the outside world. Unplug the telephone (or take the receiver off the hook). If you are outside, find a secluded park bench or some other spot where people are not likely to pass by and strike up a conversation with you.

When you've achieved this physical solitude, move toward *mental* soli-

---

3. These steps follow the pattern suggested by J. Munro Gibson in *The Devotional Use of the Holy Scriptures* (London: National Council of Evangelical Free Churches, 1904), pp. 46-52.

4. Fred J. Dorn, "Time Management for the Part-Time Freelancer," *The Writer,* April 1982, p. 24.

tude as well. Don't concentrate on the dripping faucet, the airplane passing overhead, or any other distraction. Concentrate instead on the Lord. Ask Him to cleanse all other thoughts from your mind and all anxious feelings from your heart as you wait upon Him (see Lam. 3:25,26).

2. *Realize the presence of the Lord.* He is always near, but in the devotional time you will be more conscious of Him. You are not apt to see Him or hear His voice, but you can sense His presence with you as you can sense the presence of a friend beside you in a darkened room. As you put all distractions away, you will realize more vividly than ever how near God is to you. This is what James meant when he said, "Draw near to God and He will draw near to you" (James 4:8 NKJV).

Even when you do not sense His presence, you can recognize His presence by faith. His Word says, "He that cometh to God must believe that he is, and that he is a rewarder of them that diligently seek him" (Heb. 11:6).

3. *Read the Scripture, and fix your thoughts on what the Lord clearly expresses in it.* You should avoid obscure or theologically complex Scriptures for devotional study. As Howard F. Vos advises, "The Bible student should avoid in his devotional life overemphasis on either extensive or intensive consideration of Scripture."[5] Remember, in devotional study you are not reading to gather new nuggets of information; you are reading to prepare for worship and to begin expressing your worship of the Lord. Read for the obvious (literal) meaning of the passage. What is the Lord plainly saying through these verses? What is the mood or tenor of the passage? Let your mind absorb the message and the mood. As I mentioned in Chapter 1, you will need a Bible version that is clear and easy to understand for this type of study. Awkward or erudite phrases can distract you from devotional study.

For devotional purposes, some passages (such as the Psalms, the prayers, or the *doxologies** of the Bible) are more useful than others. So choose the Scripture passage wisely before you start. Figure 16 lists one hundred Scripture portions well suited to devotional study. You may wish to use a topical Bible to locate an appropriate Scripture passage for worshipful study; for example, you may find helpful passages under topics such as "Prayer," "Praise," or "Adoration." In fact, if you use *Nave's Topical Bible* or some other that quotes most of the passages in full, you may read the passage itself from the topical Bible.

4. *Consider what the Lord is saying to you at this moment.* Here you come to the "crossing point" between Scripture and your current life concerns. As you consciously wait in the presence of the Lord, let Him speak to you through His Word. This is the final step of self-surrender. Gibson

---

5. Vos, *Effective Bible Study,* p. 173.

Figure 16—Scripture Passages Recommended for Devotional Study

God's Attributes
Genesis 15:1
Genesis 28:10-16
Exodus 34:1-7
Deuteronomy 7:6-15
Deuteronomy 33:26,27
Job 5:8-26
Job 36:5-10
Psalm 32:6,7
Psalm 33:6-12,18-22
Psalm 102:8-22
Psalm 121
Isaiah 6:1-8
Isaiah 9:6,7
Isaiah 33:16-24
Isaiah 40:10-26
Isaiah 57:15-21
Jeremiah 51:15-19
Lamentations 3:22-28
Ezekiel 34:11-17,22-31
Amos 4:13
Nahum 1:1-13
John 1:1-13
John 3:16-21
John 8:12-19
John 10:26-30
John 14:5-14
Acts 17:24-31
Romans 5:1,2
Romans 8:32-39
Romans 11:33-36
Ephesians 2:11-18
1 Thessalonians 5:8-11
Revelation 4:8-11
Revelation 21:3-6

Doxologies, Hymns, and Songs
Exodus 15:1-18
1 Samuel 2:1-10
1 Chronicles 16:8-31
1 Chronicles 29:10-19
Psalm 8
Psalm 19
Psalm 29
Psalm 71:17-21
Psalm 77
Psalm 89
Psalm 146
Psalm 147
Psalm 148
Psalm 150
Isaiah 12:1-6
Isaiah 33:5-16
Isaiah 52:7-10
Luke 1:46-75
Luke 10:21-22
Ephesians 3:20,21
Philippians 2:5-11
1 Timothy 1:17
1 Peter 1:3-9
Jude 24,25
Revelation 1:4-6
Revelation 5:9-13
Revelation 7:9-12
Revelation 11:16-17
Revelation 19:5-7
Prayers
1 Kings 3:6-9
1 Kings 8:22-61
2 Kings 19:14-19

2 Chronicles 14:11
Nehemiah 9
Psalm 5
Psalm 51:1-17
Psalm 88:1-9
Psalm 90
Psalm 143
Isaiah 61:10-11
Isaiah 64
Jeremiah 32:17-27
Daniel 9:2-19
Matthew 6:9-13
John 17
Acts 4:23-30
Acts 20:32
Romans 15:5,6
1 Thessalonians 3:11-13
Hebrews 4:9-11
Hebrews 13:20,21
2 Peter 1:2-4
Exhortations
2 Chronicles 15:1-7
Isaiah 41:10-13
Matthew 5:3-12
Matthew 7:7-11
Luke 10:19,20
John 14:1-4
John 16:33
1 Timothy 6:13-16
James 4:7-10
1 Peter 5:6-11
2 Peter 3:11-18
1 John 3:1-3
1 John 5:7-12
Revelation 14:6,7

suggests that you ponder these questions, along the lines of 2 Timothy 3:16:

Doctrine: What may I learn of God? Of myself? Of the way of life?
Reproof: Is there any sin of which I stand convicted by the Word before me, which I must confess and forsake, and for which I must ask forgiveness?
Correction: Is there any wrong path I have been following so that now I must change my course?
Instruction in Righteousness: What grace am I neglecting? And may I not be able now to add something to my life which will make it more harmonious and complete?[6]

---

6. Gibson, *Devotional Use,* p. 50.

Submitting yourself to the Lord's scrutiny is the climax of devotional Bible study. Aim to spend most of your study time at this stage. The Lord will reveal Himself as you ponder how His Word applies to you; it will be an experience that fills you with awe and adoration.

A commentary is not necessary for devotional study—not even one that is called a "devotional commentary." A devotional commentary is good for casual reading or comparison with an exegetical commentary (since the devotional commentary usually lays more stress on the practical, ethical impact of a passage). But a commentator's ideas should not have your attention in devotional study. Your chief interest should be your personal encounter with the living Lord, so that you worship Him and yield yourself to Him. Consulting a commentary may not move you any closer to this goal, and may in fact hinder you.

For similar reasons, I do not advise that you take notes during devotional study. Note-taking causes you to analyze the text; it easily becomes a mechanical task that takes the place of meditation and worship.

5. *Close your devotional time with thanksgiving and praise.* Thank the Lord for His Word. Thank Him for the specific insights He has given you today. Praise Him for making Himself known to you.

The Deductive (Synthetic) Method

For the study of a particular book of the Bible, you can use the *deductive method* to get a general overview of the book, to "get the feel" of its mood, and to note its primary themes. Some writers call this the synthetic method, because it enables you to draw together the various elements of a Bible book to form one complete picture. (Our English word *synthesis* comes from the Greek *syntithenai,* which means "to place together.") But regardless of what you call it, this method will give you a good grasp of almost any Bible book.[7] You can also use this method to study a given chapter such as Romans 8 or 1 Corinthians 13, as long as the chapter deals with one central theme.

Get a looseleaf notebook to record your findings. Figure 17 shows how you might lay out two facing notebook pages for a given book. (I have shown the Book of Ruth as an example. This format works just as well with longer books such as Isaiah, although you won't be able to note as many details.) Here is a step-by-step method that you might use for the study. I suggest that you use a pencil for writing in your notebook, so you

---

7. The deductive method will not help you get a total picture of a Bible book that is actually a collection of heterogenous parts—a "mixed bag" of subjects. The Book of Psalms and the Book of Proverbs are examples; they are collections of many short writings, with no clearly logical or chronological order in the mix. Deductive study is obviously not appropriate for books like these.

can rearrange your notes when making the final outline:

1. *Read the entire book once to get its basic theme.* Do this rapidly. Don't pause over interesting details, but skim-read the book to sense its overall thrust. Read it through in one sitting, so you are sure to get the full picture in mind at once.

(Many people shy away from deductive Bible study because they think it must take hours! But the books of the Bible are short. Dr. W. F. Crafts notes that forty-seven of these sixty-six books can be read in less than an hour, and you can read most of the New Testament books in twenty minutes or less.[8] So don't hesitate to try it.)

Remember, on this first reading you want to get the *theme* of the book: What is its chief message? What lesson of life does it illustrate? What warning or promise does it declare? When you have skimmed through the book once, you should know. Write the theme in your own words on the appropriate line of your study notes.

On this first reading, you may also get some idea of who wrote the book, who its first readers were, when it was written, and so on. If so, jot these things in your notebook as well.

2. *Read the entire book a second time, gathering information about how and why the book was written.* In other words, gather the information you need to fill in the rest of the first page shown in Figure 18. Here are some suggestions for finding the information:

Writer: Usually the writer will identify himself at the beginning or end of the book. The author's name may appear in the title, such as "The Fifth Book of *Moses,* Called Deuteronomy" or, "The Epistle of *Paul* the Apostle to the Galatians."

In some cases, the author of the book does not identify himself. Examples are the authors of the Book of Ruth and the Epistle to the Hebrews. For these books, note whatever clues you find about the author's identity. For example, the Book of Ruth nowhere identifies its author, but you can pick up several clues: The writer was a historian (since this is a book of history), a genealogist (see Ruth 4:17-22), a person well acquainted with Hebrew marriage law (Ruth 3) and quaint Old Testament customs (Ruth 4:7-9). Beyond this, we are left to guess at the writer's identity.

Readers: Again, the writer may indicate at the beginning or end of the book who his readers were. This may be stated in the title (such as the "Second Epistle of Paul the Apostle *to the Corinthians*"—i.e., Christians at the city of Corinth). But you probably will need to do some detective work to get this information, because Bible writers usually don't state who they are writing for. (So it is with the Book of Ruth.)

Period when written: You do not need to fix an exact date for the writing

---

8. Frank T. Lee, *Bible Study Popularized* (Chicago: Winona Pub. Co., 1904), p. 107.

Figure 17—Deductive Study Notes

DEDUCTIVE STUDY NOTES

Book: Ruth

Theme: A woman's Loyalty

Writer: Historian   Acquainted w/ OT laws &
Genealogist (4:17-22)   Customs (chap. 3; 4:7-9)

Readers: Jews who lived in King David's time or later.

Period When Written:
After the judges (1:1)
After the sandal custom (4:7)
King David's time or later (4:17-22)

The Writer's Purpose: To lift up Ruth as an example
to Jewish women.

DEDUCTIVE STUDY NOTES

Rough Outline (List Major Ideas/Events):

Elimelech's family flees to Moab (1:1-5)

Elimelech's widow Naomi returns to Judah (1:6-7)

Ruth returns w/ Naomi (1:8-22)

Ruth gleans in Boaz's field (chap. 2)

Ruth offers herself to Boaz (chap. 3)

Boaz takes Ruth as his wife (4:1-16)

Formal Outline (Organize Major Ideas/Events):

Intro. — Elimelech's Family Flees to Moab (1:1-5)

I. Ruth's Loyalty to her Mother-in-Law

  A. Elimelech's widow returns to Judah (1:6-7).
  B. Ruth Returns w/ Naomi (1:8-22).
  C. Ruth Gleans in Boaz's Field (chap. 2).

II. Ruth's Loyalty to Her Husband's Family

  A. Ruth Offers Herself to Boaz (chap. 3).
  B. Boaz Takes Ruth as His Wife (4:1-16).

III. God Rewards Ruth's Loyalty

  Boaz and Ruth's Descendents (4:17-22)

of the book, but you should be able to tell the *period* of Bible history to which it belongs. For instance, you know the Book of Revelation was written in the New Testament age because it refers to Jesus Christ by name (Rev. 1:1), to seven "churches" in Asia (1:4), and to all Christians as "priests and kings" (1:6)—a New Testament concept. You can tell further that the book was written in a time of tribulation or persecution (see Rev. 1:9), and that it was written after John was exiled to the island of Patmos (1:9). From a Bible dictionary's article on "John" or "Patmos," you will find that this would have been late in the first century, probably under Emperor Domitian (reign A.D. 81-96). So the book was written not only to the seven churches of Asia, but also to other Christians who were being persecuted as John was.

The Book of Ruth poses a similar challenge in identifying the readers. The book must have been written after the time of the judges, because it begins with the statement " . . . in the days when the judges ruled" (1:1), past tense. It must have been written after the Jews abandoned the custom of taking off a sandal to confirm a business deal, because it says "this was the custom in former times in Israel" (4:7). It must have been written in the time of King David, or later, because the writer traces Ruth's family tree up to David (4:17-22). This information tells us when the readers must have lived. And apparently they were Jews, because only Jews would have been interested in the king's ancestry. This process of discovery is one of the real joys of Bible study.

The writer's purpose: Sometimes the writer clearly states his purpose, as when John says, "Jesus did many other signs in the presence of His disciples, which are not written in this book; but these are written that you may believe that Jesus is the Christ, the Son of God, and that believing you may have life in His name" (John 20:30,31 NKJV). More often, you will have to discern the writer's purpose yourself. Ponder the theme of the book again. Was this book written to encourage the readers? To warn them? To teach them? To accomplish something else?

The writer of Ruth may have had several purposes in mind—to fill a historical gap in the Book of Judges; to explain how a non-Jew (Ruth) came to be a part of David's family line; to record a romantic story from Israel's past. But look at what I concluded is the *theme* of the book: "A Woman's Loyalty" (see p. 192). If this is the writer's central idea, perhaps it was written to present Ruth as an example to Jewish women, encouraging them to be loyal.[9]

---

9. Some scholars feel the book may have been written after the Exile, to protest Ezra and Nehemiah's strict policy against having non-Jewish wives. But I think that view is too speculative.

3. *Read the entire book a third time, and list the writer's major ideas.* This will require more careful reading than your first two times through the book, but it's still best to do this in one sitting in order to understand how one idea leads to another. Jot these ideas on the second note sheet, showing the chapter and verse for each idea.

Notice that you may need to do some detective work in this phase of your study, too. The writer may openly state the idea he's setting forth, but sometimes he may simply *illustrate* the idea and you must state it in your own terms. The writer of Ruth does the latter.

When reading a book of history, treat each event as an "idea"; note each major event you find. The writer may use the event to illustrate an idea that he will set forth later.

4. *Organize the major ideas into a formal outline of the book.* An outline will help you see at a glance how the book is organized, and how various parts of the book contribute to the theme.

The key to making a logical outline is to keep the theme before you as you consider each major idea of the book. Ask yourself how each idea relates to the theme. Is this a primary idea (one that declares the theme or some facet of the theme)? Or is it a secondary idea (one that explains or illustrates some facet of the theme)? To group the ideas according to major themes, you may need to reread portions of the book. Here is a list of ideas I gathered while reading the Book of Ruth:

Elimelech's family flees to Moab (1:1-5)
Elimelech's widow Naomi returns to Judah (1:6,7)
Ruth returns with Naomi (1:8-22)
Ruth gleans in Boaz's field (2)
Ruth offers herself to Boaz (3)
Boaz takes Ruth as his wife (4:1-16)
Boaz and Ruth's descendants (4:17-22)

On my first pass through the book, I concluded that the overall theme of the book is "A Woman's Loyalty." How do each of these ideas contribute to that theme? I have to do a little organizing, as follows:

The Book of Ruth:
"A Woman's Loyalty"
Intro.—Elimelech's Family Flees to Moab (1:1-5)
I. *Ruth's Loyalty to Her Mother-in-Law*
   A. Elimelech's Widow Naomi Returns to Judah (1:6,7)
   B. Ruth Returns with Naomi (1:8-22)
   C. Ruth Gleans in Boaz's Field (2)

II. *Ruth's Loyalty to Her Husband's Family*
    A. Ruth Offers Herself to Boaz (3)
    B. Boaz Takes Ruth as His Wife (4:1-16)
III. *God Rewards Ruth's Loyalty*
    Boaz and Ruth's Descendants (4:17-22)

With very little trouble, I have prepared a simple outline of the Book of Ruth. The entire process (including three readings of the book itself) took me about an hour and a half. It gave me a personal acquaintance with the Book of Ruth and (as you can see) a handy summary on paper for future reference.

Chapter 1 discusses the type of Bible version needed for deductive study. Use a Bible dictionary, encyclopedia, or handbook for the meaning of unfamiliar names. (For example, you would find that "Judah" in Ruth 1:7 does not mean the *nation* Judah, created by the civil war in Rehoboam's day. It refers to the *territory* allotted to the tribe of Judah when the Israelites first entered the Promised Land.)

An exegetical or expository commentary will give you further insight into the cultural background of this book. (For example, the comments on Ruth 3 would tell you that Boaz was following the law of *levirate marriage* in marrying his kinsman's widow. And then the commentators will explain what levirate marriage was.) A "devotional" or "suggestive" commentary would describe the theme of Ruth, in that commentator's opinion. (It's a good place to check your own conclusions!) You could also compare your notes about the authorship and time of writing with these commentaries. Compare your notes about the writer's purpose and your outline of the book with a Bible survey and a Bible introduction, respectively. Don't be surprised if you disagree with the experts now and then! But if you find a wide disagreement, take a closer look; you may have missed something important.

For instruction in using the deductive method with specific books of the Bible, see Joseph M. Gettys' "How to Study" series, published by John Knox Press.[10] At the end of each chapter, Gettys provides an exercise in "Original Study" (which generally uses the deductive method) and an exercise in "Advanced Study" (which is usually an inductive method).

The Inductive (Analytical) Method

This method has gained considerable popularity in recent years, as lay readers have taken more interest in higher-critical Bible study. The

---

10. This series of books includes *How to Study Luke, How to Study Acts, How to Study 1 Corinthians, How to Study Ephesians,* and *How to Study Revelation.*

inductive method is one approach to higher criticism; it is most helpful in analyzing smaller sections of a book (chapters, verses, even sentences) to detect subtle nuances in the writer's message or mood. Other writers have devoted entire books to this method[11]—perhaps I should say *these methods,* because there are several different techniques of inductive study. The methods described here are not as elaborate as some, but I think they will give you a good idea of inductive Bible study.

Howard F. Vos defines inductive Bible study as "the process of reasoning or drawing conclusions from particular cases,"[12] and perhaps that is the most all-encompassing way to describe it. Inductive study begins where deductive study ends. While deductive study yields a composite picture of a Bible book or chapter, inductive study reveals the various parts that make up the picture. After getting the "big picture" of the complete book or chapter, you should analyze its component parts to understand *how* the writer conveys his theme and *why* he has used certain words or turns of phrase to get the message across. Dr. Daniel J. Fuller observes that this attempt "to gain an understanding of the book requires fatiguing and often discouraging effort."[13] But the insights you receive are worth the effort.

There is some debate about what size portion of Scripture should be considered the basic unit for inductive study. Jensen and Vos say the paragraph is the basic unit; Fuller says each main proposition (statement) is the basic unit; Osborne and Woodward feel that each phrase or clause is the basic unit. I believe the paragraph is most convenient because it is the largest of these units; thus when we begin diagramming our work the notes will be easier to manage. (If you diagram each clause or phrase, or even each proposition, you will generate several pages of notes for every chapter, which is too cumbersome.)

Let's analyze the Book of Ruth paragraph-by-paragraph. You will need a Bible version that divides the text into paragraphs, not one that treats every verse as a paragraph. You can usually tell the difference by noticing

11. Daniel P. Fuller, *The Inductive Method of Bible Study,* 3rd ed. (Pasadena: Fuller Theological Seminary, 1959). Irving L. Jensen, *Independent Bible Study* (Chicago: Moody, 1963). See also Grant R. Osborne and Stephen B. Woodward, *Handbook for Bible Study* (Grand Rapids: Baker, 1979), chapters 2-4. Also Vos, *Effective Bible Study,* chapter 2.

12. Vos, *Effective Bible Study,* p. 16.

13. Fuller, *Inductive Method,* p. IV-2. By the way, Fuller advises us *not* to make a deductive survey of the book before starting the inductive study (pp. IV,9,11), because we may be mistaken in our first assessment of the writer's theme and then try to base all subsequent findings on that faulty notion. Granted, such a thing could happen. But I believe most of us will find it easier to start with a general view of the book and then analyze its many details, rather than work the other way around. Also, I believe that anyone who approaches Bible study with an open mind will reassess his first impressions if he turns up contradictory evidence in his inductive study.

the indentations on the left side of the column; an indentation usually signals a new paragraph. (Some editions of the NASB indent every verse and signal the start of each paragraph by printing that verse number in bold type. Perhaps other versions will also appear in this format.) You soon discover that each version that has paragraphs will break the material in its own way. The NEB has ten paragraphs in the Book of Ruth; the NASB has thirteen; the RSV has fifteen; and the LB has fifty-four. Obviously, the various translators had their own ideas about the organization of the book!

Let's say that you choose the RSV for this study. That gives you fifteen basic units of thought to analyze. The inductive chart (Fig. 18, pp. 200-203) shows how you might set up your notebook pages for the work. Now let me explain how to use it.

First, in the top two rows, identify the *UNITS* you are considering. In this case you are looking at paragraphs, so you write "¶" (symbol for paragraph) and its respective number in the sequence. Directly below that, write the Scripture text for that paragraph. If you were studying verses, you could write "Verse 1-Verse 2-Verse 3" and so on in the top row, and would not need to fill in the second row. If you were considering propositions (statements), phrases, or clauses, you would give each of these units an identification number in the top row and show the verse where it appears in the second row. This same format can be used for any size unit.

Second, note in your own words the *CONTENT* of that unit. Notice the two questions that will help you do this—"What happens?" or, "Who speaks, and what does he/she say?" If you are studying a doctrinal book (such as one of Paul's epistles) in which there is no real action, you might answer two different questions—"What does he say?" and "Why must he say it?" In any case, make your notes concise and clear.

Third, note any *ODD PHRASE* that appears in the passage; I've allowed room for three of these. By an "odd phrase," I mean a word or phrase that (1) is unfamiliar to you, (2) seems ironic or contradictory in the context, or (3) seems to have a double meaning of some sort. After you have noted these, refer to the appropriate Bible reference book to find the meaning of each phrase. If it's simply an unfamiliar word (such as *"Ephrathite"* in ¶1), look it up in a Bible dictionary or encyclopedia. If you encounter an unusual English word—one that is not strictly biblical terminology (such as "gleaner" in ¶5)—you probably can find the meaning in any English dictionary. For an unfamiliar biblical phrase (such as, "May the Lord do so to me and more also" in ¶3), you may need to check an expository or exegetical commentary on this passage—one that explains the meaning of every phrase in the text. Such a commentary may also help you understand a phrase that seems ironic or contradictory (such as "judges ruled" in ¶1). To check words that seem to have a double meaning of some sort, try a Bible dictionary or encyclopedia (for proper names like "Naomi") or an exegetical commentary (for common words used in unusual ways, such as the reference to God's "wings" in ¶6). Use a Bible handbook to get information about unusual customs (such as "dip your morsel in the wine," ¶7), foreign currency or measurements (such as the "ephah" in ¶8 or "measure" in ¶11), and other miscellaneous facts that you cannot find elsewhere (such as "restoring the name" in ¶12 and wives' status as property in ¶13).

Fourth, summarize the *MAJOR IDEA* or *EVENT* in the paragraph. Look again at your notes under *CONTENT* and choose the central event or idea there. This strip of the chart makes a more detailed—and more accurate—outline of the book than you could achieve with the deductive study method.

Finally, note any *UNRESOLVED QUESTIONS* posed by this passage: Does the writer say something that puzzles you (see ¶9 and ¶14)? Does he refer to some other person or incident in Scripture, without fully explaining what he means (see ¶1 and ¶10)? Does he raise some other question without answering it here (see ¶4, ¶6, and ¶9)? Note these questions at this point and look for an answer *in the Scriptures.* Scripture is its own best interpreter.

Even after reading the entire book, some questions may not be resolved, and you may need to consult a commentary or other reference book for someone else's interpretation. The type of question will determine the book you use. Generally, for interpreting an unusual word of phrase (see ¶2) you should consult an exegetical or expository commentary (assuming the expository treatment is detailed enough). For interpreting matters of doctrine, history, or motive (see ¶11), an expository or devotional commentary should help. And for questions of culture, social customs, and the like (see ¶8), consult a Bible encyclopedia or Bible handbook.

Your notes are important to the inductive method because the note-taking process: (1) forces you to fix a critical eye on every phrase of the text, (2) allows you to gather bits of information that you find along the way, and (3) gives you a permanent record of what you learn, for future review. I suggest that you make the inductive notes in ink, since you probably will not need to reorganize them in light of subsequent reading and you will have a more legible, durable record.

Doing the Word

Irving L. Jensen points out that no method of Bible study is complete without *interpretation* and *application* of what we find.[14] I heartily

---

14. Jensen, *Independent Bible Study,* pp. 157,158.

Figure 18—Inductive Study Notes

INDUCTIVE STUDY NOTES

UNIT	# 1	# 2	# 3	# 4
TEXT	Ruth 1:1-5	Ruth 1:6-14	Ruth 1:15-18	Ruth 1:19-21
CONTENT What happens?	Elimelech's family goes to Moab; Elimelech dies; two sons marry + die.	Naomi plans return; urges Orpah + Ruth to stay in Moab; Orpah does.	Naomi again urges Ruth to stay; Ruth insists on going w/ her.	They return to Bethlehem; Naomi laments her plight.
Who speaks, and what does he/she say?	—	Naomi - I am too old to bear children or marry. The Lord is against me. (vv. 11-13).	Naomi - Stay w/ your people + your gods. Ruth - your people + god will be mine.	Women - Is this Naomi? Naomi - Not anymore. I am Mara.
ODD PHRASE Meaning	judges ruled (1:1) - led volunteer armies.	Orpah (v.14) - Heb., 'youthful'.	May the Lord do so to me (v.17) - oath to die.	Naomi (v.19) - Heb., 'pleasant'.
ODD PHRASE Meaning	Ephrathite (1:2) - native of Bethlehem.	Ruth (v.14) - Heb., 'friendly'.	—	Mara (v.20) - Heb., 'bitter'.
ODD PHRASE Meaning	—	—	—	—
MAJOR IDEA/EVENT	Naomi's husband + sons die.	Naomi urges girls to stay.	Ruth insists on going w/ Naomi.	Naomi laments her plight.
UNRESOLVED QUESTIONS Answers	Why didn't family return to Judah?	Why should they seek shelter in mother's house and husband's house?	—	Why did Naomi blame god?
	Because they'd not heard famine was over (1:6).		—	Later blessed Him (2:20). Blessing proved (4:14-17).

INDUCTIVE STUDY NOTES

UNIT	A 5	A 6	A 7	A 8
TEXT	Ruth 1:22-2:7	Ruth 2:8-13	Ruth 2:14-16	Ruth 2:17-23
CONTENT What happens?	Ruth gleans barley; enters field of Boaz, husband's kin; he sees her.	Boaz invites Ruth to stay in his field.	Boaz invites Ruth to meal, tells workers to leave grain for her.	Ruth brings grain to Naomi; tells her of Boaz.
Who speaks, and what does he/she say?	—	—	—	Naomi - The Lord has not forsaken the living, or the dead (V. 20).
ODD PHRASE Meaning	gleaner - one who salvages grain.	she fell on her face - custom of respect.	dip your morsel - custom of hosp.	ephah - about 1.1 bushel.
ODD PHRASE Meaning	Boaz (2:1) - Heb., "swiftness".	God's Wings - His protection.	—	—
ODD PHRASE Meaning	—	—	—	—
MAJOR IDEA/EVENT	Boaz notices Ruth.	Boaz invites Ruth to stay.	Boaz tells workers to leave grain.	Ruth tells of Boaz.
UNRESOLVED QUESTIONS Answers	— —	Did harvesters often molest the gleaners? Apparently (2:22)	Why note that she had food left over? She would take it to Naomi (V.18)	How long did barley & wheat harvests last?

INDUCTIVE STUDY NOTES

UNIT	# 9	# 10	# 11	# 12
TEXT	Ruth 3:1-5	Ruth 3:6-13	Ruth 3:14-18	Ruth 4:1-6
CONTENT What happens? Who speaks, and what does he/she say?	Naomi tells Ruth to seek home w/ Boaz.	Ruth lays herself beside Boaz, offers to be his wife; he tells of nearer kin.	Ruth returns to Naomi w/ news; Naomi tells her to wait.	Boaz offers next kin chance to buy land + marry Ruth; he declines.
	Naomi - Go to Boaz as he sleeps, uncover his feet + lie down. He will tell you what to do.	Boaz- You are kind not to seek younger men (v.10).	Naomi - He will settle the matter today. (see #5)	Boaz- The day you buy the land you are also buying Ruth (v.5). Kin-I would endanger my own heirs.
ODD PHRASE Meaning	—	the part of... kin (v.13) - duty to marry relative's widow.	six measures- 6 × 6.9 quarts.	restore the name... (v.5) - w/o children the family name dies.
ODD PHRASE Meaning	—	—	—	—
ODD PHRASE Meaning	—	—	—	—
MAJOR IDEA/EVENT	Naomi tells Ruth to seek home w/ Boaz.	Ruth offers to be Boaz's wife.	Ruth tells Naomi the news.	Next of kin declines offer.
UNRESOLVED QUESTIONS Answers	Why should she lie down w/ him ?	What was Ruth's "first" kindness (v.10) ?	Why keep Ruth's visit a secret (v.14) ?	—
	Custom of be-trothal- he had to spread his skirt over her (v.9)	What she did for Naomi (2:11).		

INDUCTIVE STUDY NOTES

UNIT	A 13	A 14	A 15	
TEXT	Ruth 4: 7-12	Ruth 4: 13-17	Ruth 4: 18-22	
⊙ CONTENT What happens?	Boaz buys the land & takes Ruth as his wife.	Ruth bears a son; women congratulate Naomi; she nurses him as her own.	—	
Who speaks, and what does he/she say?	—	Women - Ruth has been more to you than 7 sons (v. 15). Naomi - a son has been born to me (v. 17).	The writer - lists descendants of Ruth & Boaz.	
ODD PHRASE ⊙ Meaning	Ruth... I bought (v. 10) - wives considered property.	Obed (v. 17) - Heb., 'servant.'	descendants of Perez (v. 18) Chief tribal ancestor.	
ODD PHRASE Meaning	Name... not cut off from the gate (v. 10) - family reps. sat at city gate.	—	—	
ODD PHRASE Meaning	like Perez (v. 12) - eldest son of Judah (i.e., chief heir).	—	—	
MAJOR IDEA/EVENT	Boaz takes Ruth as his wife.	Ruth bears a son.	List of descendants.	
UNRESOLVED QUESTIONS ⊙ Answers	—	Is verse 16 literal? Can an o'd woman give suck?		

agree. We need to grasp the meaning of what the Bible says (interpretation) and begin changing our lives to conform to what it says (application) if Scripture is to have any real value for our daily lives.

> For if anyone is a hearer of the word and not a doer, he is like a man observing his natural face in a mirror; for he observes himself, goes away, and immediately forgets what kind of man he was. But he who looks into the perfect law of liberty and continues in it, and is not a forgetful hearer but a doer of the word, this one will be blessed in what he does (James 1:23-25 NKJV).

In this chapter I have presented some simple, practical methods for studying the Word of God. If you faithfully use these methods, you should be able to comprehend what the Word says. But then you have a responsibility to live according to the Word. No Bible study method or library of resources can show you how to do that, but the Holy Spirit can. And I believe He will!

Glossary

ALLEGORY—a story that expresses a spiritual or moral lesson. Early Christian Bible commentators tried to interpret each Bible event as an *allegory*.

ALTERNATE READING—another way of translating or paraphrasing a Bible verse based on the accepted Hebrew or Greek text. Many study Bibles give these *alternates* in margin notes or footnotes. *Compare* TEXTUAL VARIANT.

AMILLENNIALISM—the theological view that Christ and His saints will *not* reign for a thousand years in connection with His final return.

ANNOTATED BIBLE—a simple type of study Bible with brief introductions and general outlines to the Bible books, and a few notes on significant phrases in the text. *Compare* REFERENCE BIBLE and STUDY BIBLE.

APOCALYPTIC LITERATURE—any prophetic writings concerning the end of the world and/or God's final judgment. Many books of early Jewish and Christian *apocalyptic literature* were not included in the CANON of the Bible, for various reasons. *See also* ESCHATOLOGY.

APOCRYPHA—a collection of Jewish literature from the intertestamental era (i.e., the time between the writing of the Old and New Testaments). Roman Catholics and some Protestants believe these writings are Holy Scripture.

APOLOGY—a logical defense of the gospel or of any Christian doctrine. A person who makes this kind of *apology* is called an APOLOGIST.

ARMINIANISM—a theological tradition begun by Jacobus Arminius (d. 1609), which holds that God gives each person complete freedom to accept or reject salvation. *Compare* CALVINISM; PREDESTINATION.

BIBLICAL CRITICISM—a general term that describes any objective evaluation of the Bible. This may include an evaluation of Bible manuscripts to see how authentic they are (LOWER CRITICISM) or an evaluation of the message they convey (HIGHER CRITICISM).

CALVINISM—a theological tradition begun by John Calvin (d. 1564) and his followers. *Calvinism* involves PREDESTINATION and several related beliefs — e.g., that man is utterly sinful and unable to save himself; that God is the absolute ruler of the universe and has the sole power to save man or condemn man; and that all men should follow the moral tenets of Scripture. *Compare* ARMINIANISM.

CANON—the official collection of books that make up the Bible. The Jewish Council of Jamnia (A.D. 90) formally recognized the traditional list of books that Jews and Christians had accepted as Holy Scripture (the Old Testament), while the Christian community formally recognized the accepted New Testament books at various councils, concluding in the fourth century A.D.

CANON CRITICISM—a method of HIGHER CRITICISM that attempts to trace how the Jewish and Christian communities recognized certain books as divinely inspired Scripture and rejected others.

CENTER-COLUMN NOTE—a note printed between the columns of a two-column Bible page. *Compare* FOOTNOTE and MARGIN NOTE.

CHRONOLOGY—any study of the time sequence of important events. Also, this term may refer to a dated list of Bible events that a scholar develops by studying the Bible's *chronology*. Some REFERENCE BIBLES give a *chronology* in their notes.

COMMENTARY—comments on a given piece of literature.

CONSUBSTANTIATION—the doctrine that Christ's body and blood are really present in the communion (Lord's Supper) elements, even though the substance of the bread and wine are not changed. This doctrine, held by Lutherans and certain other Protestant groups, differs from the Roman Catholic doctrine of transubstantiation, which holds that the underlying "substance" of the bread and wine are transformed into the body and blood of Christ in the ritual of the Eucharist.

CRITICAL APPARATUS—a set of textual notes that show the manuscript background and/or TEXTUAL VARIANTS that have a bearing on each passage of Scripture.

CRITICAL EDITION—an edited text of an old book, made by comparing various copies of that book to see which ones seem to best reflect the wording of the original. (*See also* TEXTUAL CRITICISM). The textual critic chooses from each copy the passages that seem most likely to have been in the original book.

CROSS REFERENCE—a reference to a related idea or Scripture passage. Many study Bibles have marginal notes or footnotes alongside every major portion of Scripture, giving the references to other verses on the same theme; these notes are *cross references*.

CULTUS—a society's religious system and all of the customs—including civil and family customs—stemming from that religion.

DIALECT—a form of a language that departs significantly from the standard language, or from the language as it is recorded in writing. A *dialect* has its own peculiar vocabulary and expressions that set it apart from the normal language of its day.

DISPENSATIONALISM—a particular view of Bible history which says that although God has but one plan of salvation, He reveals Himself to man and deals with man in different ways in each successive period (*dispensation*) of their relationship.

DOCUMENTARY THEORY—a theory of LITERARY CRITICISM developed by K. H. Graf and Julius Wellhausen. They believed that each book of the PENTATEUCH bore the marks of several writers' and editors' work, which could be identified by noting the name of God that each section was apt to use. They and their colleagues eventually noted four editorial sources of the PENTATEUCH—J (Yahwist), E (Elohist), D (Deuteronomic editor), and P (Priestly editor). This is also called the "documentary hypothesis" or the "Graf-Wellhausen hypothesis."

DOXOLOGY—a declaration of praise to God, often in the form of a hymn or prayer.

DYNAMIC EQUIVALENCE—a goal of Bible translating. A translator who strives for *dynamic equivalence* seeks to express each idea or concept of the Bible manuscripts in modern language, without trying to follow the manuscripts' written pattern phrase-by-phrase or word-by-word. *Compare* FORMAL EQUIVALENCE.

ECLECTIC TEXT—a compilation of passages from various Bible manuscripts that a textual critic may choose as the authentic text of the Bible. In other words, instead of following any single manuscript or CRITICAL EDITION the critic selects the readings he feels are most authentic.

ENCYCLICAL LETTERS—*See* PATRISTIC LETTERS.

ESCHATOLOGY—the study of things relating to the end of the world, the final judgment, and life beyond the grave. *See also* APOCALYPTIC LITERATURE.

FOOTNOTE—a note printed at the bottom of a Bible page. *Compare* CENTER-COLUMN NOTE and MARGIN NOTE.

FORMAL EQUIVALENCE—a goal of Bible translating. A translator who strives for *formal equivalence* seeks to express in modern language exactly what the Bible manuscripts say, phrase-by-phrase or word-by-word. *Compare* DYNAMIC EQUIVALENCE.

FORM CRITICISM—a method of HIGHER CRITICISM that attempts to discover who wrote a Bible passage and at what time it was written, by identifying the literary genre or *form* of the writing.

FORMER PROPHETS—the books of Joshua, Judges, 1 and 2 Samuel, and 1 and 2 Kings, which are grouped together in Hebrew Bibles because they record the work of Israel's early prophets (before the eighth century B.C.). *Compare* LATTER PROPHETS. *See also* MAJOR PROPHETS: MINOR PROPHETS.

GAZETTEER—an alphabetical list of Bible place names with code numbers keyed to an adjacent set of maps.

GENERAL EPISTLES—the New Testament letters that are not addressed to any specific individual or congregation. These are the letters of James, Peter, John, and Jude. They are also called "Catholic Epistles."

GRAMMAR—a book that introduces you to the *vocabulary* (list of words), *morphology* (formation of words), and *syntax* (patterns of word usage) in a given language.

HERESY—a denial of or a marked departure from the gospel of Jesus Christ. A *heretic* (one who espouses a heresy) contradicts the Bible's basic teaching about Christ and the salvation He brings. Note that *heresy* is always HETERODOX, but a HETERODOX teaching is not necessarily *heresy*.

HETERODOX—being different from the beliefs that Christians have traditionally accepted and taught. *Compare* NEO-ORTHODOX; ORTHODOX.

HIGHER CRITICISM—the study of the content of any portion of the Bible, in an effort to learn what the original author sought to express to his readers. *See also* BIBLICAL CRITICISM; *compare* LOWER CRITICISM; LITERARY CRITICISM.

HISTORICAL BOOKS—books of the Old Testament (Joshua through 2 Chronicles) that are grouped together in Christian Bibles because they describe the history of Israel from the conquest of Canaan to the Babylonian captivity and restoration. Hebrew Bibles refer to these books as the "Former Prophets" (except for Ruth and 1 and 2 Chronicles, which they place in the WRITINGS).

HYPERBOLE—an exaggerated statement made for the sake of vividness or emphasis.

IMPRECATORY PSALMS—Psalms that ask God to defeat or destroy the Psalmist's enemies. Some of these, such as Psalms 58 and 137, show strong hatred for the Psalmist's foes.

IMPRIMATUR—a Latin word meaning, 'let it be printed.'' A book must have an *imprimatur*—permission to be printed—from a recognized Roman Catholic official in order for Catholic readers to use it with the Church's approval. However, the *imprimatur* does not mean that the licensing official agrees with all of the book's contents. *See also* NIHIL OBSTAT.

INTRODUCTION—a review of each book of the Bible, usually with an outline of each book, that analyzes various stages of the ongoing relationship between God and man. *Compare* SURVEY.

KOINE **GREEK**—"common" Greek, the form of the language spoken throughout much of the Mediterranean area after the conquests of Alexander the Great (d. 323 B.C.).

LATTER PROPHETS—the prophetic books of Isaiah, Jeremiah, Ezekiel, and the twelve MINOR PROPHETS, which are grouped together in Hebrew Bibles because they record the work of Israel's later prophets (eighth century B.C. and afterward). *Compare* FORMER PROPHETS. *See also* MAJOR PROPHETS; MINOR PROPHETS.

LEGEND (map)—the caption for a map that describes the location and the time in history that the map depicts. The *legend* may also have a scale of measurement, an explanation of map symbols, and other information to help interpret the drawing.

LITERARY CRITICISM—a method of HIGHER CRITICISM that attempts to discover a Bible writer's identity, the date of the writing, the purpose for writing, etc., by searching for clues in the Bible text itself. A sophisticated type of LITERARY CRITICISM, known as SOURCE CRITICISM, tries to sort out and identify various authors' or editors' work in any given Bible book.

LOWER CRITICISM—the study of old manuscripts in an effort to determine which copies best reflect the wording of the original. Also called "TEXTUAL CRITICISM." *See also* BIBLICAL CRITICISM; *compare* HIGHER CRITICISM.

MAJOR PROPHETS—the longer prophetic books (Isaiah through Daniel) of the Old Testament, which are grouped together in Christian Bibles. *Compare* MINOR PROPHETS. *See also* FORMER PROPHETS; LATTER PROPHETS.

MAJORITY TEXT—a collection of the readings given by a majority of all the Bible manuscripts that have been handed down. With a few exceptions, the *TEXTUS RECEPTUS* is the *Majority Text*.

MARGIN NOTE—a note printed in the side margin of a Bible page. *Compare* CENTER-COLUMN NOTE; FOOTNOTE.

MASORETIC TEXT—a Hebrew text of the Old Testament that contains vowel signs, breathing marks, and other "pointings" added by late Jewish scribes (*Masoretes*) to aid in pronunciation. These "pointings" are vital to our understanding of the text, since the early scribes wrote their manuscripts as a continuous stream of letters with no spacing between words.

MILLENNIALISM—a particular view of Bible prophecy about Christ's return. People who hold this view believe that Christ will reign on earth with His saints for 1000 years. *See also* AMILLENNIALISM; POSTMILLENIALISM; PRE-MILLENNIALISM.

MINOR PROPHETS—the twelve shorter prophetic books (Hosea through Malachi) of the Old Testament, which are grouped together in Christian Bibles. *Compare* MAJOR PROPHETS. *See also* FORMER PROPHETS; LATTER PROPHETS.

NEO-ORTHODOX—being in harmony with the beliefs that Christians have traditionally accepted and taught, but reinterpreting those beliefs to fit modern concepts of the nature of God and man. *Compare* HETERODOX; ORTHODOX.

NIHIL OBSTAT—a Latin phrase meaning "nothing is offensive." It indicates that a book does not contain anything that contradicts or offends Roman Catholic dogma. Normally, a Catholic censor will review a book's contents and decide whether to grant his official approval (the *nihil obstat*). If he does, the book then goes to a higher Catholic official for his *IMPRIMATUR*. However, neither of these approvals mean that the reviewers agree with all of the book's contents. *See also IMPRIMATUR.*

ORTHODOX—being in harmony with the beliefs that Christians have traditionally accepted and taught. *Compare* HETERODOX; NEO-ORTHODOX.

PARALLELISM—a literary device used by Hebrew poets. Instead of using rhyme or rhythm to match the successive lines of a poem, Hebrew poets used *parallel* thoughts. That is, they expressed the same idea in different words in each successive line.

PARAPHRASE—the task of rephrasing a piece of literature in the same language. Also, this term refers to the material that results from such rephrasing. *Compare* TRANSLATION.

PASTORAL EPISTLES—the New Testament letters (1 and 2 Timothy and Titus) that Paul wrote to individual pastors, dealing largely with pastoral concerns.

PATRISTIC LETTERS—letters written by leaders of the Christian church who lived before the Council of Chalcedon (A.D. 451). Some of these letters, called ENCYCLICAL LETTERS, were meant to be circulated to all the churches in that leader's district or province. Many of the *patristic letters* contain Scripture quotations that help us know what Bible manuscripts the early Christians were using.

PAULINE EPISTLES—the New Testament letters written by the apostle Paul.

PENTATEUCH—the first five books of the Bible (Genesis, Exodus, Leviticus, Numbers, and Deuteronomy).

POSTMILLENNIALISM—the theological view that Christ and/or His saints will reign on the earth (or in heaven) *before* His final return.

PREDESTINATION—the theological view that God chooses some persons to be saved, even before they are born. The doctrine of *double predestination* further holds that God chooses some people to be damned, even before they are born. *See also* ARMINIANISM; CALVINISM.

PREMILLENNIALISM—the theological view that Christ and His saints will reign on the earth for a thousand years *after* His final return.

PROGRESSIVE REVELATION—the gradual process by which God reveals more of His truth to man.

REDACTION CRITICISM—a method of LITERARY CRITICISM that attempts to trace how a Bible writer's work has been edited by various scribes and editors (German, *redakteurs*) as it was handed down.

REFERENCE BIBLE—a general term for a Bible with certain study "helps." It may refer to an ANNOTATED BIBLE or a STUDY BIBLE.

SEMITIC—referring to the people who are thought to have descended from Noah's son Shem. In biblical times, the *Semites* included Babylonians, Assyrians, Arameans, and Phoenicians as well as the Jews. The languages of these peoples were remarkably similar.

SEPTUAGINT—a Greek version of the Old Testament, translated for the Library of Alexandria just before 200 B.C. Seventy scholars (Greek *septuaginta,* "seventy") are said to have worked on the project.

STUDY BIBLE—a Bible with a fairly elaborate system of study "helps," including detailed introductions and outlines to the Bible books, notes on nearly every verse, a concordance, and other study tools. *Compare* ANNOTATED BIBLE and REFERENCE BIBLE.

SURVEY—a general descriptive review of Bible history which explains how various events revealed more of God's nature and advanced His relationship with man. *Compare* INTRODUCTION.

SYNOPTIC PROBLEM—a problem in HIGHER CRITICISM concerning a number of seeming discrepancies in the first three gospels (Matthew, Mark, and Luke). These three books give such similar accounts of Jesus' life that scholars say they are *synoptic* ("seeing together"). And yet there are differences — events in different sequence, sermons in different order, etc. These differences pose the *synoptic problem.*

TEXTUAL CRITICISM—*See* LOWER CRITICISM.

TEXTUAL VARIANT—a different phrasing of a Bible verse, according to another Hebrew or Greek manuscript that the translator felt was not as reliable as his chief textual source. Many study Bibles give these *variants* in margin notes or footnotes. *Compare* ALTERNATE READING.

TEXTUS RECEPTUS—the "received text," or the text traditionally accepted as being the most authentic text of the Hebrew or Greek Testament.

THEOCRACY—a form of government in which God is the supreme ruler. The king, priest, or other national leaders are supposed to follow God's guidance as they shape national policy.

THEODICY—the doctrine that God is righteous and omnipotent in spite of injustice, disease, and other consequences of evil.

TOPOGRAPHY—the describing and/or picturing of geographic features in a given area. An atlas or geography text are two kinds of *topography* books.

TRANSLATION—the process of expressing the meaning of a word, a phrase, or idea in another language. Also, this term refers to the translated word, phrase, or idea itself. *Compare* PARAPHRASE; TRANSLITERATION.

TRANSLITERATION—the process of expressing the pronunciation of a word in the letters of another language. Also, this term refers to the transliterated word itself. *Compare* TRANSLATION.

TYPOLOGY—the study of Old Testament people, events, or objects as a prediction or "type" of similar people, events, or objects in the New Testament.

UNITARIANISM—a theological tradition that holds that only one God is worshiped by all the people of the earth. *Unitarianism* denies that Jesus Christ was God in the flesh, and it denies that a person must be saved only through Jesus Christ. *Unitarianism* also denies that the Holy Spirit exists as a distinct Person of the Godhead.

UNIVERSALISM—the theological view that all people will be saved or all people will be annihilated at death, regardless of their religious experience. Many people who follow the tradition of UNITARIANISM have also embraced the idea of *Universalism*.

VERSION—a translation of a book into language other than the original. There are versions of the Bible in Latin, German, English, and other languages (both ancient and modern).

WORD STUDY—a book that explains the meaning of significant Hebrew or Greek words that appear in the Bible. Also, this term refers to any individual's study of a particular Bible word.

WRITINGS—the remaining books of the Old Testament that are not included in the HISTORICAL BOOKS or the PROPHETS. Hebrew Bibles group these books together at the end of the Old Testament.

General Bibliography

Albright, W. F. *Archaeology and the Religion of Israel.* Baltimore: Johns Hopkins Press, 1946.

_____ . *From the Stone Age to Christianity.* Baltimore: Johns Hopkins Press, 1946.

Alexander, Pat. *Eerdmans Family Encyclopedia of the Bible.* Grand Rapids: Eerdmans, 1978.

Baly, Denis. "What to Look for in a Biblical Atlas." *The Biblical Archaeologist,* Winter 1982.

Bruce, F. F. *History of the Bible in English,* 3rd ed. New York: Oxford Univ. Press, 1978.

Castagno, Anthony J. *Treasury of Biblical Quotations.* Nashville: Thomas Nelson, 1980.

The Compact Edition of the Oxford English Dictionary. New York: Oxford Univ. Press, 1971.

Daniélou, Jean and Henri Marrou. *The First Six Hundred Years,* trans. Vincent Cronin. New York: McGraw-Hill, 1964.

Dorn, Fred J. "Time Management for the Part-Time Freelancer." *The Writer,* April 1982.

Foster, Lewis. *Selecting a Translation of the Bible.* Cincinnati: Standard, 1978.

Freedman, H. and Maurice Simon, eds. *Midrash Rabbah,* vol. 1. London: Soncino, 1939.

Fuller, Daniel P. *The Inductive Method of Bible Study,* 3rd ed. Pasadena: Fuller Theological Seminary, 1959.

Gaebelein, Arno C. *The History of the Scofield Reference Bible.* New York: Loizeaux, 1943.

Gibson, J. Munro. *The Devotional Use of the Holy Scriptures.* London: National Council of Evangelical Free Churches, 1904.

Glassman, Eugene H. *The Translation Debate.* Downers Grove, Ill.: InterVarsity, 1981.

Goldin, Judah, trans. *The Living Talmud.* New York: Mentor, 1957.

Harrison, Everett F., ed. *Baker's Dictionary of Theology.* Grand Rapids: Baker, 1979.

How to Sell the Right Bible. Nashville: Thomas Nelson, 1980.

James, Edgar C. *The Open Bible Owner's Guide.* Nashville: Thomas Nelson, 1976.

Jensen, Irving L. *Independent Bible Study.* Chicago: Moody, 1963.

Kraeling, E.G.H. *Rand McNally Bible Atlas.* New York: Rand McNally, 1956.

Lee, Frank T. *Bible Study Popularized.* Chicago: Winona, 1904.

Lockyer, Herbert. *All the Apostles of the Bible.* Grand Rapids: Zondervan, 1979.

_____ . *All the Children of the Bible.* Grand Rapids: Zondervan, 1979.

_____ . *All the Kings and Queens of the Bible.* Grand Rapids: Zondervan, 1961.

_____ . *All the Men of the Bible.* Grand Rapids: Zondervan, 1958.

_____ . *All the Women of the Bible.* Grand Rapids: Zondervan, 1979.

Martin, Walter. *Walter Martin's Cult Reference Bible.* Santa Anna, Calif.: Vision House, 1981.

Massey, James E., ed. *The Christian Brotherhood Hour Study Edition.* Nashville: Thomas Nelson, 1979.

Metzger, Bruce M. *Lexical Aids for Students of New Testament Greek,* rev. ed. Princeton: Theological Book Agency, 1970.

Olivier, Edith. *The Eccentric Life of Alexander Cruden.* London: Faber and Faber, 1934.

Petty, Jo. *Apples of Gold.* Norwalk, Conn.: C. R. Gibson, 1965.

Pritchard, James B. *Ancient Near Eastern Texts.* Princeton: Princeton Univ. Press, 1955.

_____ . *The Ancient Near East in Pictures.* Princeton: Princeton Univ. Press, 1955.

Ramsay, William M. *The Bearing of Recent Discovery on the Trustworthiness of the New Testament,* 2nd ed. London: Hodder and Stoughton, 1915.

Recommending and Selling Biblical Reference Works. Grand Rapids: Eerdmans, 1980.

Robert, A. and A. Feuillet. *Introduction to the Old Testament.* New York: Desclee, 1968.

Scofield, C. I., ed. *The Scofield Reference Bible.* New York: Oxford Univ. Press, 1945.

Sellin, Ernst and Georg Fohrer. *Introduction to the Old Testament,* trans. David Green. Nashville: Abingdon, 1968.

Skilton, John H., ed. *The New Testament Student at Work,* vol. 2. Nutley, N.J.: Presbyterian and Reformed, 1975.

Strack, Hermann L. *Introduction to the Talmud and Midrash.* New York: Harper Torchbooks, 1965.

Vos, Howard F. *Effective Bible Study.* Grand Rapids: Zondervan, 1956.

Wallace-Hodrill, D.S. *Eusebius of Caesarea.* Westminster, Md.: Canterbury, 1961.

Wiseman, Donald J. "The Chronology of the Bible," *The Holman Study Bible.* Philadelphia: A. J. Holman, 1962.

The Words of Jesus. Nashville: Thomas Nelson, 1982.

Wright, G. Ernest. *Biblical Archaeology,* rev. ed. Philadelphia: Westminster, 1962.

Bible Rebinders

Bookshelf Binders, Box 310, Ridgetown, Ontario, Canada NOP 2CO—(519) 674-2801

Dobbs Brothers, 301 Dobbs Road, St. Augustine, FL 32084—(904) 824-0821

Ginesta Eudaldo, 49 W. 27th Street, New York, NY 10001—(212) 689-3866

Heckman Bindery, 1010 North Sycamore, North Mancester, IN 46962—(219) 982-2107

Hill Book Bindery, 2409 Manor Road, Austin, TX 78722—(512) 472-2225

National Library Binders of Georgia, P.O. Box 11838, Atlanta, GA 30355—(404) 233-9442

Northeast Library Binders, 101 Mystic Avenue, Medford, MA 02155—(617) 396-8900

J. L. Perkins Book Binders, Ltd., 1212 Scarth Street, Regina, Saskatchewan, Canada S4R 2E5—(306) 527-2216

Sources For Out-of-print Books

Alec R. Allenson, Box 31, Naperville, IL 60540.

Baker Book House, Used Book Division, 1019 Wealthy St., S. E., Grand Rapids, MI 49506.

Basil Blackwell, 49 Broad St., Oxford, ENGLAND OXI 3BP.

Christian Used Book Exchange, 6943 Grange Court, Cincinnati, OH 45239.

Kregel Publications, Used Book Division, 525 Eastern Ave., S.E., Grand Rapids, MI 49501.

The Lamp Press, Ltd., 29a Ludgate Hill, London E.C. 4, ENGLAND.

Jumbo Mendham, Lampe Press, 6 Old Town Street, London, ENGLAND.

Nelson's Bookroom, Lydbury North, Salop, ENGLAND, SY7 8AS.

Richard Owen Roberts Booksellers, 205 East Kehoe Blvd., Wheaton, IL 60187.

The Theological Book Center, 99 Brattle St., Cambridge, MA 02138.

University Microfilms, Inc., 313 N. First St., Ann Arbor, MI 48103.

Index